Celtic Submari

A new model of football relationships based on affection and respect, not hatred, bitterness or sectarianism.

Alan

Best wishes

Sandy Jamieson

Sandy Jamieson

Ringwood Publishing
Glasgow

First published in Great Britain in 2011 by
Ringwood Publishing
PO Box 16298 GlasgowG13 9DD
www.ringwoodpublishing.com
e-mail   mail@ringwoodpublishing.com

ISBN 978-1-901514-03-2

British Library Cataloguing-in Publication Data
A catalogue record for this book is available from the British Library

Typeset in Times New Roman 11
Printed and bound in the UK

Dedication

This book is dedicated to the Boixader family.

To Ernesto Boixader, the finest man I know; to his wife Maria Dolores; and to their two children, young Maria and Ernest.

Ernest's life was unfortunately a short one, but the Celtic Submari has ensured he has an enduring legacy.

"Of all the things in life that are not important, football is by far the most important"

Pope John Paul II

"People are by far the most important thing in life, and football is only a game"

Ernesto Boixader

Chapter One   Introduction

While rightly classed as a football book, this book is more the story of remarkable people than an account of past games of football. It is the tale of the attempt by Spaniards living in the small Castellon town of Vila-real, to develop a new and better way for football supporters to relate to each other. One based on affection and respect, not hatred; one based on friendship rather than hostility. Their approach includes a determination to exploit the potential of football to be a positive and beneficial force for good in a complex troubled world. They were inspired in this ambition by the example given to them in 2004 when their peaceful little town, population 50,000, was invaded by 10,000 Celtic supporters.

The book considers the amazing and unique love affair that has developed over the last few years between the supporters of Villarreal and the supporters of Glasgow Celtic. The values behind this friendship, and the determination to make football a force for good in the world, have important lessons far beyond the confines of Vila-real and Glasgow.

In April 2004, Vila-real was entirely unprepared for the invasion of almost 10,000 people that accompanied the UEFA Cup quarter-final second leg game against Glasgow Celtic. It was less than 12 months after around 100,000 Celtic supporters had descended on Seville, and the Spanish travel mood was still high in the Celtic camp. Overnight the population of Villarreal increased by 20%. The invasion proved a benign one. Every Villarreal supporter has a clear memory of that amazing day, 14th April 2004, and a colourful story to tell. They were emotionally blown away by the magnificence of the Celtic support; their friendliness, their cheerfulness, their kindness, their generosity, their magnanimity in defeat, their capacity for unlimited enjoyment along with unlimited drink.

And it might have ended like that, an unforgettable day in the history of Villarreal and Vila-real, but nothing more tangible than a set of happy memories. But the particular circumstances of a very remarkable man, Ernesto Boixader, fed an ingredient into the brew that created a lasting outcome from the heady mix. Ernesto's young son had died from a cancerous brain tumour just 2 weeks before the Celtic invasion. Heartbroken and devastated, Ernesto turned his back on life. But over the 24 hours of the Celtic invasion something happened to Ernesto that rekindled his belief in people and his faith that goodness existed, and led to a recognition that football could be a powerful force for good in a troubled world. He determined that the goodness he had seen enacted by the Celtic hordes should not be dissipated. He wanted Villarreal people to apply those lessons in a way that would link them for ever in friendship with the Celtic nation. He formed the Villarreal Celtic Submari Penya, which quickly grew to be the biggest supporters club in Vila-real, and so began an ongoing friendship and alliance between the two sets of supporters dedicated to promoting the best Celtic virtues of friendship, respect, and practical help for those in need. The remarkable friendship between Celtic Supporters and Villarreal supporters has continued to grow, and inspire, many years on.

This book also explores the reasons why the subsequent visit of Glasgow Rangers to Villarreal did not result in a similar outburst of mutual friendship. It will examine whether there are any lessons for modern Scotland, with its troubled history of sectarian sourness, in the events and friendships developed in Vila-real, and the model of behaviour developed by the Celtic Submari. It will provide an explanation of the differences between Celtic and Rangers supporters that explains their radically different behaviours abroad. It offers an enhanced understanding of some of the elements of the sectarianism that so scars Scottish football, and suggests radical solutions drawing on the Villarreal model.

Celtic supporters everywhere can take pride in the story told in "Celtic Submari". But the book does not flinch from examining the hard questions which demonstrate that Celtic supporters have no room for complacency, and that a major dichotomy exists between the positive face of Celtic supporters presented to and appreciated by the outside world, and the less admirable behaviour sometimes exhibited in their own back yard.

Rangers supporters who care about the standing of their famous club in the eyes of the football world should find considerable cause for thought in this book.

It provides a never before articulated theory to explain the incontrovertible reality that over the past 50 years, Celtic supporters have behaved far better than Rangers supporters on excursions outwith their native shores.

All those Scots, of all religious persuasions and all football allegiances, who have despaired of the vile atmosphere that has poisoned top flight Scottish football for the past century should find much in this book of interest, both in terms of analysis, and in terms of lessons that can be learned from the Celtic Submari experience.

Most of the people involved in the story told in this book can be defined as good, i.e. they unselfishly help others. While this still remains a book legitimately to be classified as a football book, it contains far more descriptions of people and their good actions than descriptions of football games. Football provides the context and the common bond that brought these people together. Football provided a mechanism within which they could focus and channel their goodness into good actions.

This story of how the Celtic Submari were formed and how they have gone on to offer a new model of relationship for football supporters everywhere, was originally due to be one thread in the story of a modern miracle; the remarkable rise of Villarreal CF from being a wee club from a small town of 50,000 people, to become one of the top clubs not just in Spain but in all Europe. However the particular story of the Celtic Submari demanded the telling in its own right as a separate phenomenon from the rise of Villarreal CF. The story of the Celtic Submari can make a major contribution to the debate about how to restore health and vitality to a body riddled with the cancer of sectarianism. So "Celtic Submari" is a book in its own right, and should be seen and read as a companion volume to the "Yellow Submarine - the Miracle of Villarreal CF", also published by Ringwood Publishing.

Celtic Submari   Cast of Characters
Vila-real
The Boixaders
Ernesto, ex player for Villarreal CF   President of Villarreal Celtic Submari
His wife **Maria Dolores** and their two children **Ernest** and **Maria**
His brothers **Jose Manuel**, **Javi** and **Julio** all founder members
His parents **Ernesto Senior** and **Conchita**
Vicente Andreu, founder member, writer, his wife **Marie Carmen**, daughter **Paula** and son **Vicente**
Jose Luis Broch first Secretary of Celtic Submari
Saul Ramos current Secretary
Pepe Mansilla founder member, legend and sports shop owner, wife **Antonia,** and daughter **Laura**
Luis Broch Banker, founder member
Enrique Navarro original Committee member
Vicente Llop original Committee member
Jesus Del Amo Bort   founder member
Estrella, who never stops, brother **Pablo**, husband **Miguel**, sister **Pili**
Sisilia Nuno writer
Angel and Encarnita leading lights
Juanma and Carmen leading lights
Pascual and Monica Broch, sons **Alex** and **Javier**
Fermin and Claudia Font, and father **Jose Maria**, Supporter Number One
Ioan Nelu Bordean Romanian
Key individual members   Ximo, Domingo, Felix, Tofal, Carlos, Javi Vilar, Javi Sales Javi Serralbo, Pedro
All the other members of the Villarreal Celtic Submari

Celtic Supporters
Gerry Martin a key player in the founding of the Celtic Submari
His son **Matteo** and brother **Terry**
In Scotland
Derek Rush and **Damien Kane**
The Carfin Crew - Hope and Willie Wightman, and son **Paul**
Pat and Francis McGorry and daughter **Francesca**
The Hamilton lot - Linda Orr teacher and trailblazer
Tosh McLaughlin   John Ogilvie High School, **Tam McCabe The Abuelo**
Bill Alexander, Mairi McNeill and their children **Liam** and **Caitlin** from Inverness
Richard Fowles Gooner and regular visiter to the Penya
The ten thousand Celtic supporters who went to Vila-real in 2004.
The thousands of Celtic supporters who have proudly mingled with the Celtic Submari since its inception.

Chapter Two Ernesto Boixader

Somewhere in the yet to be written history of Villarreal CF will be a small footnote mention of a young attacking midfielder, Ernesto Boixader, who played for Villarreal CF for three seasons in the mid 1980s, while they were in the Third Division. But it is not his exploits on the Madrigal pitch that have gained Ernesto Boixader his place as one of the true heroes of this book.

"Quite simply, Ernesto is the best man I know." Thus Vicente Andreu put it. You don't have to be around Vila-real long to know that is a judgement shared by many.

Certainly Ernesto Boixader is one of the finest men I have ever met. His goodness shines brightly, illuminating everywhere he goes. It seems that within minutes, everyone who meets him is captivated. Certainly everyone who knows him, loves him. As someone almost totally devoid of the commodity, and glad of it, I have always been suspicious of charm, the immediately appealing but superficial exterior presentation that often glosses over less attractive realities. However Ernesto's immediate attraction is not one of charm but an intense combination of integrity and niceness. Ernesto doesn't have the kind of matinee idol good looks that renders most women vulnerable. Even Maria Dolores, his doting wife, makes jokes that acknowledge he is not the most beautiful man in the world, but he has an attractiveness that shines from the inside out and makes him irresistible to both sexes.

Ernesto was born on the 30th January 1964. He was not actually born in Vila-real. There was no hospital in Vila-real at that time, so Ernesto was born in Castellon. He grew up in the cramped streets of the sleepy town of Vila-real, and has seen it grow markedly in size since his youth. Ernesto is the oldest of four brothers. His parents wanted a daughter but produced four fine sons, Ernesto, Jose Manuel, Javi and the 'baby' Julio. They stopped trying, disillusioned, before they had enough for a great five a side team. Ernesto enjoyed a very happy family life, with loving parents who were god-fearing, churchgoing and proper but not strict. Also both parents were always very committed to charitable efforts, not just the usual church charities but humanitarian ones too, like Manos Unido, a particular favourite of his mother. It is clear that the happiness of his childhood, and the values he absorbed from his parents, have been key ingredients in creating the man he has become.

Through mutual friends he met a young woman Maria Dolores. They hit it off immediately. Ernesto was surprised to find it possible to be in a relationship of affection and trust, but within which he was able to be allowed to spend time with his friends. They set up home together and eventually, 7 years after they met, they were married, in August 1992.

For the last 10 years Ernesto has been a teacher, a job he loves and one at which he excels. With his strong empathy and interest in others, especially young people, it is no surprise he has ended up as a teacher. However he took a roundabout route into this seemingly obvious profession for him. When the time came for him to go to University he did not want to leave Vila-real and his new love Maria Dolores. This from the boy who against his family's wishes insisted on leaving home aged 12. The apparent contradiction can be explained in two words, Maria Dolores. The courses he really fancied, in Physical Education, could only be got in academic institutions too far away from his home for him to continue living there. So he did it the other way round, selected the local University in Castellon and then chose from the courses available there. He took a degree in chemistry, then further studied biochemistry.

After finishing his studies he wanted a job in Vila-real, which meant the Ceramics industry. He worked for Zirconia, one of the more enterprising Ceramics firms. He enjoyed the work but found the hours, often 8am to 9pm, too demanding. Around this time he began tutoring his youngest brother Julio and some of his friends, who were all struggling with their chemistry work for the Baccalaureate. He proved to be a natural as a teacher and the group made great progress. Word of his achievements got around, and he was approached by his current employers and offered a full-time job as a teacher. He knows now that this is the only job for him, one at which even his natural modesty cannot prevent him from acknowledging he is very good.

In the midst of this education and employment history is a year of torture and misery, when he did his national military service in an army base near Betera. He hated that whole experience. The only time I have ever heard Ernesto being negative and critical is in describing the bullying and waste of time involved in that whole experience. Although his natural authority and leadership got him a position of rank, he hated the whole hierarchical structure and was eventually disciplined for treating the men below him as equals rather than directing them as a superior.

Ernesto was football daft from as soon as he could toddle, playing football in the streets from dawn to dusk before graduating onto Football Sala, the Spanish equivalent of indoor 5 a side football. At that time there was no organised football for young children in Vila-real. No structure of youth football of the kind that Villarreal CF have put in place in the past few years, and which would have guaranteed a young kid of Ernesto's ability and enthusiasm, the framework of coaching, training, education and support that would have helped his considerable potential develop to its greatest. Indeed the facilities and possibilities were so sparse, that the young Ernesto felt forced at 12 years of age to make an extremely difficult decision, in order to advance his chances of attaining his dream, of a football career. He made up his mind that he wanted to go to a boarding school, in Cheste some 10 miles south of Valencia, which specialised in physical education. This school did not allow even weekend leave for the first three months, and thereafter only the occasional weekend home visit was permitted, but he saw that as a sad but acceptable price to pay for the education and play opportunities he would receive. Both parents, and most of his wider family, cautioned him against this move, and wanted to keep him closer at home until he was a little older.

When I asked him to tally both his strengths and his weaknesses, stubbornness featured nowhere in either list, but it is obviously a quality he has always had to a highly developed extent. So the 12 year old, who had always been extremely happy at home with his close loving family, insisted on packing his bags and moving away. And ultimately they let him go. Before his school career was over he did return to Vila-real at the weekends, but only to play for the Villarreal CF juvenile team.

His father, also called Ernesto, was a Valencia supporter, had been all his life, and his sons followed in his footsteps and gave their support and devotion to the Ches. So like most of the young boys in Vila-real, Ernesto grew up supporting a First Division team rather than his local side. As a young boy Ernesto seldom saw a real game of football live. He didn't go to Mestalla often, but neither did he often walk the half mile up the road to El Madrigal to see the Villarreal CF play in the Third Division.

His first real contact with his local club was to sign for them as a Juvenile. He developed quickly, starred, and soon worked his way up the limited hierarchy of reserve and youth teams. In those days, the early 1980s, the Spanish Third Division had a version of the SPL under 21s rule that Strachan so disliked. This one stated that every team must start with at least 2 under 20s in its line-up. The good part of this rule from Ernesto's position was that as one of the most promising young players at the club, he was picked for the starting lineup before he otherwise would have been. He made his first team debut aged 18 in the last match of season 1981-82 against Paterna. The bad news was that the coach, having fulfilled his obligations under the rule by starting the under 20s, would, cynically or otherwise, bring them off after 20 minutes to replace then with more experienced, stronger players. Ernesto described how demoralising this was to his confidence. However by season 1982-83, gradually he progressed to the point where he got his place in the side on merit. The turning point was one game where he started on the bench but was brought on early in the second half when his team were losing 1-0. Ernesto scored the equalising goal, then laid on the winner. Thereafter he was a regular starter and finisher in the Villarreal team. That season the Villarreal CF finished 14th in Group III of the Spanish Third Division. The next season, 1983-84, with Ernesto contributing more, they climbed to 13th in Group VI. Ernesto's finest hour and a half in a Villarreal shirt was when he scored both goals in a 2-0 victory over local rivals Burriana. He was on song that day, everything he tried came off. He and his family and friends, really enjoyed that stuffing of the hated 'pig snouts'.

In his fourth season with Villarreal in 1984-85, Ernesto started as a regular in the team. The new trainer, Causinilles, decided that a more professional approach was required and that the days of training only two nights a week had to stop. He instituted a regime of 4 training sessions a week. Ernesto at this time was a student at Castellon University, and he struggled with the implications of Causinilles's new regime for his academic life. He describes it as the hardest decision he has ever had to make in his life. Ernesto's decision was that he could not continue to be a Villarreal player. It was a decision that reduced him to tears for the only time in his adult life. Later of course there would be many more tears, for Ernesto Junior.

When he so reluctantly left Villarreal, Ernesto dropped down a league into the local Regional Preferente, the 5th level, with Almassora, but after leaving Villarreal, football was never the same for him, and his heart was never really in it.

From talking to as many older Villarreal supporters as I could, only some of them his friends, I was able to get an insight into Ernesto the player. I have always believed people show their true character in the way they play football, and Ernesto was no exception to that rule. Ernesto was an honest player, a clean player, a trier, a team player. He had skill, talent, ability, desire, application and a sense of the importance of the team. He also had a sense of modesty that inhibited him from being as good as he might have been.

Like many a proud father, Ernesto's dad had become a season ticket holding supporter of Villarreal while his son played for them, and his socio number is in the low 200s. He continued to be a season ticket holder after his son stopped playing for them, while continuing to maintain an emotional attachment to Valencia. The three younger brothers by this time were also Villarreal supporters. Ernesto started to join them, even becoming a season ticket holder himself when the club were promoted to the Second Division in 1992. Ernesto gave up his season ticket for a while in the mid 1990s when he became a coach with the Villarreal Alevin team, a youth level between the youngest Benjamins and the slightly older Juvenile team. By the time the team got that first promotion to La Liga in 1998, he had stopped coaching and had become a season ticket holder again. Although as a coach he got into the ground for nothing, he still regrets the loss of his low Socio number because by the time he resumed, there were a couple of thousand ahead of him in the numbers allocation. He has remained as season ticket holder ever since, but it was only after Fernando Roig took over as President in 1997 and Ernesto realised he was serious, did he become an emotionally committed regular follower of the side. His St Paul moment of conversion when he realised he was truly a Villarreal supporter came in 1998-99, the first season in La Liga. He went with the team on an away trip to Zaragoza. Villarreal were humped, 4-0, and through the pain and the tears he realised he was Yellow all through. Thenceforth, after that trip to Zaragossa, there was no ambiguity or mixed loyalties, no lingering love for Valencia, he was definitely committed 100% to the Yellow Submarine. His wife Maria Dolores came to occasional games when Ernesto was playing, "just to look at his legs", but it was only in 2006 she too became a season ticket holder.

Chapter Three   Villarreal CF supporters before Celtic Submari, before Roig, and before God

Most of the 25,000 people who form the season ticket holders and other regular watchers of Villarreal CF have only ever seen their club perform in La Liga and the major European club tournaments. And for a town with a population of 50,000 that is an amazing number to enjoy an unprecedented experience for a club from so small a town.

But there is a smaller group of several thousand Villarreal supporters who have had the even more amazing experience of first watching their club in a seemingly lifelong diet of mediocre football in the Regional Preferente, Third Division and Segunda B Divisions, when the greatest dream permitted was to hope for a brief period of promotion to the national Second Division. Then they have watched, entranced, their club ascend from these depths to become one of the top clubs in Spain, the last one to split Real Madrid and Barcelona in La Liga as Sub Campeones. They have also watched their club come within a missed penalty of being Finalists in the Champions League, while establishing itself as one of the top ranked clubs in Europe with 3 InterToto Cup Finals, one Champion League Semi final, and one Semi final and Quarter final in the UEFA Cup in its record. This small group have lived the dream of every supporter of all small clubs throughout Europe and the world, that their little club will one day somehow be transformed into one of the giants of the game.

These Villarreal supporters are a unique group in top class football, and over the next few chapters it is worth getting to know a few of these 'livers of that great dream' in some detail, to get a sense of what such a transformation can do to the human soul. And also to see in this examination, what special qualities they possess that have helped the Villarreal Celtic Submari Penya, which they all subsequently joined, to become so positive a force for hope and good in an often cynical world.

Are the supporters of Villarreal 'better' than other people? Is the success of Villarreal CF a miracle? Has divine intervention played any part in the recent success of the club? Who better, you might think, to answer these kind of quasi theological questions than the man who acts as the official priest of the club, and is also one of their keenest supporters. However it soon becomes obvious in conversation that Mossen Guillermo (Mossen is a title somewhere between Priest, Father and Monsignor) is no ordinary priest. He is of a radical persuasion, and I suspect the only reason he has both stayed in, and been tolerated in, conservative Vila-real is his active love of the football club and the people who support it.

The day I interviewed him, he was sitting outside his house, in one of the narrow Vila-real streets dressed in a bright yellow shirt and check bermuda shorts, with gangster type sunglasses shading his eyes. Given a 100 guesses you would not have pegged him for a priest. He was born Guillermo Sanchis in Picassent, near Valencia in July 1937, making him over 70 years old at the time of the interview. Mossen Guillermo came to Vila-real in 1965 and has been a parish priest there ever since. That means he knows everybody and they all know him. It also means he knows all their secrets and they know he knows. He married several of the Penya members, and through christenings and first communions, weddings, and the second cycle of the same for their children, he knows most of the 1960s generation and their families very well. It should be said they all love him. He is one of them, but also something special and different.

Asked to describe himself for me, he gave me four concepts "happy, faithful, loyal and 'a good sense of humour'" which fitted in well with much that I had heard of him. When I asked him for 3 words that his Bishop might use to describe him, he laughed uproariously and could produce only one, "Rebel", fit for a Bishop to use, and several unfit ones that the Bishop might privately think but could never say out loud.

Among his professional interests are supporting College students and helping people with drug dependency. Among his personal interests are a love of Literature, particularly of the 16th and 17th Century when Spain led the world, Theatre and Music.

But it is football that is his true passion and where he has managed to combine professional duty with personal obsession. Mossen Guillermo played football, passionately, as a young man. He was a right winger as a player, a position that causes him some amusement given his subsequent political leanings. His Uncle played for Valencia, and it was the Valencia club that made first claim on his heart and his affections. He has been associated with the Villarreal football team, on religious duty, since the early days of Font de Mora, a man he obviously admired enormously. Mossen Guillermo gave him support through his long illness and was with him when he died a few years ago. Over the last 30 years Mossen Guillermo has given spiritual support and counselling to the Directors, staff and players of Villarreal, and given passionate support to the football club. It did not take long for Villarreal to replace Valencia in his heart.

One of the fringe benefits of his job is that he gets to travel with the official Villarreal CF party to all away European games. Several of the Submari who have been able to afford this as an occasional treat, like Luis and Jose Luis, have told me how Mossen Guillermo takes this responsibility seriously, acts as a MC on the flights, keeping up spirits with a succession of funny stories and outrageous tales, while providing philosophical and spiritual guidance for the whole party.

With only a small and excusable example of the sin of pride, Mossen Guillermo revels in the fact that he has become an international media star, particularly in South America. Many hundreds of South American TV crews have come to Vila-real over the recent years, drawn first through the Palermo and Belletti super signings; sustained by the continuous further signing of excellent South Americans; and bolstered by the appointment and success of a manager from Chile, famous and successful in Argentina. All these TV crews, and the many more from Europe and North America, have quickly learned that an interview with Mossen Guillermo was a compulsory part of their itinerary.

With his vivid imagery, his facility with words, his radical views on both football and life, and his wicked sense of humour, he never lets them down.

Like all Villarreal fans he has vivid memories of the Compostella promotion night. He uses the words 'suffering' to describe the experience of watching the game, and 'joy' to describe the events after the game. He celebrated it as enthusiastically as did his flock. He has enjoyed the successes of the past 10 years. When I asked him to explain that amazing success for a club from so small a town, he did not give any of the credit to divine intervention or even use the word 'miracle'. He did not claim any of the credit for himself, but admitted to having intervened in some of the struggles to persuade local and regional politicians to do their civic duty by doing right to the club, especially around areas like upgrading the Stadium to its present magnificent state (his words) and facilitating planning and other permissions for the Cuidad Deportiva. He had actively supported the proposal to make Fernando Roig an adopted son of Villarreal, an honour shared with himself.

Mossen Guillermo was clear that the success of Villarreal CF had been very good for the spiritual health of the town. He spoke of older citizens given an interest in life. Given the remarkably high percentage of the town actively involved with the club, as season ticket holders or active supporters, he felt the population were much happier than they would otherwise have been if the club had continued as a minor one. He does not believe in the "Football as the opium of the people" diversion argument, rather he believes that football success has made the whole population happier, and therefore spiritually healthier. When I asked if people were really happier overall because of their football team, he looked at me almost sadly (the shades were off for the interview) and said "Of course we're bloody happy." Without delving too deeply into cause and effect, Mossen Guillermo said that the population of Vila-real are spiritually happier than most other populations, and provided support, based on the evidence of his 35 years there, for my theory that there are a disproportionate number of 'good' people in the town. Mossen Guillermo is no soft idealist, he is well aware of the existence of sin and evil, but he genuinely believes that Vila-real has more than its fair share of goodness, decency, integrity and compassion. And that there was some connection between that fact, and the success of its football club that could not be easily separated into simple cause and effect.

A cultured, highly intelligent and self educated man, Mossen Guillermo is capable of engaging in theological discussions at the highest intellectual and philosophical level, but as a natural populist he likes to keep things simple. He was very keen to stress to me that he has never, would never, ask for divine assistance for the team. He told me parishioners would often ask him, in all seriousness, to "put in a prayer for the team", particularly at keys moments of success or danger. He has developed a standard line of response including a pious statement that of course he would not do so, always adding "God has so much more important things to concern himself with." But I suspect he strongly approves of the statement of his last but one Pope, "Of all the things in life that are not important, football is, by far, the most important."

He gets into all matches free because of his official role with the club and had been indignant when one local radical journalist attacked him as a freeloader, partly because he normally agreed with most of what that journalist wrote. "I have been going since the days when the crowds were very low, and the football was so bad they should have been paying me to go. I earn my free seat." he said, with only a slight trace of defensiveness.

At the end of the interview his phone went, and I recognised that his ring tone was the Champions League Hymn signature tune. That seemed to sum up well the fusion of football and religion in this remarkable man.

Chapter Four   Vicente Andreu Socio 1259

Vicente's book, "El Trebol de Cuatro Hojas" (The Four Leaf Clover), although geared at the older juvenile market, should be of great interest to all Celtic fans, whatever their age. It is about a young Spaniard playing for Celtic. There is a Holy Grail element too in the book. Football and religion, with a dash of thwarted love interest, making it ideal for any young Scottish Celtic supporter. The book might yet be translated into English but is currently available in Spanish via Ringwood Publishing (www.ringwoodpublishing.com). It won a prize in Barcelona in 2009 for the best adolescent novel with a sporting theme.

Vicente was born in 1965 and has lived in Vila-real all his life. He was the eldest of 5 siblings and had a very happy childhood. In typical Vila-real manner, all his siblings and their families live close to each other, still in Vila-real. In 1992 he married Marie Carmen and they have two children, a son also called Vicente and a daughter Paula.

Vicente played football as a boy, and says he was very enthusiastic but not very good. He remembers that facilities were very poor, no grass, only waste ground, filled with stones. And the club at that time only ran one team for boys, restricted to some 15-20 15 and 16 year olds. His father was a Barcelona supporter and Vicente grew up supporting both Barcelona and Villarreal. They were many divisions apart, and all his life they never played each other, so there was no conflict.

Vicente used to go to the Madrigal regularly from an early age, as young as 5 or 6 years of age. He was taken by his grandfather. Although his father loves football, he has never been to a football stadium in his life, he just watches games on TV. When Vicente went first, it was to see Villarreal in their two years in the Second Division, 1970-71 and 1971-72. His abiding first memory is of the brown pitch. His grandfather first took him to the only stand, the Tribuna. This was a small stand, with only 7 or 8 rows but a least it had a little cover if it rained. At that time the main part of the ground was what is now the Fondo Sur, which had a built-up concrete terracing, with no seats. The Fundo Norte had just a few rows, of standing only. Vicente remembers as others do, the half time trek to the other end so they were always behind the Villarreal goal. His grandfather stopped going when Villarreal were relegated back to the Third Division but after some years Vicente started going again, with his friends.

He claims to remember some games when the crowd was measured in tens rather than hundreds. "At some games, there were more players than spectators. There would be the 22 players, 2 journalists, the President and about 20 of us."

Vicente, Jose Luis and their other friends would go to away games too. Vicente in particular remembers a trip, probably in 1982, to Olimpico of Xativa. With Villarreal doing well that season and Olimpico top of the league, 5 buses had gone with some 300 people on them. Villarreal lost 1-0 and the pain was made worse because they had to go to the police station in Xativa after the match because they had lost one of their group, and the bus couldn't leave without him. They hung about looking for him for 3 or 4 hours but it finally turned out he had gone home with another group.

Both Ernesto Boixader and another friend of theirs Mezquita, a defender, had begun working their way into the Villarreal first team after several seasons with the juvenile team, so they watched as they made their debuts, in the Third Division in the early 1980s.

"I met Ernesto for the first time, at school, when I was 4 years old. Although Ernesto was one year older, for a year he, his brother Jose Manuel and me were in the same class. Then Ernesto jumped up a year but Jose Manuel and I stayed in the same class together until we were 9. I have been friendly with Ernesto for over 40 years. It is impossible not to be friendly with Ernesto." Vicente showed me a photo of a party where a very young Ernesto, Jose Luis who has also known them both all his life, and Vicente were celebrating a pal's birthday. I recognised immediately Ernesto and Jose Luis but not Vicente, but we agreed he has improved with age.

Vicente described Ernesto as "a clever player, smart and speedy but lacking strength. He was an attacking midfielder, a bit like Messi", he paused dramatically, "in terms of position only" he added laughing.

With both Ernesto and Mezquita in the first team, Vicente and Jose Luis would go to every game, but around the same time Ernesto abandoned Villarreal, Vicente went to Valencia to University and was unable to come home at weekends to watch his team. He was still living in Valencia when Villarreal finally made it to Segunda B and then in 1992 won promotion to the Second Division. Vicente returned to Vila-real around this time and became a season ticket holder again. The crowds in the Second Division were significantly higher, as many as several thousand people, and the Stadium had been upgraded slightly to reflect their new position as a Second Division club.

Vicente remembers going along to the club's office in Plaza Maior to renew his season ticket, and having Jose Manuel Llaneza himself take his money and write out the new season ticket personally. Vicente and Jose Luis got their season tickets together and have consecutive numbers. Vicente remembers Fernando Roig becoming President and welcoming him as a man with money and business experience. He said there were no major worries that he was an outsider from Valencia. Vicente and his friends were amused rather than anything else by the extravagant promises made by Roig from the start.

He describes the night Villarreal got their first promotion as "unforgettable. It was a Sunday, the last day of the Fiesta in May. There was a great screen in the Plaza Maior. We had dinner in a Fiesta Penya then we went to the square which was full. Canal Nou was present filming the scenes. Alberto scored a great goal, then we hung on defending. We were under pressure all the time after that but finally it was all over, and we were promoted. Unbelievable. Wonderful." "I immediately thought, next season Barcelona will be here, Real Madrid will be here." A relative was in Santiago, watching the match. We phoned him excitedly and said "We saw you on TV." "People were walking in the fountain, climbing the giant statue of the King, Jaume. There were firecrackers and fireworks. My daughter was one year old, loving it, wanted to stay on and on."

Vicente enjoyed the season in the First Division but was clear that Villarreal were not really good enough to survive. Vicente remembers thinking, "We are going back where we belong. It is unthinkable a town with only 50,000 people could maintain a team in the First Division."

"Since we finished 3rd bottom, we had to playoff against Sevilla who had finished 3rd top in the Second Division. They beat us. Vicente remembers that they struggled a bit that season back in the Second Division, but like most supporters he believed they would eventually make it back up. He remembers well the last home against Las Palmas who had already secured promotion. Villarreal played very nervously but eventually got a 1-1 draw which was enough to secure 3rd place and promotion, without a play-off.

There was a party again in the Plaza Maior this second time, but it was not the same. "The first promotion was unexpected. No-one ever expected Villareal could play in the First Division, before Compostela. By the second one it was expected, so psychologically it was different. But there were some similarities, fireworks, much drinking, dancing and singing."

Since that second promotion, Villarreal have been there ever since, have consolidated themselves as a First Division club, and have become a force in Europe. Vicente still finds it hard to take in the scale of the transformation. Vicente is one of the more intellectual and thoughtful of the Villarreal supporters I know, but even he struggled to provide me with an explanation as to how this miraculous transformation happened. The best he could do was to say that the club were "well-managed, like a very successful business." He gave the full credit for this to Fernando Roig and his partnership with Llaneza. "Roig is the brains, the mind, and Llaneza the hands" was how he put it. Vicente also gave credit to the son, Fernando Roig Negueroles, who worked well in partnership with Llaneza. "The three of them know how to manage people as well as issues. And, most importantly, unlike at all other Spanish clubs, they do not do silly things."

Vicente struggled to explain how the club had managed to reach the incredible number of 20,000 season ticket holders. "They don't all come from Vila-real, many are from other parts of Castellon province." Vicente believes that the fact that Villarreal have always played very attractive, attacking football has been an important factor in persuading people from neighbouring towns and villages to give their affiliation to Villarreal. "It is not really glory hunting, because after all we haven't actually won anything, it is about watching good football. The way Villarreal play captivates people".

When I asked Vicente for help in understanding why Villarreal have such a high percentage of women supporters, he surprised me by telling me that when he first became a season ticket holder, nearly 30 years ago, you could bring your female partner into the ground for free. That had been one of the articles of the original constitution of CD Villarreal in 1923, but I had not realised it was still in force 60 years later, despite the club having gone through two transformations since then.

Vicente would take his girlfriend along to games in the early 1980s and his recollection was that about half the males going to games would also do so, adding 50% to the attendance. He does not remember exactly when this stopped, sometime when he had been away living in Valencia. Certainly by the time he renewed his season ticket in 1993 it was no longer the case, but he reckoned that by then the practice was ingrained that many women attended. Vicente's wife has been a season ticket holder for several years, since early in the La Liga years, but not for 2009-2010 "because of the economic crisis".

Vicente had not been too excited by the first couple of years in Europe in the Intertoto Cup, but qualification for the UEFA Cup had really got him excited with games against great teams like Galatasaray, Roma and Glasgow Celtic. Vicente had come to Glasgow in 2004, to see the first leg game against Celtic at Parkhead. He had come with his wife and 2 children, Jose Luis and his wife, and another family. They rented three cars at the airport "and two of them managed to find the hotel no problem!" They stayed in a hotel in Great Western Road and Vicente remembers the hotel staff, all Rangers supporters, wishing them luck enthusiastically before the game. They took taxis right to the front of Celtic Park. At that point Vicente had been a little worried about possible hostility and hooliganism from 'British' supporters. As they stood in a family group just outside the main gate, Vicente noticed this huge fat Celtic supporter wearing the hoops coming right towards him, and remembers thinking, "This is it, the end." But the man just very politely asked if they would swap a Villarreal scarf for his Celtic one. Unfortunately the only Villarreal scarf they had belonged to his then 5 year old son and the boy refused to swop it, saying, not unreasonably, that he had come to support Villarreal and he was keeping his scarf. The big man took this refusal well and insisted on taking a photograph of the family group. As other Celtic supporters saw this taking place, they joined in, and many photos were taken of the Andreu family. Vicente always remembers how moving he found his first experience of the sight and sound of almost 60,000 Celtic supporters singing "You'll never walk alone" with scarves raised. He utilised the memory well in his novel about Celtic.

The UEFA Cup semi-final game was only 40 miles down the road against Valencia. Vicente had decided not to go to the second leg game in Valencia, but a friend had bought him a ticket and pushed him into going. It was as grim as he had feared, with Valencia beating them . "Very sad."

The night they first qualified for the Champions League the party was the closest they have ever come to recapturing the magic of the Compostela promotion night. "Plaza Maior full, party, fireworks, children jumping, wanting to stay up all night, all the players on the balcony of the Town Hall, the crowd singing and chanting, magic night."

Vicente was in Italy when the first leg of the qualifying round against Everton took place, sitting having dinner near Lake Como. Jose Luis Broch was sending him texts every 10 minutes, and one came "Josico has scored". Vicente had never doubted they would dispose of Everton "Our fate had predetermined we would be in the Group Stages" and so it proved. As a long time student of top class European football, Vicente was thrilled when top clubs like Manchester United and Benfica came to the Madrigal for Group Stage games. That Villarreal finished top of the group and Manchester United did not even finish second, was a particular source of pride for him.

Vicente returned to Glasgow in 2006 for the Knockout Round first leg game at Ibrox. The other two times he has gone to away European games he has taken his wife and his two children, but he decided this time that it would be too dangerous to take his wife and children to Ibrox. He described the atmosphere as being entirely different from two years previously at Parkhead, with Rangers supporters showing no friendliness, and a sense of latent hostility all around. He saw no direct violence or active aggression on the away trip, but both he and Jose Luis were shocked by the nastiness and aggression, both verbal and physical, that they saw Rangers supporters exhibit in Vila-real for the second leg.

Another classic moment was meeting and defeating aristocrats Inter Milan in the Quarter Final, with the iconic moment being Arruabarrena's goal in the home leg that secured qualification for the Semi-Finals. Then the semi final games against Arsenal. Vicente went to London for the first Arsenal game with his wife and children, and was fairly confident after it that they would win the second leg and get to the Final. Not that he thought they were robbed in the first game, he acknowledged Arsenal deserved to win. But he did think "We can beat this team." So confident was he, that he told his son that whatever his mother said, he would take him to Paris for the Final. "The second leg was one of the great days in our life, a Champions League Semi-final." An unthinkable dream made reality.

Vicente described Arsenal as a physical team, who came to Villarreal to defend, to get a 0-0 draw. He can't remember much of the game, being in a state of nervous tension throughout, so nervous he can only really remember the penalty. He will never forget the image of his son crying copiously after the match.

When the whistle went for the penalty, Vicente first thought it was the other way, a foul for Arsenal. "I am not sure it was a penalty". Jose Luis beside him, had no sliver of doubt "Penalty!" However as a philosopher by nature, Vicente quickly rationalised that since Villarreal had played much better throughout the match, the penalty was just, and that was maybe even what had inclined the referee to give it. Vicente knew Riquelme was the normal penalty taker and would take it. He instantly had the view, later confirmed by Robert Pires, that the Arsenal players were knackered and extra time would bring Villarreal triumph. He remembers also thinking, all this in a few seconds, "We could beat Barcelona in the Final."

Vicente had thought Riquelme would score. His 7 year old son said "He's going to miss it", but Vicente thought that was just his way of coping with the pain of possible failure. Then Riquelme shot, the keeper saved it, and Vicente's dream was over. In the immediate aftermath, his main thought was to console his broken hearted son who was sobbing uncontrollably, and his broken-hearted wife who was also crying. It was only later his own pain and sadness kicked in.

So when I asked Vicente who his favourite Villarreal player of all time was, I did not expect and did not get the answer "Riquelme". His loyal answer was "Ernesto Boixader", his other answer was the whole hearted Argentinean full back Arruabarrena. When Jose Luis Broch answered "Martin Palermo" to the same question, Vicente tried to dismiss him as the greatest success of Villarreal but only as a marketing ploy rather than a great player, but Jose Luis was insistent. "Palermo was an honest and a great player and it was really unfortunate that Villarreal did not persist and see the best of him."

Chapter Five   Sisi

Sicilia Nuno, known to all as Sisi, began writing her book, an autobiographical novel, about the same time I started writing this book. She finished her book before I finished mine, and a very good read it is. To any readers who can already read Spanish, or are in the process of learning to do so, I would recommend Sisi's book. It is called "Metamorfosis de una Mariposa" (Metamorphosis of a Butterfly) and is a very honest and amusing account of a difficult period in her life. It can be purchased either from Ringwood Publishing in Glasgow (www.ringwoodpublishing.com) or from Spain via the Internet at bubok.es .

I first met Sisi one Friday night in the Celtic Submari Penya. She is a divorced single mum with a 15 year old son she adores. She lives in a flat in central Vila-real that she has decorated in a very positive contemporary manner. Sisi is a strong Villarreal supporter, and has been a season ticket holder for many years. Sisi has such a distinctive voice, and such a unique way of saying things, that I have put in her comments, unaltered, as she produced them. In her words:

"My experiences of and memories with Villarreal C.F. go back many years, to about 1980 or 1981. I have always been a great fan of football. The first team that I followed with enthusiasm and admiration was F.C. Barcelona. The reasons were several, first because I was born and grew up in Barcelona, and second because Barcelona was a team of the first division and in those years Villarreal C.F. was in divisions very inferior, and I only visited this town two weeks in my vacations every summer. In 1980 I came to live in Vila-real, and since then, my great liking for football helped make me a full time supporter of the team of the town, Villarreal C.F.

I still have a first memory of the stadium. We used to go to the Fondo Sur, that great concrete terracing, in which there were no seats, simply one wide stone staircase that rose like a giant edifice towering over the rest of the ground. You sat down on those steps wherever you decided to stop for the game. When the match finished, after two hours with the bum lodged in the cold concrete, not knowing if still you had buttocks or if they had become one with the concrete terrace, you would stand up with a certain discomfort, testing if they continued being of meat and bone and still belonged to you, bemused with the so intense pain that you felt in your noble parts. As for the rest of the ground, it had a small stand, covered with a slight awning, that when early summer came with the last games of the league and the sun began to shine strongly, made you sweat, and in winter it protected you neither from rain, nor from the cold, rather you were frozen. And then there were the other two sides, the Preferencia and the North goal, where concrete terracings did not exist to anything like the same height nor any overhead covering, and simply you had to remain standing up, and if the day were rainy, you got wet without remedy, if you did not wear a good rain-cape with hood, or umbrella. And that is the stadium where the players, Sunday after Sunday, struggled in duels with the opposite teams. There was only a light greenish hue to the pitch, given the baldness of the turf and the brown earth predominating over the green grass in the playing field. In spite of all that, we were many, the fans who went to the stadium to support Villarreal and to spend pleasant times with our team. Although sometimes we returned to our house with more pain than glory, by the following Sunday we were there again supporting our team.

I have a good memory of an occasion, when the Club put on buses, I believe that they were able to fill two, so that we could go to an away game. The displacement was to Novelda (Alicante). My memory is that Villarreal C.F. won and the return trip was quite a celebration, although given my young age, about fifteen or sixteen years, and because I went with celebrating girlfriends, I cannot remember what it was that was at stake, but it had to be something very important by the joy that was present amongst the fans. But what I do remember, to this day, is the muscular legs of the players, and a certain Rafa that was guapísimo (very handsome). At that age my hormones were in the heat of full splendour.

I also remember another very important day, it was the visit of the Real Sociedad who played Villarreal in the Copa Del Rey. There was much sense of expectancy in the town, and the stadium that day was full to overflow. Nothing less than we received the visit of a team of the top division, La Liga!! Everything was an event that day.

It was sunny, it was a Sunday like another anyone, the thing that only could make it different, was that if Villarreal C.F. won at Compostela, they would be promoted to the First Division. The whole town was summoned to meet in the Plaza Maior, where a giant screen had been installed, to allow us all to follow all together the incidences of the game. The day began calmly, but as the hour of kick-off approached, a river of people wound its way to the Plaza and at the arrival of the hour of the game, that square was filled to capacity and not a single soul more could have been fitted in. The hour of kick-off arrived, the referee blew his whistle and the game began. Faces of expectancy, faces of suffering during the game. Things were not tranquil, people protested decisions of the referee, requested freekicks, demanded penalties, to help Villarreal win the game and, finally, the goals arrived. People exploded in a shout, the only one that was heard, the only one that could leave the thousands of throats in unison "GOOOOOOOOOOL!!!!!!. At last, after an eternity of suffering, the end of the game and WE ARE OF THE FIRST DIVISION. The cars sounded their horns, firecrackers were set off, drums were beaten, trumpets were blown, people jumped up and down, everybody kissed everyone else, the euphoric shouts "WE HAVE OBTAINED PROMOTION".

After this great celebratory party, on the following day we continued the celebration, and the Club organized in one of the great avenues of the town, a fireworks display. It was spectacular, beautiful, the sky illuminated in honour of those players who had obtained promotion, and in honour and gratitude to the thousands of fans who had been supporting their team Sunday after Sunday, and in honour of our President Fernando Roig and his team, who had made possible the miracle with their unconditional support and their knowledge and skill.

That same summer, the Stadium of Villarreal C.F. had to transform itself into a stadium that satisfied the requirements of a stadium of the First Division, facilities, turf, stands and terracing with seats. So in record time, our Stadium underwent an impressive transformation. Before it was that one small but closed stadium, and when the new season began there, rising in its place, was the magnificent new stadium of Villarreal C.F. For the inauguration of the new Stadium everyone was present, directors, players, president and the whole support. This inauguration and the presentation of the team for the new season, was closed with the new Hymn of Villarreal CF, that was the emotional high point. The dark sky was illuminated with fireworks and the wind carried to the last corners of the town the sounds and notes of the Hymn that would accompany us in our new adventure in the First Division.

The first year in the Division of Honour was very good. On the Sundays that Villarreal played at home, at the time of the game the town was a swarm of excited people who went to the stadium. In the streets the yellow and blue colours predominated, the colours of the first team of Villarreal CF, and thus we sang our Hymn "El nostres colors son el Blau i el Groc". Unfortunately on the pitch we could not fulfil the expectations. Villarreal was not succeeding, we lost many games, we left the stadium somewhat saddened, but it did not matter, we understood, hope remained in our hearts, and the following Sunday we were there again. As I had expected, Villarreal C.F. could not maintain itself in the First Division, we all understood it. We went back down to the Second Division. It was a hard blow, but necessary so that we realized that everything could not be wonderful all the time, that this is true of football as of life. You cannot relax and think that everything is done, and if you fall you have to rise and to attack with more force.

And that is what Villarreal CF did. They passed like a hurricane through the Second Division and by the end of the following season we were able to rise again to the First Division. The joy returned, the euphoria returned, and this time Villarreal knew how to cope at this level. The team won games, beat Barça, only Real Madrid resisted us. We stayed in the First Division, with the big clubs. And not only that, we were able to enter European competitions, to win the "Intertoto Cup" twice, were placed in the UEFA Cup. Indeed thanks to this competition, the town of Vila-real made contact with the people of Glasgow Celtic. What a wonderful experience, that so many marvellous people accompanied this team, the Glasgow Celtic, when they came to Vila-real. Such was the interaction and bond that was created between the two sets of supporters, that even a Penya (Supporters Club) was born from fans of Villarreal C.F. and the Celtic. A Penya that, apart from football, had a very important purpose, more important than football itself. A Penya that ensured that everything that was collected at the events organized between the two sets of supporters, would be donated to an Association for Children with Cancer. This aspect of the Penya is very important. I am a member of this Penya, I participate in all the events that my time allows me and I am proud to belong to the "Celtic Submari". Proud firstly of all of the work that the Penya does and secondly that so many wonderful people belong to this Penya, beginning with its President, Ernesto Boixader. I think that the hands of a certain personita, from the sky, unites us and gives strength to all the members of this Penya, to proceed with this work and to follow our Villarreal CF, even at the moments at which we feel tired. I believe that we have a Guardian Angel with us.

The Champions League

I was scared to wake up, it could not be happening, Villarreal C.F. with the great teams of Europe. I did not wake up, I was already wide-awake, it was real. The euphoria returned again, more fireworks displays, more celebrations in the Celtic-Submari Penya, more optimism in the streets. Was there more joy now, than when the team was promoted to the First Division? Yes, it was madness, lovely madness. That year the people of the town were made more international than ever. I travelled with the team, I encountered new countries, there came people from other countries to our town, the town was opening itself to a new adventure. Villarreal C.F. had a very good campaign in the Champions League, reaching the Semi Final. I remember with pride and raised hair the first time that I listened to the Hymn of the Champions League played in our Stadium "the Madrigal", the moment in which that gigantic fabric ball was put in movement, carried by the volunteers, in the centre of the field, the moment in which the players of Villarreal C.F. came onto the pitch splendid and proud, to appear before their supporters as players in the elite of Europe, proudly displaying their yellow strips. That yellow that shone like rays of sun in summer, and that turned the cold night of winter into a night warm and full of indescribable emotions.

At the present time, Villarreal CF are still in the First Division, still playing in Europe, continuing to fill the Madrigal Sunday after Sunday with their almost 20,000 season ticket holders, in a population of 50,000 inhabitants. This is magic, this is joy, this is something that helps us all to feel better in the moments of our lives in which we could feel badly. There we have Villarreal C.F. our club, and there Villarreal C.F has us. There we are when we are needed, the Club and the Supporters, the Supporters and the Club.

In this final part, I only want to say that Villarreal C.F. is very important in this town of Vila-real. Thanks to this team, in all Spain and many sites of Europe they know us, know where the town of Vila-real is. The Club has become well known in Europe and in Spain, and all this is thanks to the great work of one person, our President Fernando Roig. I have not had the honour to have been able to ever speak with him. I have only seen him in some official acts and of course in the Stadium following the team every Sunday, but the concept that I have of Fernando Roig, is the one of an intelligent, serious person, who knows what he wants and who has surrounded himself with a good team of professionals. And thanks to his wisdom he has been able to make of a dream a reality, with great personal and economic effort. Thanks Fernando Roig for trusting us and for having chosen this modest town to carry out your dream, that at the same time has become the dream of all of us".

Chapter Six   Saul Ramos Socio 351

You can tell within seconds of meeting Saul Ramos that he is a warm, caring human being who has a natural ability to treat other people well, and believes that is important always to do so. It is no surprise that he is a teacher, who loves his job and does it very well. Whenever I have taken friends from the United Kingdom to the Celtic Submari Penya, it has always been Saul who has been the most attentive to them and their needs. That is partly down to the fact that he is one of the few Penya regulars who feels confident enough in their English to talk to strangers in that language, but more to his caring welcoming nature.

"What a lovely man, that Saul" has been the undisputed general consensus of all these visitors, one shared by the many Celtic supporters who have met him over the last few years.

Saul is slim, slight and looks younger than his years. Saul was born in 1969 and has lived in Vila-real almost all his life. His father died when Saul was only 8 years old, and he and his sister have been brought up by his mother and his Aunt and Uncle, forming an extended household with two cousins. The whole family live in different flats, up what in Glasgow would be termed the same close. Now the Aunt and Uncle have one flat, his mother another, and Saul himself has a small flat above them. This kind of 'same family, several flats up the same close' is quite a common pattern in Vila-real. Even the ones who do leave home do not move far, and visit every Sunday, if not more frequently.

Saul spent all his school years in Vila-real. He started teaching unqualified, easier to do in Spain than in Scotland, but was determined to earn enough to be able to put himself through University and become a teacher. He has been a qualified teacher for over 16 years now, teaching English. As part of his professional training he spent 6 months studying in England, a source of happy memories for him. He currently teaches young adults, and prefers them to the less disciplined and less motivated younger pupils.

He likes teaching, loves the contact with young people, and sees himself being a teacher for all his working life. It was through teaching that Saul got to know Ernesto well. Before that he had been aware of him, through football and his own friendship with Ernesto's younger brother Julio, but it was only as professional colleagues that Saul and Ernesto became really close. Saul is proud that one of his former pupils is Hector Font, one of the first of the very promising footballers produced by the Villarreal Cantera.

Saul has loved football all his life. His father was a Barcelona supporter and Saul can remember him talking positively about Johan Cruyff. When Saul was 6 years old, his father started taking him to the Madrigal. After his father's death, Saul continued to go, and has been a regular attendee at the Madrigal since the age of 10. He first got became a season ticket holder aged 17, in season 1986-87, and has renewed it every single year since then. His current number is 351 and he expects that to fall as older season ticket holders die. Saul is proud of the fact that a cousin of his father was Herrero, the He in FOGHETECAZ as in CAF Villarreal, Club Atletico Foghetecaz. The whole family support Villarreal and his sister and cousin are also members of the Celtic Submari Penya,

When I asked Saul to describe himself, he used words like "honest" and "hard working" which seemed accurate. But he also had enough insight when asked about his defects, to describe himself as "inclined to take on too much responsibility", and "to take things too seriously". Despite this latter self criticism, the Saul I know is always laughing. Replaying the tapes of all my interviews with the Celtic Submari, the interviews with Saul were the ones that rang most with almost continuous laughter. He has that gift, rare in my listeners, of knowing when I am making a humorous remark, and always appearing to find it amusing.

His happiest memory of his early days at the Madrigal was when Villarreal beat Valencia in the Copa Del Rey. Valencia were going through a rare bad spell, were in the Second Division and had brought in Di Stefano as their manager. Villarreal drew 2-2 and eliminated Valencia on a penalty shootout. That year they were eventually eliminated before a record Madrigal crowd, by Real Sociedad, who went on to win the Cup that season. Saul also vividly remembers an away game a few seasons later when they went to Nastic, Tarragona, were under pressure all game, had one shot and won 1-0, but still got relegated that season back to the Third Division.

"I remember Ernesto Boixader as a Villarreal player, a fast right midfielder but not a world beater" Saul said laughing gently. Like Angel he actually has a stronger memory of another Villarreal player of that time, the defender Mezquita, also now a member of the Celtic Submari who took his one year old daughter on the 2005 trip to Glasgow.

Saul still has happy memories of the 1992 promotion to the Second Division and the party that took in the Plaza Maior to celebrate it. He describes that as "the first part of the dream, to play in the second division." Saul enjoyed watching his team in the Second Division even though they struggled most of the time. "It was still a dream come true, to watch them in a national league."

Saul could remember his feelings when Fernando Roig first took over the club. "We doubted him at first, a man from a different city. But he did make it clear that if anyone from Vila-real wanted to take it over, he would stand aside and no-one did, so in the end we thought, yes this could be a good thing." When Fernando Roig, immediately after taking over the club, began to talk of taking Villarreal into La Liga "we thought at first he was drunk. Then when he added the Champions League I thought, maybe this man is mad. But he has proved himself to be neither a drunkard nor a mad man. He has delivered on every promise he made to us. And soon we were living a second dream, as he began signing real good players, for our little club."

Saul was about the only Villarreal supporter I interviewed who mentioned the first Compostella game as well as the famous second one. The game finished 0-0 in the Madrigal, with Compostella missing a penalty, blazing the ball well over the bar. Saul had not been too depressed by that result, knowing a score draw in the second leg would be enough to see them promoted. Unlike most of Vila-real he did not watch the match on the giant screen in the Plaza Maior. Instead he watched the game on a TV set in his mother's lounge along with about 25 family and friends. He still remembers vividly the pain and suffering that ensued after the famous Alberto goal put Villarreal ahead. He remembers "Compostella did all the attacking and after they got one back, everyone knew another one would do it. We suffered and suffered, and it seemed to last forever, but finally the end came and we were promoted." His somewhat hazy recollection of the rest of that night is summed up in one word "Great".

He has three particular memories of that first season in La Liga. In their first home game, Villarreal played Celta. When Villarreal scored, their first ever league goal in the top flight, Saul describes how "The whole place went mad, not just cheering, but shouting, stamping. What a racket, it seemed to last for ages." No-one really seemed to care when Celta equalised and the game finished all square.

Then there was the trip Saul made, along with 6000 other Villarreal supporters, to the Nou Camp on 13th December 1998. Like many of the Villarreal supporters Saul had grown up supporting Barcelona as his "Big team". But by then, 1998, "suffering had conquered my soul and I knew I was a Yellow Man through and through, no contest, no divided loyalty". He tells the story of how "Barcelona supporters near us were saying 'you have to help us'. I didn't realise what they meant until they explained they hated Van Gaal (the Dutch manager of Barcelona) and wanted him out. When Villarreal got our first goal 6,000 people cheered. When we got our second goal 12,000 people cheered and when we got our third goal the whole crowd cheered. It was surreal."

The third memory was less pleasant. When on-loan goalkeeper Palop made a terrible mistake to cost Villarreal a 2-1 defeat against Alaves, Saul knew they would be relegated even though there were 7 more games to go. Saul was not hopeful that they would make a swift return but when he heard Fernando Roig telling all the supporters at the start of the next season, "Promotion is going to happen again. I have made some mistakes but I have also learned how to solve them", he suddenly knew they would be all right. Once again the man proved right, and Saul has never worried about relegation ever since.

Chapter Seven   Pepe and the other Mattress makers
Pepe Mansilla

It is a mistake generally to be avoided, to lumber any one individual with all the claimed key characteristics of a whole species. But there are exceptions to every rule and Pepe Mansilla is an exception to almost every rule. If one of the central theses of this book is that there is a special gene of friendship abroad in the Vila-real population, then the best personification of that claim is probably Pepe Mansilla, known in Vila-real and the environs of Celtic Park as "the legendary Pepe Mansilla".

I wondered at first if Pepe's joviality was forced. Surely no-one can be so relentlessly friendly and cheerful all the time. But I know now, having observed it never let up in three years, it is natural. He is a man who truly lives his own philosophy of friendship, to everyone he meets. Certainly it is impossible to fail to engage with Pepe's enthusiastic personality and be welcomed immediately as a new friend.

Pepe is always voluble in his regular claim that for him "friendship is the most important thing in the world" although if his wife and daughter are anywhere within earshot he will quickly add "after family, of course". Pepe claims that he has always been interested in the concept of friendship. When he was 10 years old, he wrote a poem on friendship containing the immortal lines "friends for today, tomorrow, next week and always", which he claims Ernesto Boixader plagiarised for his "Friends Forever" Submari slogan. At the slightest invitation, Pepe will recite this whole poem, usually from on top of a bar counter. But unlike many other frequent talkers, Pepe Mansilla lives his words. Interviewing the Celtic supporters who have had encountered the Celtic Submari on their trips to Glasgow, they all of course know, and respect, Ernesto. But while all the other regulars of the Celtic Submari crew, Saul, Angel, Jose Luis, Vicente, Domingo, Pascual, Monica, Juanma, Carmen, Encarnita, Estrella and the rest are known by some, there is only one other Celtic Submari member known to everyone, and that is Pepe Mansilla. - 'The wee guy', 'the legend', 'the one who never stops talking or drinking'.

The "Four faces of Pepe Mansilla" photos will generate recognition in many, revive happy memories for others. Or frightening ones perhaps, in those who tried to keep up with him. Gerry Martin, no slouch on the binge-drinking front, describes Pepe as "the only man I am scared to drink with. I tried to keep up with him one session and my liver was calling me names for a week afterwards."

Pepe is another, if probably the youngest, of the generation, born over 40 years ago that have lived in Villarreal all their life. His parents first came to Vila-real, for their honeymoon, because a close relative lived there. They liked it so much the family moved here. Pepe was the first born, to be followed by a sister and then a brother. His father was an administrator in the Medical Centre. Pepe described it as a very happy family background.

Pepe was good at football as a boy and played for Castellon Juveniles, the top youth team in the club, between 8 and 14 years of age. He also played for one season with the top Villarreal youth team. At that time Villarreal did not have a range of youth teams, and no teams at all for those players who outgrew the youth system. Pepe campaigned to change this but the then President Font de Mora did not see it as an affordable priority so Pepe formed his own team, Vila Aficionados. It was geared at giving a game to those players like Pepe himself who would otherwise have been lost to the game because Villarreal had no reserve teams for them to play in once they were too old for the Juveniles. According to Pepe, the team were pretty good and did well at a local regional level. When Fernando Roig took over in May 1997, he engaged in a process of consultation with people in the village about what the priorities might be. At one meeting, after everyone else had been overly polite to him, Pepe had taken the floor and said "Fine if you are Real Madrid, and want to get rid of a player, there will 50,000 others wanting to take his place. But here, 50,000 is the total population of the place. You need to work hard to ensure the Club has enough young people to replace them". Roig seemed impressed with the set up Pepe had created and bought over Pepe's club for the grand total of nil pesetas. "No money changed hands but I was just glad Roig recognised that I had been filling a vacuum". According to Pepe, who might not be the most unbiased witness, his team became the nucleus from which Villarreal B were formed, and the rest is glorious history.

Pepe went to local schools, most latterly with the Carmelitas. He attended the Francesc Tarrega school later to pair up with John Ogilvie High of Hamilton. He left aged 17 and studied accounting at a local college, following in his father's footsteps. However to his father's distress, he did not wish to become an accountant, and by the time he was 19 he started up a Sports shop in Vila-real with a friend, borrowing the equivalent of 6,000 euros as his initial investment. His partner was a fellow player with Vila Aficionados. Pepe claims he and his partner have never had a single argument. The shop was an instant success and he has owned it and worked full time in it ever since. He loves the job, mainly because of the opportunities to talk to people. He also claims that in over 20 years he has never had a row with a customer. Even with the most obnoxious or agitated customer, he uses calm words to talk them round. On his skill in handling customers, he compared himself to one of his beloved bullfighters, "Dodging from the right, ducking from the left, staying on my feet, and winning them over." Normally the shop is proud to display Celtic jerseys prominently but Gerry managed to persuade him to put them out of sight during the visit of Rangers fans. Pepe had refused to believe that his windows might have been smashed, until he heard what happened to the Villarreal team bus. A few years ago Pepe married a beautiful local girl Antonia, and has a five year old daughter, Laura, to whom he is obviously devoted.

Pepe's father had grown up as an Atletico Madrid supporter and passed on this affiliation to his son. Pepe always remembers an old Spanish cartoon with a father and son, both in Atletico colours. The son asks the father "Why am I Atletico?" and the father says "Because I am Atletico." In Spanish it is a witty pun about being athletic, but it summed up a truth for Pepe who idolised his father. On settling in Vila-real his father adopted the local wee team. Pepe's father, now aged 65, is still a Villarreal season ticket holder. He took Pepe to watch Villarreal from when he was about 7 years old. Pepe has been a season ticket holder most of his life. However he no longer buys a season ticket. Since his shop pays quite a lot of money to the club as part of Llaneza's marketing initiatives, he gets free admission. "I no longer buy specific advertising for the shop. It is now too dammed expensive. I have stayed Third Division level while the club has become First Division, but I still contribute to the general pot, so I get corporate hospitality and free entry".

Pepe was a right back, and is still built a bit like a slim Bobby Shearer. How good was he? I asked. "Good enough to play for Celtic" he told me straight-faced. "I played the British way rather than the Spanish way, more physical. Now defenders have to play football, I would have been lost." I took from that, confirmed by others, that he had been a dirty bastard, well worthy of the Shearer comparison. After playing with the Aficianados for several seasons, he took over as a coach/trainer but that stopped with the Roig takeover.

The day before the Compostela promotion game in 1998, Llaneza came to him and ordered 50 Villarreal flags for those going to the game. Llaneza also suggested Pepe should sell scarves to all those who were going to watch it in the main square. Pepe took this advice and sold over 1,000 in that one day. And all the remainder he had, he sold the next day to the people going in convoy to the airport to greet the returning heroes. Before that day there was no real tradition of scarf wearing in Villarreal, but since that day it has become the norm and scarves have stayed one of his staple items.

Pepe as a natural party man had one of the great nights of his life celebrating that first promotion; much partying, much drinking, much dancing.

Pepe is not the only Villarreal supporter who grew up as a "Colchonera" (mattress maker) as Atletico fans are generally known. Others include one of the grand old men of Villarreal and two of the original starting eleven of the Celtic Submari Penya

Juan Luis Botelha Socio Number 6

When I interviewed Juan Luis Botelha, who had been described to me as one of Villarreal's most passionate and most knowledgeable supporters, I was delighted to find that Juan Luis has converted his ground floor room into a veritable shrine to Villarreal CF. This one was equipped with a wealth of material to satisfy my lust for knowledge about the Club. Juan Luis gave me books, articles, photocopied newspaper reports, photographs, even most wonderfully a video of season 1998-99 that allowed me to feel I had been there then. He was born in July 1940 in a small town called Montanar. He spent some of his early life in Toulouse in France but settled in Alcoy before moving to Vila-real for good over 40 years ago. He spent his working life in the construction industry, which meant he was always fit. Since retiring he has made a point of keeping fit and every day he runs 8 kilometres in the morning. He married in 1965 and had two children, Yolanda and Juan Luis. He now has two grandchildren, one of whom has a cultured left foot and plays for a youth team at a good standard. He comes across as a serious thoughtful person, who has a good respect for other people, with a dry sense of humour. According to his wife, he is stubborn, devotes too much time and mental energy to football, and is an incorrigible ladies' man, although he assures her and told me, that he never goes beyond mild flirtation, at least now he is in his late 60s.

Juan Luis always was a football fan as a boy. He has been a season ticket holder at Villarreal for over 40 years and has a very low number, 6, of which he is very proud. When he started supporting Villarreal, they were in the Third Division. He remembers well the promotion to the Second Division in 1970 and how the club proved incapable of sustaining itself at that level, returning quickly to a further 20 years of lower fare.

His recollection of the size of crowds at Third Division games is higher than of most other people, claiming that crowds of up to 2000 were not unknown if the team was doing well, and never went below several hundred. He showed me a series of photos demonstrating the massive changes in the Madrigal over the past 50 years, some of which appear in the Yellow Submarine book.

When Villarreal won promotion to La Liga he said "I could die happy now". He described how the whole town went crazy that night and the next few days. He felt a deep sadness when it only lasted one season. He remembers the second promotion party in 2000 being a more sedate affair. Since then life has been "wonderful" but he has no desire to die yet. He was not able to provide any reasons for the 10 years of success other than to heap praise on Roig and Llaneza, both of whom he has got to know quite well over the past decade. He is not a hero-worshipper by nature, and does not offer them uncritical acclaim, but even so he admires them both, and knows they are the architects of the success without understanding exactly how they have done it. "They know the correct direction" he concedes. He is a great admirer of Riquleme the player and does not blame him at all for 2006. "How can we be disappointed at a semi final place in our first attempt" he says displaying impatience for those greedy for more and blaming the wee Argentinean for failing to deliver it. "He was our star player that season, a great player, one of the best in the world." Unlike some of the Riqulemistas in the town, Juan Luis has come to terms with his loss and thought that the team that did so well to be runners up - "Who would have believed it?" - could yet have further success in the Champions League.

Enrique Navarro

Enrique is another child of the mid 1960s, born just a few months after Ernesto whom he has known almost all his life. His father was an Atletico Madrid supporter, and Enrique took this identification from him. But his father also would occasionally go along to the Madrigal in the bleak Third Division days and his young son can remember begging his father to take him. At last, his father agreed and a very young Enrique was thrilled to be attending his first football match, even if it was in the Third Division. After 5 minutes, Villarreal made a terrible defensive mixup and went 1-0 down. Furious, his father decided to storm off home and despite all his desperate protests, his son was dragged away with him. Within 5 minutes of leaving the ground they were back in the comfort of their home. His father did return to later games with his son, and then Enrique went on to become a regular attender in his own right.

Enrique tells of the poor state of El Madrigal and how there was only a slight fence between the spectators and the side of the pitch. He used to be one of those ruffians who would occasionally spit at the near side linesman if his decisions went against Villarreal. Despite this interesting diversion, his favourite position in the ground in those days was the Fundo Sur, with its concrete terracing.

Enrique was a good student and went on to develop a successful career in computing, and new technology, and is currently a Managing Director of a small IT firm. He has two children, a son and a daughter, and is that rare thing in Vila-real, a divorced man. He has dark hair and the face of a romantic gypsy, and there is generally a smile paying around his lips.

Enrique is at a loss to explain the success of Villarreal, although he gives great credit to Llaneza as "very good at directing the club, very important to its success". Enrique knows that not even being the capital of Castellon Province and not having the power of mass media behind them, it has been something of a miracle that Villarreal have been able to compete with the big clubs of Spain. How they have been able to become one of the big clubs is a miracle too far for explanation, but one he is prepared to keep enjoying.

Luis Broch

Born in 1968, Luis is another who has lived in Vila-real all his life. A Bank Manager, he knows Llaneza and most of the players professionally, but was careful to maintain professional discretion. Luis claims he has a memory of the 1970 promotion to the Second Division, which lasted two seasons. Although he was only two years old, he swears he can remember waiting for the coach to come back with the victorious team. He started going to the Madrigal in the mid 1970s, as a 6 year old with his father. The Club was then stuck in the Third Division or worse, the Regional Preferente. Luis memory is that the club were getting crowds as low as 500, at most 2000. One of Luis stronger memories of these early games, was that the crowd was so small that they were all able to change ends at half-time to move behind whichever goal Villarreal were attacking, almost always Fondo Sur first half, Fondo Norte second half. He got his first season ticket in 1984 aged 16 but didn't renew it every year and lost his original place in the number queue. When he got his season ticket in 1995 it was around number 3,000.

Like all his generation, one of his happiest memories was being in the Plaza Maior, with most of the population of the town, the night Villarreal drew with Compostella and finally won promotion to the First Division. He describes it as "an outcome beyond my wildest dreams as a child." Luis did not expect Villarreal to survive in La Liga, but he remembers being impressed with Roig's assurance after the relegation that the mistakes had been learned from and the club would come again.

Luis enjoys being a Villarreal supporter. He feels the journey he has made from watching behind the goals at a Regional Preferente game as a young boy, to jetting around Europe on the official plane or with the Celtic Submari, has been a fantastic voyage. He still has painful memories around the Riquelme penalty, and sometimes gets disappointed at the quietness of the Madrigal crowd and the lack of vibrant atmosphere there. He was entranced by his trip to Celtic Park in December 2008, and would love to see and hear some of that atmosphere at the Madrigal. "That is one area where we can definitely learn from Celtic supporters. The atmosphere at Celtic Park, the attitude of the crowd, is immense."

However Luis is very positive about the future of the club. As a man whose profession is money, he does not see Villarreal as having serious financial problems. He thinks the Villarreal B team will be a net earner for the club and while he recognises Roig can no longer take money out of Pamesa as he did in the early days of his Presidency, he reckons he is such a shrewd and forward thinking businessman that the future is assured. He knows the assets of the club, including the Cuidad Deportiva and the playing staff, are hundreds of million of euros more than when he first began watching the team.

Chapter Eight Other pre Roig Socios
Angel Socio 1532

Angel is the big solid dependable one in the Submari. Built like a colossus, and always working like a Trojan, he always reminds me a little of Boxer, the horse in Animal Farm whose broad shoulders were capable of carrying any burden. Angel was not born in Vila-real. His father moved to Villareal when Angel was two, to work, but liked it so much he stayed for the rest of his life. Angel is married to Encarnita, who along with Maria Dolores is one of the natural leaders of the women of the Celtic Submari. Their two children are now in their early twenties. Angel grew up with the 'Big Team Wee Team' syndrome, supporting Real Madrid as well as 'wee' Villarreal. He used to go to the Madrigal often. He has been a season ticket holder continuously since the mid 1990s, with his current number 1532. He is annoyed that he had a few years break which lost him a much lower number. Angel knew Ernesto, had played football against him in company games. But at that point they were not close. Angel does remember him playing for Villarreal, as did another of Angel's friends Mezquita, who impressed him more.

Angel has vivid memories of the night Villarreal first won promotion to La Liga. He watched the game leaning against a palm tree on the main square the Plaza Maior, where a giant screen had been set up to cater for the many thousands who thronged there. He used a complicated metaphor involving vividly feeling like a chicken skin, which best translates as remembering the feeling of the hairs on the back of his hand standing up when Alberto scored the crucial goal and staying up all the way to the final whistle. Angel was one of the people who piled into their cars and went to Valencia airport, to ensure the team was well-received on their return. He spoke of the sense of excitement around the airport, and of the delight of the players at so many of their supporters making the effort to be there for them. Then there was the fabulous convey of honking cars that escorted the team bus back to Vila-real to the Plaza Maior "where it seemed the whole village had turned out to greet their returning heroes". Angel vaguely remembers that the party went on for another whole day and night.

Villarreal's first game ever in La Liga had particular resonance for Angel since it was in Madrid against his own "Big" team Real Madrid. The Agrupacion of Penyas had made arrangements for two special trains to make the journey and Angel as the President of one of the bigger Penyas was in charge of one of the trains. Both trains were fully filled with excited Villarreal supporters. Before the trains were halfway to Madrid, all the beer and other drink brought in ice packs was finished. Angel remembers that someone had got on the train wearing a Real Madrid shirt, but Angel, in charge of ticket distribution for the game, refused to give him one.

From the station, some 4,000 Villarreal supporters had marched in unison to the Bernabeu. In Spain, they do not do away games, so this was quite an unprecedented sight for the Madrid natives. Angel remembers the Madrid police, on horse back, taking the piss out of the country yokels, saying things like "That'll be the whole village here then, who's left looking after the sheep?"

Any residual feeling Angel might have had for Real Madrid disappeared quickly into the match "I watched in growing disgust as the Real Madrid players bullied the referee, and so blatantly thought they had an inherent right to every decision going in their favour. I was disgusted by their arrogance and their contempt and from then on, I lost all affection for Real Madrid and knew that only Villarreal was the club for me". Even a 4-1 drubbing didn't spoil the experience, and the return journey was just as happy and memorable, and better stocked with alcohol.

Angel didn't get too sad as the season progressed and it became clear that the team would be going back down after only one season in the sun. But he was not one of those who never doubted there would be a quick return, he was more in the "At least we got one year there" camp.

The great sadness for him as a Villarreal supporter was the Riquelme penalty miss. But despite the sadness and the pain, Angel did not blame Riquelme. He was philosophical "Sometimes you score, sometimes you do not. Sometimes you con the goalkeeper, that time Riquelme did not." Angel had firmly believed before the second leg that Villarreal would beat Arsenal and get through to the Final. He made arrangements before the Arsenal game to go to Paris for what would be the greatest day of his life. Although broken hearted he and a few others had decided since the arrangements were made and fares paid he might as well go anyway. The trip had cost him 1300 euros. Which was still less than the 1500 euros he had spent going on the plane with the official Villarreal team party to Manchester. An expensive season but he did not grudge it to see his team so successful in the Champions League. And he still believes one day they will make the Final.

Angel's wife Encarnita, although now one of the keener and more active members of the Celtic Submari, used to hate football and used to give him regular aggro for the time he spent on it. Even when they were promoted that first season in 1998-99, she refused to join in. However when she saw him continuing to support them back in the second division, and not getting into any trouble, she decided to start coming along to games with him and their two children, and very quickly became hooked, to the point she really celebrated the second promotion in 2000 and then signed up herself as a season ticket holder for the next season, back in La Liga. She has become both enthusiastic and knowledgeable ever since, as well as a very active member of the Penya. When asked if he had any explanation why Villarreal have the highest % of female season ticket holders of any Spanish club, indeed probably the world, Angel cited Encarnita's conversion as typical and told of a massive culture shift in Villarreal. "15 years ago, watching football was an anti-social habit and those who wished to do so were banished to the kitchen and the smaller television, while the majority of the family would watch a film on the bigger TV in the main lounge. Now throughout Vila-real this has changed, and if a minority want to watch a film rather than the football, they are banished to the kitchen, but in most families in the town almost everyone, from the oldest granny to youngest baby, prefers to follow the football".

Jose Luis Broch Socio No 1258

Every organisation needs a member like Jose Luis Broch – solid, reliable, dependable and efficient. If Jose Luis is given an important job to do, as he frequently is, he can be totally relied upon to carry it out promptly and perfectly. If he is not given a job to do, he can be relied upon to find something important to do, and do it quietly and efficiently. He is always there, quiet, available, and always, enjoying himself.

Jose Luis was born around the same time as Ernesto and Vicente Andreu and has known both all his life. They grew up together as close friends, a Vila-real version of the three Musketeers. Jose Luis and Vicente would always go to watch Villarreal together, so they share the same memories and the same stories. They have kept this double act up all their lives and even today their season tickets have consecutive numbers, with Jose Luis always making sure he keeps the lower one. Jose Luis is one of those people of whom Mossen Guillermo can say "I married that man". Jose Luis has two children from that marriage.

Jose Luis has loved the glory years of the past decade. Having suffered all his childhood and thereafter in the third division, he has revelled in success in La Liga and Europe. He really thought the dream was going to come true and that Villarreal were going to win the Champions League in 2006. When the penalty was awarded against Arsenal, he knew it in his bones. Unlike Vicente who was sitting nearby, Jose Luis had been in no doubt that it was a penalty. When Riquelme missed it, he felt "Jodido", a phrase perhaps best left untranslated. He stated "I passed from Heaven to Hell in a second."

Jose Luis has happy memories of his first visit to Glasgow in April 2004 with his family to see the first leg at Parkhead, but less happy memories of the visit two years later to Ibrox. On the first visit they had met several groups of Rangers supporters and they had all been friendly and wished them luck. But not the second visit. Jose Luis still shakes his head when he talks about the Rangers supporters who came to Villarreal in 2006. He talks about the ones who charged the bus, with disbelief still in his voice. "Incredible, absolutely incredible". He had never seen such naked hate and aggression.

Jose Luis went to Milan for the Inter game, but his strongest memory of the trip is of Tam O'Hare, the Abuelo, the grandfather, drinking beer, lots of beer and for once, getting drunk. Jose Luis claims he is learning English with his principal teacher being the Abuelo. He attends the classes run by the Penya. He always maintains he speaks no English but like many Spaniards, this claim obscures a far better grasp of the language than he confesses to.

Ximo, Socio 1526

Ximo is a solid, serious man, whose religion is very important to him. He has lived in Villareal 46 of his 47 years, his parents moving to Vila-real from a neighbouring village when he was one year old. Both parents were very religious and Ximo grew up with religion a very important part of his life. He studied at a Carmelite College for his secondary education. He went to a seminary aged 17 and almost became a priest before going onto University where he did a degree in mathematics and psychology. His wife of 29 years marriage is a teacher in religious studies. They have a 15 year old son who attends the English school in Vila-real. Like many of the population of Vila-real, Ximo works in the Ceramics industry, for Zirconio, where he is a middle manager, having worked his way up from the shop floor. Other family members, including one of his two brothers, also work for Zirconio.

His family, including his father and grandfather, were all Valencia supporters so Valencia became his big team from an early age. From when Ximo was about 8 years old, his grandfather began taking him to the Madrigal to watch Villarreal. He saw them initially in their brief two year spell in the Second Division but his main memories are of the long grey spell in the Third Division. Ximo remembers average crowds of about 300, and he too remembers fondly first halves watched behind the South goal, followed by the long half-time hike up to the North end for the second half. His grandfather lived to be 98 years of age and remained a Villarreal season ticket holder to the end. Ximo became a season ticket holder at an early age and has remained one ever since. His wife and son are also season ticket holders, his wife from the late 1990s (Socio No 5760) and his son from as soon as he could walk.

Ximo remembers Ernesto Boixader playing for Villarreal. He was not a personal friend of his at the time, so claims his scoring of a 7 as a player on a 1-10 scale is an unbiased view.

Ximo had been one of the few people in the whole of Vila-real who had been working during the second Compostela game, but he listened to it on a radio at his work, where nobody had really believed they would get promotion. After work finished, he had hurried over to the Plaza Maior, very happy, to take part in the unforgettable all night party.

Ximo described his conversion toVillarreal as his main team in arithmetical terms, befitting a maths graduate. He said that until Villarreal were promoted he had been maybe 80% Valencia 20% Villarrreal, but from that first season in La Liga he had switched to 80% Villarreal, 20% Valencia. By the time the two met on La Liga business he knew he was 100% Villarreal.

Ximo had not been surprised the team were relegated in their first season. "The players were just not up to it, not good enough" he remembers. He remembers believing Roig when he publicly said "Regressaremos" (we shall return). Ximo has enjoyed the last ten years immensely, as Villarreal confirmed themselves as a top club in La Liga and began to conquer Europe, "All as Roig had promised us in his first few days and weeks."

Like many Villarreal supporters, Ximo's saddest memory of this time was the Riquelme penalty. "I was standing exactly behind the goal. I saw Riquelme's face clearly as he bent down and put the ball on the spot. I knew he would miss, you could just tell from his facial expression." Despite his enormous respect for the man, Ximo does not go as far as Mossen Guillermo and believe the miss was a deliberate part of a massive UEFA conspiracy to prevent an all Spanish final. Ximo was behind the goal with his wife and son. All three of them took it badly.

His wife took it hardest of the three of them. Ximo had thought Villarreal would beat Barcelona in the Champions League Final, so he believes the penalty miss cost them the trophy. "I am certain of it. We would have beaten Barcelona. See how they struggled to beat a ten man Arsenal. We would have won the Final."

Chapter Nine   Some other Villarreal supporters
Estrella, a true star

Estrella is a genuine pulsating force of nature. While everyone else in the Penya or the bar is standing, or sitting, Estrella will be dancing. She is one of these very rare creatures for whom the much misused word 'continuously' is appropriate, as in "Estrella dances continuously". And often throws in raucous singing and chanting as an added bonus. Always with a smile on her face, often a wicked smile. I don't think I have ever seen her still. She does not do still, she does perpetual motion, and she does it well.

Estrella was born in 1965, to parents who both supported Villarreal. Her mother was the keener of the two, having been an active supporter from the age of 14.

Her parents moved to Castellon to live, so Estrella grew up there with her sister Pili, and did not have much opportunity to watch Villarreal as a child, although she always, thanks to her mother, followed their progress with interest. But she was in Villarreal the night in 1998 they clinched promotion. She describes it as one of the best nights of her life, partying, drinking and dancing until well after dawn. She cannot remember too much of the detail, but she remembers the pride and the enjoyment. When she eventually awoke late the following day she discovered her legs were all bruised, and she had to be reminded that she had ended the night "pushing cars, dozens of them" as part of the general euphoria. She signed up for a season ticket for the first season in La Liga and has been an active supporter for the past 12 years. Estrella was one of the 6,000 who went to Barcelona that first season. She describes a whole fleet of over 60 buses leaving the town, an unforgettable sight. She remembers Barcelona fans asking if the whole village were there, and saying with grudging praise "the village shakes" so animated were the Villarreal supporters. She was very sad when Villarreal were relegated at the end of that first season. "But not too sad, for too long, because our President Fernando Roig, promised us we would go straight back up, and I believed him, and knew he would deliver."

Estrella had been very disappointed in 2006 in losing out to Arsenal in the semi-finals. She went to Highbury and had been very impressed with the stadium and the experience of watching a game there. "One minute we were surrounded by houses, the next minute there was this great stadium." She had felt confident Villarreal would beat them in the second leg. She told how she cried when Riquelme missed the penalty, and said many of the people around her were crying too.

She said Riquelme was not a nice man, not a good personality, and that he had not been good to either the club or the fans. She compared him very unfavourably to Josico whom she knows well, and loves. Josico had danced with her several times, at the Penya, at Alaska and most recently when he was back in Villarreal for the game between his current club Las Palmas and Villarreal B.

Estrella was very proud that her niece, Pili's daughter Paula, was playing with one of the Villarreal youth teams. She was doing well and had recently been picked to represent the Valencia Community team at her level. Paula had wanted to wear her Villarreal top that day, and been upset they wouldn't let her. Eventually a solution was agreed where she was allowed to wear Villarreal CF underwear. I asked Estrella, and Pili and Claudia who were there with her, to explain why so many women watched Villarreal compared to other teams. They felt it was something to do with Vila-real being a village still, with a very strong sense of community identity. All were definite Vila-real was definitely still a village, not a town and definitely not a city. Everybody felt a part of everything important that happened in Villarreal, and the football club was the most important thing that was happening. So the whole family would go to the games, babies, children, parents, grandparents, and everyone felt a part of the miracle that was happening around them.

Estrella actually still lives in Castellon, where she and her husband run a bar, but feels emotionally part of Vila-real. She keeps a ball signed by all the Villarreal players in a prominent place in the bar, which doesn't please all her regular customers. "The Castellones always wanted to throw rocks and stones at anyone from Vila-real." Estrella does not hide her affiliations, which must make life hard in hostile Castellon. Maybe that is why she is always on the move, dodging imaginary rocks.

Her other brother, Miguel, lives in Mexico where he formed the Mexican Villarreal Penya, the Amarilla Taquilla Grocs. One game he promised them all tacos every time Villarreal scored, from that point on they all became ardent Villarreal supporters.

Domingo   Socio Number 4000 mas or menos

Many Celtic supporters will have a sharp recollection of Domingo, from the time he turned up at Celtic Park in April 2007 wearing a red toreador's outfit. That can only have happened once, so if you remember it, that was Domingo you saw. Domingo is one of the few males who can even try to compete or keep up with Estrella, in terms of perpetual motion and positivity of outlook. He will dance with her in the Penya but always gives up before her. He spent one year in London as a young man, but claims he only speaks English, "a very little". However he always tries to talk to me about football and we generally can make ourselves understood on that universal subject.

In some ways Domingo is the most 'Scottish' of the Penya members, in that he drinks a lot and often gets drunk when he does so. Not in any bad or problem way, just much more like an average Scottish footballer supporter than most of the Penya members, who drink all right, but who stay sober most of the time and never seem to get drunk. The Vila-real pattern of drinking seems more sensible than the Scottish one.

Although the same age, mid-forties, as most of Celtic Submari males, Domingo is not one of the 'lived all their life in Vila-real' crew. He was born and brought up in Gandia, an hour south of Valencia and came to Vila-real aged 23, through his work as a telephone engineer with Telefonica. He has lived happily in Vila-real for the past 20 years with his wife and his daughter, now aged 14.

When he arrived in Vila-real, the team had just been relegated from the Segunda B Division (third level) to the Third Division(fourth level) but Domingo signed up to support them anyway. His first two years as a supporter saw successive promotions, and when they reached the Second Division in 1992-93, he became a season ticket holder, and has remained so ever since. Domingo got into games free, early on, as a technician/cameraman with a small TV channel Canal Treize, which has long since disappeared. He remembers celebrating promotion from Third to Segunda B against a Mallorca team. For him that was the best celebration, other than the night they clinched the first promotion to La Liga. He remembers banners, flags, singing, Fiesta, but little detail, since he ended up very drunk.

His best memory is "The day people got their eyes opened, 3-1 in the Nou Camp, that first season in La Liga". Domingo had supported Barcelona since he was a child but felt no conflict that magical day. He was one of the ones who made the trip to Barcelona in a fleet of buses and according to him, he was the happiest of the whole 6,000, in what he still describes as the best day of his life. According to Domingo there was a party even when they got relegated, at the end of that first season. He totally believed Fernando Roig when he said they would come back. "In one year we will return." The party was special because of that belief. They did come back, in one year, and then there was a third great party.

Domingo has very good memories of the 2006 Champions League. He admits he dreamed of going to Paris and the Final. And dreamed of Villarreal winning there. He really felt the dream coming true until the Riquelme penalty miss, which broke his heart. Unlike some of the others, he didn't go to Paris anyway. "Reality put us back in our place" was the way he put it about the shattering of his dream. He has no lingering resentment of Riquelme. Domingo feels most Villarreal fans have dealt with it, it was a case of "Great player, shit person, complicated and problematic person." For Domingo it was Riquelme who couldn't deal with it, hence the problems a few months later.

Since his first introduction to Celtic supporters, Domingo has had some positive experiences with them outwith the Penya orbit. He went to Benidorm for a wee break (yes, some Spaniards do go there, too), and met up with Celtic supporters, in a Celtic Bar. Seeing his Villarreal top, the whole company sang a song for Villarreal. Domingo found it a very moving and strangely emotional experience. When Celtic came to Barcelona a few years ago, Domingo organised tickets for his Celtic supporter friends, amongst the Barcelona crowd, and went up to spend a few days with them around the game. All his memories of times like these with Celtic supporters, are good memories. He laughed and said "I am always drunk, trying to keep up with them, drinking faster than I do normally. Before every game, after every game, always more partying, more drinking. I try to keep up but never seem to manage to stay sober, like most of the Penya do." Domingo feels that Celtic supporters have taught him a great deal. "They have taught me that football is about more than football. They don't just go to a game, they take an interest in kids, hospitals everything around them. I have learned from Celtic fans how to act like that. They have made the Villarreal Celtic Submari Penya a mirror to allow others to witness it too."

Fermin and Claudia Font

Fermin, the son of the number one supporter, is one of the regular members of the Penya. He is a quiet thoughtful man. He has written a book on Spanish castles. Fermin is a generous man, to give just one example, it was he who offered Gerry Martin a bed when he wanted to stay at a Penya do and I insisted on driving back to Naquera. Claudia, his second wife, is a lovely person, with a very warm friendly manner. Claudia is that village thing, an outsider, one of the few around the Penya not to have spent her whole life in or around Vila-real. She came to Vila-real in December 2005, from Nicaragua. She found the Penya a wonderful way to make real friends in what can otherwise be a fairly closed community. Her warm personality has ensured that she now has many friends within the Penya.

Ioan 'Nelu' Bordean

Unlike most bigger Spanish towns, Vila-real does not have a lot of immigrant workers, the few that do tend to be South American, like the Boca Juniors supporting barman in Lluisos. But one stalwart member of the Celtic Submari Penya club does come from outwith Spanish culture. Ioan Petru Bordean, known to his friends as Nelu, came to Spain over 10 years ago, from Romania, seeking work in the construction industry. He ended up in Vila-real by pure chance through a friend, but liked it so much he decided to stay. In Romania he was a supporter of Steaua Bucharest, so he knows about the joy of winning the Champions League. He immediately bonded with Villarreal CF, partly because of the Romanian international forward Giga Croiveanu. He has followed them avidly ever since, and has only ever known them as a La Liga club. He watched with some amazement as the club from the small town became a top club in Spain and Europe.

Pascual and Monica Broch

Pascual is the other one in the Toreador photo, turning up at Parkhead in traditional Valencian costume, to the great delight of the Celtic crowd. I first met Pascual and his wife Monica at the January 2007 Celtic Submari Three Kings Children's Party, where they were there with their sons Alex and Javier.

Pascual speaks no English at all, much to his wife's despair, and although she enrolled him in the Penya English classes his commitment proved insufficient to produce progress. Monica grew up supporting Barcelona and only had her conversion to supporting Villarreal when the club reached the First Division. Her two sons Alex and Javier who both speak good English, have only known Villarreal as a big team, one which they support passionately. But Pascual who has lived in Villarreal all his life belongs to the same generation as Ernesto, Angel, Jose Luis, Vicente, Luis, Saul, Pepe, Juanma and the rest that grew up together, and well remembers Villarreal as a wee team.

The rest

The Penya has over 700 members and it is not possible to name them all but I want to give at least a passing mention to several whom have been part of my interviews and discussions. Juanma and Carmen have always been friendly, even though language has remained a barrier to the fullest communication. Pablo, brother of Estrella, has also always been helpful. Carlos, the grumpy faced accountant, and his more jovial English lookalike, the Orient supporter, have brightened several Friday nights. The three old men who volunteer most for bar duty have done their part in ensuring I have enjoyed my Friday nights in the Penya. Javi Salas, Javi Serrebro, Felix, Tofal and many others have helped generously with stories, memories, views and opinions. To them, and the other 700 members, thank you for the kindness and friendliness you have shown me and I am sorry I have not quoted you directly in the book but I hope you find the portrait of your Penya a fair and positive one.

Chapter Ten   Ernesto Junior

Ernesto and his long time girlfriend Maria Dolores married in 1992 after several years of living together. They did not rush to have children but were both delighted three years after the wedding when Maria Dolores became pregnant. Unfortunately Maria Dolores suffered a miscarriage after 4 months, and it was to be another 12 months before she became pregnant again. The pregnancy was a source of great happiness to them, and their families, and the birth was an eagerly anticipated event. Despite the inevitable anxieties after the earlier miscarriage, the pregnancy was straightforward, and on 30th August 1997 Maria Dolores gave birth to a baby boy. They had already agreed that if it was a boy then he would become Ernesto too, but be known as Ernest to differentiate him from his father.

Sometimes it is best to avoid clichés like "the proudest day of my life" but both parents use the phrase with such sincerity and intensity, you know it was true for both of them. Young Ernest was a beautiful baby, a view widely acknowledged outside the biased immediate family. Indeed so good looking was the young male baby, that it became a family joke that Maria Dolores had to fend off some never openly expressed but quietly whispered doubts about the paternity of her beautiful baby.

He demonstrated a personality of his own from birth. Ernest was a very calm baby, 'muy tranquilo', and definitely 'guapo', highly attractive. When he was about 3 months old, both parents became concerned about irregular and unusual movements of his eyes. They were concerned enough to ensure he was seen by a specialist, who assured them everything was normal and there was nothing to worry about. However the eye movements continued, and there were also growing concern about aspects of his head development, so he was taken back to hospital. This time the distraught parents were taken seriously. The first diagnosis they were given was Hydrocephalus. However after a full scan was undertaken, they were given a much more serious and concerning diagnosis, of a cancerous tumour on the brain. This diagnosis was soon confirmed by a biopsy on the tumour. Maria Dolores gave up her work completely and devoted herself to the full time care of her baby. They were warned that the first thing that would happen was that his sight would go completely. Young babies can see and recognise things, particularly the faces of their parents, from a far younger age than used to be thought possible. Ernest was fully sighted for the first 5 months of his life but after that lost his sight completely.

There was a debate amongst hospital staff as to whether an attempt should be made to remove the tumour. One neurosurgeon wanted to operate to try to do so, but the overall medical consensus was that the operation would have too high a chance of failure with fatal consequences. So from the age of 5 months, young Ernest received chemotherapy every week. He had no less than 8 operations, some of them involving the placement and subsequent replacement of a valve in his brain. The chemotherapy seemed to adversely affect the functioning of the valve and regular readjustments were required. During the year of the most operations he and Maria Dolores spent much time in hospital. At the age of three, the treatment was changed to radiotherapy, again on a weekly basis, for the next 3 years of his life. The radiotherapy seemed to produce better results. Ernest responded well and it seemed to be helping him. It was an awesome responsibility for the family to cope with. Maria Dolores provided care for him 24 hours a day, and hardly slept a full night for 6 years.

What helped both parents was the personality of their son. He developed a unique character of his own. He coped with all the medical attention, demands, pain and discomfort without complaining. He taught Ernesto and Maria Dolores humility, that he could be so strong, so brave and so happy under such adversity. They learned from him, not to complain so much about unimportant things.

Ernest also showed a great sense of fun, loved to play games of all kinds. 'Alegria', happiness, was a word that cropped up regularly in their descriptions of their son and his personality. He was always very keen on communicating with people. He grasped languages quickly, learning to speak both the local Valenciano language as well as Spanish. He received education through a combination of attending a day centre and getting home tutors brought into the house. He proved to be a willing and quick learner. Although he clearly qualified for the phrase 'learning difficulties', he demonstrated that he had a keen intelligence and a good memory. He used both assets to memorise many songs, both in Valenciano and Spanish. He loved singing, song after song, either alone or with anyone else who would sing along with him. When I asked Ernesto and Maria Dolores to share with me their happiest single memory of him, they both came up with episodes involving Ernest singing in a family setting.

He could turn his disabilities to his advantage too. The Spanish equivalent of Santa Claus is for a family member to dress up as one of the three Magic Kings and visit bringing presents. The carefully applied King's disguise fooled the young cousins, but Ernest, relying as always on sound rather than sight, was not fooled, and said "It's Uncle Jose", to the pride and delight of his parents.

Ernesto and Maria Dolores tolerated, just, the ignorant but kindly enough outsiders who assumed that the enlarged head, the blindness and the physical awkwardness must be accompanied by an equal amount of mental handicap, but they knew their son and his capabilities.

Ernest received the full Villarreal CF treatment from an early age, with endless presents of scarves, football tops, the works. He was given an oral history lesson in what it meant to be one of the Villarreal family. On 22nd June 2003, aged 5 years old, he was taken to his first game in the Madrigal by his mother, father and maternal grandfather, to a game against Real Betis, in what was the last game of the season. Unfortunately it turned out not to be a happy experience for the young Ernest. The noise, the unending cacophony of sound produced by excited football supporters, was just too much for the unsighted young boy and he had to be taken home, early, slightly distressed by the experience.

Ernest was to visit El Madrigal one more time, in what proved to be an experience more distressing for the mother than the son. Villarreal, with Roig's eye for involvement and engagement with the community, always have a preseason session where young supporters can come along and be photographed in groups alongside the first team players. Young Ernest, dressed up in his best Villarreal top, was taken along by his mother and maternal grandfather. He seemed to enjoy the experience and be happy enough to be part of it. Some member of the Villarreal staff, at the point the group photograph was about to be taken, apparently sensed some discomfort on the part of one or two people about Ernest's disabilities and removed him from the group, so that he was not actually a part of the final group photograph. Maria Dolores was livid with anger and rage. Ernesto too became upset when he heard of it from his return from work. It is bad enough to suffer ignorance and insensitivity from strangers, but from the football club of your heart brings an extra dimension of pain. Someone from the club phoned up the next day to apologise to Maria Dolores, but the damage had already been done. Even talking about the incident five years on, her anger and her hurt are still strong. She has forgiven the club, become a season ticket holder in her own right, but has never, and will never, forgive the individual involved, luckily for them no longer part of the club.

Maria Dolores and Ernesto expressed to me in eloquent terms a philosophy they had developed over the years of Ernest's life. "If you cannot see the beauty in a gorgeous child because of an obsession with disabilities, then shame on you, but the loss is yours, because the child is beautiful." They determined early on never to hide Ernest away, involved him fully in their world, and were rewarded by the obvious pleasure he brought to so many of their friends as well as their family.

Ernest had confounded so many of the more pessimistic prognoses of early death, that they had begun to half-believe that he might indeed live on into adulthood, but the end, when it came, came very quickly. Aged 6 years old, he came down with flu, deteriorated very rapidly and suddenly within 15 days he was effectively gone. The decision was made to let him go peacefully and on 22nd March 2004 Ernest's life ended.

When Ernest died, Maria Dolores was 3 months pregnant. She gave birth to young Maria on 10th September 2004. Maria has grown up always knowing she has a brother who is in heaven. Maria Dolores whenever asked, always says she has two children, one here and one there.

Chapter Eleven Gerry's Story   and the lead-up to 14th April 2004

Gerry Martin, the unlikeliest hero in this book, could only come from Glasgow. Christened Gerard Martin, he has always been known in the wider Celtic community as Gerry Martin, but as Ged to closer friends and family.

He was born in Shettleston and is a true son of the Dear Green Place. He is the personification of that Glasgow phenomenon known as Gallus. He is a mass of contradictions; being both charming and rudely cheeky; funny and capable of intense seriousness; cynical and principled; devious and wide; generous of spirit, mean of money; big hearted and big headed; very intelligent and occasionally stupid; sensitive and crude. He routinely tells the most enormous whoppers while being devoted to the importance of the truth. He treats everything as a great joke but takes life very seriously. And those are just the more obvious surface contradictions. Underneath that public exterior lies a mass of internal contradictions. On first impression almost everyone likes Gerry but wouldn't buy a used car off him. Those who get to know him better, soon learn to trust him too.

Gerry had a complicated family background, not that unusual in Glasgow terms. He grew up with his mother and four siblings and never knew who his father was until well into his thirties, by which time it was too late for any relationship. His relationship with his mother was difficult, and due to her mental health and alcohol difficulties, he spent some of his early years in care. When the family were reunited with their mother when Gerry was around 9 years old, the oldest sibling, Pauline then just 16, had the sense not to join them, though she stayed in touch and did the best she could to help her 3 younger brothers survive what were often quite torrid times. Social workers remained involved in Gerry's life and when the Children's Hearing offered him the choice of respite and education away from the family home, or continued social work supervision at home, he chose the former, getting some of his education in a school approved by the state but run by the Catholic Church.

As the older boys, Terry and Alex, turned 16 they too left home, leaving Gerry alone in an uneasy relationship with his mother, by then confined to a wheelchair. Pauline has done well for herself, pursuing a successful career in Social Work where she is now a senior manager with an English authority. One of the brothers Alex is no longer alive but Gerry has kept in contact with Terry, who has become a legend in his own right with Celtic Submari members following several action packed contacts. Like all his siblings, Gerry left home as soon as he could.

Pursuing dreams and mad plans took Gerry to London where he learned his trade in music and video, scraping by without finding true happiness or fulfilment. Marriage to Susanna, the classy daughter of a rich Italian businessman, and mother of the light of his life, Matteo, did not quite work out for him but with his friendly personality and his undeniable charm he was never short of partners or friends. When I suggested to Gerry that more detail was required, he offered to fill in the 25 year gap with a brief biographical profile.

"I arrived in London aged 15 to the flourishing punk scene, earning a living by selling evening newspapers to pub customers. I would buy 12 copies from the wholesale shop, then with the tips from selling them, buy 18 more and repeat the process until a handsome profit was made. Life was a series of punk concerts and parties. Then at 19 I went travelling around Europe, busking to earn a living. I did France, Italy and Spain. Later, returning for a 2 week holiday in Spain, I stayed for a year. It was the time of the ' La Movida' in Madrid, an explosion of youth culture coming on the back of Franco's death and the return to democracy. It was a great way to spend part of one's youth, and it was then I fell in love with Spain and its people.

Reluctantly I came back to the UK and took on a series of jobs, like tourist information, barman, and roadie, before joining a band and playing the pub circuit. Some acting jobs followed before setting up as a freelance cameraman. I started off by doing wedding videos, local government information videos etc. On the advice of professional friends, and after the stinging break up of a five year relationship, I decided I would go to Film School for 3 years to take a degree in 'Independent Film Making and Cinematography.' My career began to take off with work in short films, pop videos working with MTV and Music Box and a full length documentary for the BBC, 'The Merry-go-round'. Unfortunately it all came to a halt after a car accident that left me in a wheelchair for over a year, and with accompanying mental scars from the accident. I slowly started doing location scouting for film production companies, and some post production editing. It was then I met Susanna, the mother of my son Matteo. Although the relationship did not work out, I have remained in a civilised relationship with her, as we are both devoted to our gorgeous son Matteo".

With his usual dryly intelligent wit, Gerry headlined the above text as "Becks, Hugs and Sausage Rolls", a wry improvement on the more conventional sex, drugs and rock'n'roll.

In early 2000, he picked up a Spanish girl in a London bar. He thought she looked very like a Spanish girl he knew, and as a chat-up line asked Rosa if she had a sister Anna. She said she did and their relationship was up and running. It turned out the Anna Gerry knew, was not Rosa's sister Anna, but another Anna altogether, although by coincidence Rosa's Anna had also lived in London, but by then the link was forged and the relationship was on. When Rosa decided after a couple of years to return to Spain, to the small town of Betera near Valencia, she invited Gerry to come back with her and he could think of no strong reason not to go. Rosa took over running the family Ferreteria business (an ironmonger's shop) and Gerry settled down to improving his already very workable Spanish. He set up as freelance Media Consultant working between the UK and Spain for production houses with projects in either country. He spent much of the last 8 years doing this, working on several audio-visual projects.

Gerry has a real facility for languages. He speaks Spanish like a native. Most English speakers who speak even good Spanish, tend to speak it as English speakers, slower and more distinctly than the natives, which makes them more comprehensible to the likes of myself who struggle to hear the language well. But Gerry speaks like a local, so I find him just as hard to understand.

Gerry has mastered Gaelic for a combination of musical and political reasons. And to the great delight of staff in the Betera Chinese restaurant, he has also taught himself to speak Chinese Mandarin, a skill he hopes one day to use to improve links between Celtic Football Club and the huge enthusiastic Chinese football market. There is a clip on You Tube of Gerry singing, in Chinese, his own translation of "You'll Never Walk Alone", which is well worth a watch.

"Then one day Celtic went to Villarreal to play in the UEFA Cup". Gerry was always of the Celtic faith, fanatically so. Even when his travels took him to London and further afield, he remained green to core and kept in touch through internet forums like the Huddleboard. On arriving in the Valencia Community, with the usual Celtic love of the under-dog, he assumed he would become a Levante man, a notion confirmed when they signed big Johan Mjallby from the Bhoys in green. He did watch them once or twice, but before true affiliation could occur, came the link with Villarreal that would convert him into one of the captains of the Celtic Submari.

From his new base in Spain, Gerry went to Seville in May 2003 where his exploits were worthy of inclusion in any one of the myriad of books written about that amazing week when the city turned green. His brother Terry was in Seville too, but despite some attempts they never actually met. "I'm on a corner, near a big church, wearing a Celtic top, right!" Gerry didn't have a ticket but tried to get into the ground by offering his translating services to the local police, attempting to persuade them that their interpreters who spoke perfect English would be little use and what was needed was his expertise in the Weegie tongue. They seemed to consider the point valid and said they would think about it and call him back, but his involvement in the new found Celtic sport of Seville fountain dancing with mobile phone in pocket meant he will never know if they called or not. It is one of the enduring Celtic myths about those magical Seville days that despite almost 100,000 Celts being there (the figure grows every year as repressed memories add to the numbers recollecting their attendance) only wan was arrested, and he turned out to be a half Spanish Juan from Valencia. Gerry knows from his contact with police that day that that number of one arrested is a slight under-estimation, but in truth most who were arrested inside were put outside without formal charge and there was a complete absence of malicious or destructive behaviour. Gerry got into the ground briefly before being thrown out, and watched in a crowded bar as poor Celtic were outmuscled and outplayed out of the trophy they had been sure was theirs, by Jose Mourinho's Porto.

It would be no great exaggeration to say that the Celtic supporter made happiest by the 2004 UEFA Cup Quarter Final draw was Gerry. Despite Vila-real being just 40 minutes down the road from Betera, Gerry had never actually been to Vila-real, or seen Villarreal play other than on television. Indeed he had not even clocked exactly where it was, and had to check a map to discover with delight it was only 30 miles up the road. Within hours of the draw he had made promises to around 30 of his family and friends, that of course they could get a bed, or at least crash with him, for the second leg. Gerry immediately set about planning for the second leg which as well as his host duties included getting in touch with Villarreal supporters over the internet using websites like Forza Groguet to see about arranging joint activities.

From the minute the draw was made and he realised he lived close enough to play an active planning role in preparing for it, Gerry had two main notions in his mind. A friendly football match between supporters of both clubs, and a collection that would raise money for a local charity. Both concepts came from his innate sense of what Celtic supporters do best, and what is the right way for them to behave.

One of the first Villarreal supporters he linked up with through the internet was Julio Boixader, who responded enthusiastically to Gerry's request that a team of Villarreal supporters be recruited to play against Celtic supporters on the day of the game, and began to make the necessary arrangements at his end.

Gerry, like most Celtic supporters, did not see the 1-1 draw at Celtic Park on the 8th April 2004 as a bad result. Okay, Villarreal had been the better team on the night, but there was still all to play for, and the club that eliminated Barcelona should have little to fear from a smaller Spanish club. In the days before the return leg, Gerry worked hard along with his new found friend Julio and his brother Jose Manuel, and they finally agreed to meet in person. Gerry went to Vila-real for the first time ever 5 days before the game. He still vividly remembers his initial impressions "When I got off at the train station, it was like something out of a Sergio Leone western, one platform, a swinging sign, windswept and empty streets, a one horse town." Arrangements were finalised for the supporters game to be held in the afternoon of the main game which would have an 8pm evening kickoff. Together with Julio, Gerry organised the supporters' game. On promises made over the internet through Huddleboard where he called himself "Chalkie Armani" in honour of the old Gerry Adams joke. There was the usual Gerry pattern of initial enthusiasm and effort, followed by lack of applied attention to the detail.

Gerry learned to his delight that the locals, led by the Agrupacion of Penyas, (the umbrella group of the various Villarreal Supporters Clubs) were already planning to run two separate communal parties to offer beer and paella to the Scottish hordes.

After talking to Gerry, Julio spoke to the Agrupacion, and alerted them to the likely scale of the imminent invasion. The Agrupacion were also organising a giant screen, in the Casal De Festas where the main Paella Party would be held, for those Celtic supporters still without a ticket at kick-off time.

Gerry was keen also to carry out a particular Celtic tradition, inherent in the club since its very foundation, that of using games to raise money for local charities. Gerry found it harder than he had anticipated to translate this tradition into practical action on this occasion, partly because the concept was not one known to his Villarreal contacts. The Church tends to deal with all local needs not catered for by the state. There is no great tradition of non-church charitable organisations like Barnardo's, or Quarriers. However, after long discussion with Julio and Jose Manuel, it was agreed that all monies raised would go to a local special needs centre for children and young adults. Gerry had to hustle, bustle and work quite hard, organising raffles and competitions and other moneymaking devices and ensuring prizes would be available on the day, but in the end, thanks partly to generous support from Huddleboard members, he ended up with enough to make the concept viable.

Gerry went back to Vila-real a few days before the game, helping with hostels and other accommodation arrangements, organising tickets, preparing written directions and all the other last minute preparations required before the Celtic forces arrived.

He remembers 2 Daily Record reporters with thick Glasgow accents wanted a photograph of a girl in a Celtic bikini. So Gerry helped recruit a willing local girl, Gisella Trini, the 21 year old daughter of a local bar owner. Gerry drove down to Burriana beach with them and held the jackets as the photos were taken. With Julio, Gerry went to the Vila-real police station 2 days before the game. Gerry reassured the main man that there would be nothing to worry about, he checked the boss had already been in touch with their colleagues in Sevilla and got very positive feedback. Gerry assured him there was no need for wood to be placed in town centre shop windows and that plan was abandoned. Officially the game was still categorised as high risk but that was due more to the recent terrorist climate. Partly reassured by discussions with Gerry, the police officer in charge put out a public statement the day before the game saying they were not expecting any trouble and were looking forward to meeting the famous friendly Celtic fans, "We welcome them." Privately he admitted the sheer scale of the likely invasion still caused him some concern. His men had never had to cope with more than 1,000 away supporters in all his time in post. But he did seem somewhat reassured by Gerry's confidence all would be well.

Gerry's brother Terry and some pals arrived in Betera but Gerry had to be in Vila-real to help organise. Poor Rosa. I can just imagine the telephone conversation with Rosa the late afternoon of the day before the game. "Sorry, darling, I know I said I would be back, I know you've got all my relatives and friends to cope with, but they need me here, there is just so much to do. You'll be all right. Love you." then off to the bar for more work.

The night before the game, the advance guard of a few hundred Celtic supporters had arrived in Vila-real and the fun began. As did the singing of Celtic songs. Community singing in bars is not part of the Spanish culture so "The people in this pub they cannae sing, cannae sing, the people in this pub cannae sing" became a regular challenge in different bars in the town. As Gerry put it later, "there was a wee party the night before, a lot of singing, a little drinking, much friendliness on all sides, touring all the bars".

That night after many happy hours partying and drinking with Celtic supporters, Gerry Martin went to bed, eventually, tired and emotional, but happy, looking forward to the next day. But as he drifted off to sleep, he had no idea just how much the next day would set off a train of events that would change his life forever, for the better.

And leave him with a major legacy he would later describe as the best thing he has ever done in his life.

In May 2003 Celtic just failed to win the UEFA Cup, losing out in the Final to Jose Mourinho's Porto. Yet disappointing though the actual result of the Final was, in many ways May 2003 remains one of the great positive memories for almost all Celtic supporters. The 100,000 plus supporters who congregated in a sun-drenched Seville will never forget the experience of being there. The hundreds of thousands of Celtic supporters who had to settle for watching on television have fewer direct positive memories, but even for them the predominate emotion was not so much disappointment as pride. Pride that so many Celtic supporters made the journey to Seville. Pride that so many Celtic supporters behaved so well, bringing world wide credit to the club and its support.

So many books have been written about the Seville 2003 experience that even many of the stay at home supporters feel that they were there, were part of the carnival of happiness and good behaviour that so impressed not only the people of Seville, but observers from all over the world.

This pride received further boosts when the two primary football bodies in the world, FIFA and UEFA, both acknowledged the excellent behaviour of the Celtic supporters by giving them awards for fairplay and excellence. These awards strengthened the notion already well-established in the collective Celtic mentality, that the Parkhead club have the greatest supporters in the world. Supporters whose innate friendliness and good behaviour make them a considerable credit to the Club.

In March 2004, Celtic once again were marching on the UEFA Cup, if through the back door of finishing third in their Champions League Qualifying Group behind Lyon and Bayern Munich. After easily disposing of a Czech team Teplice in the first knockout round, they drew the mighty Barcelona in the next round. I was at Celtic Park the night of the first leg when Celtic outfought if not outplayed Barcelona and probably narrowly deserved their 1-0 victory. The second leg was a desperately heroic defensive operation, which succeeded in achieving the 0-0 draw required to gain them a notable overall victory, thanks mainly to an inspired David Marshall.

The Quarter-Final draw matched Celtic with a Spanish team called Villarreal. Some 99% of all the Celtic supporters interviewed for this book confessed freely that before the draw they had never heard of Villarreal and not one, including even the 1% that had vaguely heard of them, could have pointed to a map of Spain with any clue as to where Villarreal might be. Even Gerry Martin, living in the same province, didn't know where Villarreal was. After disposing of the great Barcelona, it never occurred to Celtic supporters that their team could be beaten by a side they had never heard of, with only three players Belletti, Riquelme and Sonny Anderson, that even the better informed and most erudite Celtic supporters knew of.

They all thought after the draw that they had pulled the weakest team left in the competition, and that none of the other 6 clubs were as powerful as Barcelona. So there was much confidence in the general view that this time justice would be done and Celtic would win the UEFA Cup they had been so unfairly denied the previous year by the bully boys from Porto. So they signed up for the trip in their eager thousands, hoping to repeat some of the Sevilla sunshine and happiness. The great mass of optimistic Celtic supporters were not too downhearted after the first leg, on 8th April 2004, when Villarreal played them off the park at Celtic Park and were unlucky only to get a 1-1 final result. "No", the collective rationalisation went, "most wee teams tend to raise their game to unnatural heights given the grandeur and history and atmosphere at Parkhead. However, the inevitable superior force of Celtic will be bound to prevail over the 180 minutes, particularly in a small ground where Celtic supporters might even be in the majority. Viva Espana, here we come again".

So almost all of the 10,000 Celtic supporters who made the trip to the Villarreal game were quietly or noisily confident that their team would win the tie overall and would proceed to the semi-final draw. Many of the travellers had already made at least tentative preliminary arrangements to travel to Gothenburg for the UEFA Cup final due to be played there in May 2004. The 10,000 strong invasion force was divided into four main battalions. The advance guard of a few hundred Celtic supporters who arrived in Vila-real the night before the game and made the first contacts with the locals.The second battalion, the largest of the four, flew to Spain on the Tuesday and stayed in Valencia the night before the game. Many did so in the mistaken belief that Villarreal were a team from the suburbs of Valencia, the rest because there are not the hotels in Vila-real to cope. This second force decamped to Vila-real by train and bus on the day of the game, in time to partake of the various events laid on for them, including the supporters game and the massive Paella Party organised by the Agrupacion of Villarreal Penyas. Plus, of course, the mandatory drinking in and outside the many bars dotted around the main square and the streets around the ground. The third force, a smaller more select group, were the supporters who came with the official party. They too spend the night before the game in Valencia but were not transported to Villarreal until just a couple of hours before the kick-off thus missing out on the events and parties organised. The Celtic team itself stayed in La Calderona a luxury sports resort near Betera. The fourth group, of several thousands, arrived in Spain a few days before the game but decamped to Benidorm and similar Costa Brava resorts for a bit of Spanish culture before making their way to Vila-real on the day of the game.

I have talked to many Celtic supporters who were there in Vila-real that eventful day, the 14th April 2004. Many of them used a phrase writers hate to hear, the ultimate challenge, "It is impossible to explain exactly what happened that day. You cannot adequately convey to people who were not there, just how mind blowing and astonishing it was."

The events

The Supporters game

The notion of a game between the two sets of supporters, first conceived by Gerry Martin, was picked up at the Villarreal end by Julio Boixader, who put a great deal of work into organising the game. The Villarreal team was composed of eleven fit young men recruited from the whole resources of the Agrupacion of Penyas, the Association of Villarreal Supporters Clubs. They had proper Villarreal CF strips, donated by the club. The Mayor and the local Minister for Sport were in attendance along with a reporter from the local paper, plus a good crowd of locals, and an ever growing number of inebriated Scots. It had been organised that the game would be played in the magnificent Cuidad Deportiva with all its resources. The Villarreal boys took it seriously, many of them had abstained from alcohol the night before, and none of them had touched a drop the day of the game.

They were expecting a tough game, against a disciplined Celtic supporters side.

Half an hour before the game was due to start, Gerry Martin was panicking. He could only find 7 of his players, and that was after a thorough trawl of all the nearby bars, where all of them had been drinking quietly for hours, so none of them were exactly sober. So Gerry went back to the nearest bars and press ganged six new players, promising them all they would only be substitutes. None of the 6 had been expecting to have to perform, not on a park anyway. He couldn't find anyone sober enough or drunk enough to volunteer to be a goalie but Julio managed to come up with a big Spaniard for that role. Gerry hadn't organised a set of strips so they had to make do with what they had. Celtic tops were not a problem, most of the team were already wearing one, and those who weren't had plenty of people to chose from to find one roughly their size. Boots were more of a problem since only one or two of even the magnificent seven volunteers had brought a pair. However, again many were wearing trainers, some were able to borrow other trainers and one or two played in their shoes. Some had shorts on, others borrowed shorts from pals or Spaniards, and some played in their trousers.

So there you had it, 11 fit, athletic well equipped sober Spaniards against what politely could be called a ragbag of mostly drunken Scots, all the worse for wear, most out of shape. Three of them looked good, the rest rough. Some of them even continued drinking during the game from carryouts in the goal. To make matters worse, the hot Spanish midday sun was beating down, and words like boiling, dehydrated and even melting were used by the Scots in the crowd. Gerry Martin has regularly tried to rewrite history over the years by claiming he did not take part in this first game, insisting that he was the manager organising from the sidelines. But he lies. He did play, or at least he was on the pitch. Shortly after Gerry missed a sitter, he did substitute himself.

There are two versions of how the game went. The Spanish version is that the natural ability and natural competitiveness of the Celtic supporters made it something of a game at first but the Villarreal side were not just the better team, they were the only team. Once the Villarreal boys realised that, they relaxed, didn't try too hard and were happy to allow the game to end a draw, even though they could have won comfortably if they had so desired. The Scottish version is slightly different, a stirring tale of bravery and defiance against the odds, of character and determination saving the honour of the tribe, with a draw being a fair and hard fought for result. What is not in doubt is that the final score ended up 4-4. The crowd, swelling all the time as more and more Celtic fans arrived, loved it from beginning to end. No-one felt cheated and everyone agreed honour was satisfied.

Scott McCorry was the only player from that first game I was able to track down. He had vivid memories of the experience which I am happy to include almost verbatim.

"Ok, so my name is Scott Peter McCorry, I was born and have stayed in Cambuslang all my days in a Celtic minded family. Father, uncles, aunties, cousins, all tims, the sister stays with a Hun, but we don't talk of her ha ha. I was taken to games in my early life by my Dad, Peter, alongside my older brother Mark. My first cup final was the 1988 Dundee United match. My Dad stopped taking me in the early 90s, but I went back on my own accord when Fergus took over and got my first season book in the 1994 Hampden season. Since then I have really tried my best to make every game I can, be it home, away or Europe."

"My Villareal story really all happened by chance. I answered an SOS by Gerry Martin, Valenciabhoy from the Huddleboard, with an invitation to play in a charity bounce match versus a Villarreal team, bunch of fans v fans it was to be. The thing was, he put the invitation up once the draw happened, I replied saying yes, okay, but then I heard nothing back. So instead of me and my mates, heading to the game with my bag filled with boots, shorts in tow, I had 10 cans of Tennents and a bottle of the finest monks' wine, all of which had been severely depleted during the trip from Valencia to Villarreal itself. When I met Gerry in Villarreal, he found me and my mates being interviewed by a local paper. I don't think that interview ever did find print, unsurprisingly, since we were already well on. Gerry was touring the bars looking for his players and when I told him who I was, he said "Come on, you're playing". So with 3 new players pressed into action from nearby pubs, the game was ready. We turned up, basically playing with what we were wearing. One of my mates, Martin Kearney had to get a loan of shorts off someone, and trainers off another who had came along to watch. While the opposition stood, all tanned, long haired and ready to rock, in their full kit. I laughed wryly. We never had a keeper so we enlisted a Spanish lad from the sidelines. Now picture a big guy, same shape as Frankenstein, with jeans and massive doc martins on, and a glaiket looking smile. I swear every time the ball came near him, SMASH a big toe poke back up the pitch.

A mate on the side, who would have been a bit too rotund to play, helped himself to the lads' carry out during the match. I knew something was up when he was dancing on the sidelines with a penny whistle.

Of the match itself my memory is pretty hazy. My main moment was playing a beautiful through ball to Gerry, only for our new leader to miss the ball, trip up and rattle into the fence at the back. Another was of a wee young Spanish lad skinning me time and time again, so I took up my enforcer role and launched him into the air. Needless to say he didn't come near me again. It also meant when we played the return match at Barrowfield the following April, there were more than a few fingers directed at me. The match finished 4-4, a young lad called Tam Beckett being the stand out for our lads. I think the wee man scored 2 that day. After the match, a shower and put the same clothes back on, I know, I know!"…

After the game everyone, players, officials, politicians, spectators all marched off down to the Paella Party just down the road headed up by the same bagpipe player who had piped them into the Cuidad Deportiva.

This football match gave an early illustration of the pluses and minuses of the organisational skills of Gerry Martin. The pattern seen here, of great vision, immaculate conception, strong initial enthusiasm and much expenditure of energy, poor follow through and low attention to boring detail, would be repeated often. Yet it also illustrates the other side. With Gerry Martin in charge things that would not otherwise happen, happen and many people are better –off as a result. Disaster often seems minutes away, but somehow Gerry muddles through and everything works out. This football match was proof of that, and the large crowd was well pleased.

The Paella Party
Originally the Agrupacion had intended to charge a small fee to cover the costs, but were soon persuaded to abandon that notion, mainly by the provision of free smaller alternatives all around. A few unfortunate early Scots did have to pay, and felt conned and frustrated at this injustice, but the later arrivals were catered for free. Anyway, the Agrupacion are well subsidised by the club, so no financial harm was done. And other sponsors, like the local paper, had also chipped in, so both big Paella Parties provided the food free and the drinks at a very cheap price if not free. Paella, the traditional Valencian meal of rice with chicken and rabbit, is a dish well suited to mass production so there was more than enough to cater for the thousands of delighted Celtic supporters that turned up over the course of the afternoon and early evening. The Agrupacion had advertised the availability of the Paella Party with flyers at the Airport and the station, so most of the 10,000 Celtic supporters heard about it, and about half of them attended. Many Villarreal supporters attended as well, attracted not by the food and drink but by the company and a desire to make friends.

Entertainment was provided at the main party by a local group, whose music had a celtic flavour, even if their name, Govanon, did not. Although the Casal site is a huge cavernous barn, most Scots chose to stay outside, in the midday sun. Many of the initial friendships made at the Paella Party were carried on into bars before and after the match. It was at the Paella Party that people first started the mass exchange of clothes that was to be a main feature of the day.

The Collection
It was there at the Paella Party that the bulk of the collection took place. All afternoon after the match, Gerry Martin ran around asking for money from people, for charity. Others like Scott McCorry saw what he was doing and pitched in to help. In Scott's words "Gerry began collecting money off everyone who moved. He would say 'Gie me money, Gie me money, it's for a local charity'. I didn't quite know what he was doing, but I decided it was a good idea,

and me and one or two others soon joined in saying 'Gie us money, it's for charity'." Gerry had managed to get various items donated as prizes and several raffles were organised. Prizes included a signed Celtic top, and a Chewing the Fat DVD. Gerry remembers wondering what any Spanish winner might make of "Gonnae no do that". Most Celtic supporters present responded well to Gerry's enthusiasm and gave generously of their Spanish currency. The respectable sum of around 400 euros was raised and, after the party, Gerry and Julio led a large ragtag procession to the agreed local children and young people's centre to hand it over. The woman in charge was confused by the notion and the commotion, and wouldn't take it. Two days later Julio went back, and they did take it, graciously and gratefully.

Scott, who has been to just about every Celtic trip abroad in the last 20 years, said that while charity collections were a major part of Celtic activity in Scotland, it was not something that ever until then formed part of the trips abroad, but he sensed Gerry Martin was genuine and gave him enthusiastic support. Scott later was told by one or two fellow supporters that they had thought originally that he and particularly Gerry "were at it", but they had been convinced by the procession and regretted their initial suspicion and meanness of spirit. Scott, who is well aware of the subsequent importance of that original collection, is proud to have been part of it. "I think Gerry deserves a huge amount of credit for kicking starting the whole relationship."

The Drinking in the Square and surrounds

As the Paella Parties came to a natural close, everyone began to gravitate towards the main square near the Madrigal Stadium, and the dozens of bars that surround it. The Plaza del Labrador (the Workers's Square) is particularly suitable for the political inclinations of the Celtic supporters. It has a massive statue of three workers plus a plaque that glories the contribution of real workers. The square became a sea of green and white and yellow. Bar after bar ran out of beer but there was always another bar to try. There was never the slightest hint of trouble, anger or aggression, only the happy sounds of people making new friends and enjoying themselves immensely. As kick-off grew nearer, the crowds in the Square swelled as late comers of both persuasions arrived to join the party. But the atmosphere remained remarkable and positive.

The game

The Celtic end, the part of the Fundo Norte allocated to away fans, was full. The Glasgow club had been allocated 3,800 tickets for its supporters and all these seats were taken. But it was also obvious many more Celtic supporters, several thousands of them, had managed one way or another to get tickets allocated to Villarreal supporters. Since there had already been a lot of scarf and shirt swapping colours alone were not a reliable guide to affiliation, but it was still obvious many Celtic fans were mixed in with the bulk of the Villarreal supporters. Quite a few Villarreal fans gave Celtic supporters their tickets. When I was first told this I thought "Aye, Right", but I have since heard sufficient stories of this phenomenon to know it to be true. Others, for similar or more mercenary motives, were happy to sell their tickets. Remember too, this was by far the biggest game in Villarreal's short European history and very important to the Yellow Submarine followers, so such acts say a great deal about the remarkable atmosphere of that day.

Inside the ground, the lack of segregation proved absolutely no problem, the spirit of friendliness continued. Most Villarreal supporters have told me how amazed and impressed they were by the singing of the Celtic supporters. Several commented on how they experienced a physical manifestation of an emotional response, with the hairs on the back of their necks or hands standing up, especially at the renditions of "You'll Never Walk Alone".

Gerry forewarned Julio and other Villarreal supporters that they would be outnoised by the minority from Scotland. Some had listened to his warning and turned up with pans and spoons, that they used as drums to generate some noise of their own. But they lost the noise battle. El Madrigal is a small, intimate and compact stadium that is usually pretty quiet. But that night it rocked. "The atmosphere was brilliant the whole game, everyone was friendly, positive. There was no tension, only friendly banter and great singing."

The most emotional single moment for Gerry was at the final whistle when all the Villarreal fans stood up and chanted 'Celtic, Celtic'. "I was really choked with emotion. The hairs on my arms stood up. It was so wonderful. I never thought in my life I would hear something like that, opposition fans chanting our name. Magic." The announcer had requested all the Celtic supporters to stay behind for 15 minutes after the final whistle. They did, but the desired benefit was lost because the Villarreal fans stayed too, chanting "Celtic Celtic" in between the many Celtic songs the supporters of the Hoops belted out.

Gerry was aware after the game that Villarreal fans had lined up to applaud the Celtic supporters all the way back down into the centre of town. "They were amazed at how well the Celtic fans took defeat, stayed positive and sang their club songs, so they wanted to applaud such warm hearted and generous people." Gerry managed a few drinks in the town celebrating with both sets of fans, who were still intermingling, still swapping clothes and other mementoes, but when the special supporters train back to Valencia finally left after midnight, Gerry was on it, with his brother and other pals, heading back to Betera, blissfully happy at the end of an almost perfect day, but still unaware of the train of events he had helped set in motion. Even years later Gerry still feels surges of pride and pleasure thinking of that day and how well everybody on both sides behaved. He is proud of the role he played in the events of the day.

And the game itself. Oh yes, Celtic were totally outclassed and beaten 2-0.

Some other memories from Celtic people

Robert Wilson is a typical representative of the invasion army, second battalion. Robert looks what he is, an honest and decent man, now in his Seventies but sharp as a tack. Robert has been a supporter of Celtic for 65 years, and sees being a Celtic supporter as his principal identity, rather than his job as a joiner, or any other form of identity. Robert has been going to away games all his life, and easily moved into following Celtic across Europe as well as Scotland. So he happily signed up for the 2004 trip to Villarreal even though he hadn't a clue where in Spain it was. He came that time by bus, a 3 day trip. I met Robert in Valencia the night before the 2008 Champions League game in Vila-real, and he was happy to talk about his previous visit in 2004. He told me he had loved the hours in Vila-real before the game, watching the football match between the two sets of supporters and seeing the two groups of fans mix so well and so happily before the game. He was struck by the numbers of women and children who were part of the pre-match celebrations and obviously going to the game. His ticket was amongst the home fans, at the Villarreal rather than the Celtic end of the ground, but it was not a problem and he spent the game happily chatting away to Villarreal fans. "Although I was in with the home support, it was no problem at all, they were all very nice. Some could speak English and we chatted away, but the others around me tried to communicate to, it was all wonderfully friendly."

Robert knew that Villarreal were by far the better team and had deserved their 2-0 victory, but somehow the result had not spoiled his good feeling. He recounted that at the end of the game "All the Villarreal fans clapped and cheered the Celtic supporters" which he found remarkably touching. After the game he was amazed by the way the two sets of supporters had walked arm in arm, into the town (actually Robert used the word village rather than town, as do most locals), singing together and somehow communicating together. "It was the best time I ever had at an away game in my life and believe me, over 65 years as a supporter, I have been to very many away games, but that was the best, ever."

Robert remembered that a collection had been taken amongst Celtic supporters for a local charity and that he had been happy to contribute to it. His wife had died of cancer, and one of sons had died of a heart disease and another was affected by the same disease. In Valencia he told me he had subsequently heard about the Celtic Submari being formed in Vila-real, and had read in the Celtic View about the story of Ernesto and his son. Having lost a son himself to illness, he had identified with Ernesto and said he would like to meet him. He had seen Ernesto on the pitch at Parkhead and had been proud that so many Villarreal supporters had come to Glasgow to see Celtic. When the two clubs had been drawn in the same Champions League Group he had been very happy, and immediately signed up for a return visit.

Brian McGowan, a happy go lucky charmer with a warm wry smile always playing around his face, had similar happy memories of the 2004 trip. Brian, a delivery driver, never really takes long holidays, preferring instead to take his annual leave in sufficient small doses to allow him to accompany Celtic to all their away games in Europe. He had been doing this for over 10 years when Celtic were first drawn against Villarreal. He had been over in Valencia when Celtic played them several years before and so in 2004 was happy to base himself in that beautiful city a second time. The day of the game, he left Valencia about 11a.m., arriving in Vila-real just after midday with 8 hours to enjoy before kick-off. He remembers it as being a beautiful day in terms of the weather, but one which became even more beautiful as the friendliness all around grew. He quickly found the Paella Party organised by the Agrupacion of

Villarreal Supporters. "I had a great time there, eating drinking and making pals. All the locals were very friendly, they could not have been nicer." After the Paella Party came to a natural conclusion, Brian and his pals had managed to find a few bars, and a few beers, and a few songs. Then it was on, in a state of grace, to the game. His original ticket had been for the Celtic end behind one of the goals, but he had taken part in the ticket swopping process prevalent in the bars, to allow him to go, to a much better seat at the halfway line, with his new Spanish pals. He was overwhelmed with the kindness of the Villarreal supporters after the game and proud of the way his fellow Celtic supporters responded, despite their disappointment in their defeat. "The people could not have been nicer. We could not have asked for anything more."

When I asked him what was his single most powerful memory of the evening, he told me "At the end of the game I had felt a bit depressed, a bit down, so I sat down somewhere, probably looking very sad, for a bit of a rest. This Spanish woman came up to me, put her Villarreal scarf round my neck, and gave me a wee kiss and said 'Good luck'. Magic, pure magic."

Martin Wilson, self-described as a long haired hippy vegetarian, had also ended up at the halfway line rather than behind the Celtic end goal. Although he achieved a different route, claiming "I took my own ticket to an empty turnstile after seeing the length of the queue for the Celtic end and deciding I was too drunk to wait. I was admitted without problem and found an empty seat with a wonderful view, surrounded by Villarreal fans who treated me like royalty". His predominant memory was of the Villarreal supporters eating birdseed rather than pies, but as a vegetarian his attitude was of quiet approval rather than the more normal Scottish ones of dismay and disbelief. He also claimed to have been very moved by having seen swarms of bats floating over the stadium eating the smaller insects. When it became obvious to him that it would be Villarreal rather than Celtic that would be advancing to the Semi-finals after the game, he began passionately exhorting the Villarreal supporters around him about the need to book cheap airplane flights to follow their team to the semi-final, unaware that the draw would pair them against Valencia some 40 miles down the road.

As a people loving pacifist, his mind had been blown by the friendliness of the natives, before, during and after the game. Martin is a seasoned European traveller, having seldom missed an away game since his first trip to Cologne in 1992. But while he was clear Celtic supporters were always well behaved and peaceful, he reckoned the response from the Villarreal supporters was the most positive he had ever encountered in all his travels, just marginally ahead of the welcome given to Celtic supporters by St Pauli fans. To put St Pauli in second place was quite a complement from Martin to the Villarreal fans, since he claimed he was the first Celtic supporter to wear a St Pauli scarf to Celtic Park, having picked one up in Cologne in 1992.

Scott McCorry recovered from playing in the supporters' game and found the real game another amazing experience. "I remember after the match being amazed, walking through the streets gutted, but being applauded by the opposition fans from the pavements and balconies. I had been in many places with Celtic, but never seen anything like that. It to an extent made up for the previous 90 minutes action."

Not all Celtic supporters came away with happy memories of their trip to see Celtic play Villarreal. Francis McGorry was a seasoned traveller to Celtic's away European games and he rated the trip to Vila-real as one of his less happy memories. He had gone with the official party so he did not arrive in the town until just before the game, missing out on all the pre-match conviviality and intermingling. He had come across with his long term pal, Martin Kane. They had put themselves down as helpers to Hope and Willie Wightman, disabled supporters but not in a wheelchair. At that time, before Diego Marza's mother wrote to Fernando Roig, the club did not really provide special facilities for disabled supporters. The best they were able to do for Hope and Willie was to put a bench out at the far end of the pitch, near to the by-line. Francis and Martin had to sit at the end of the bench, not quite what they expected for the money they had paid Celtic for disabled supporter facilities. They were alongside the benches for the firemen and ambulance men. There were also some disabled Villarreal supporters beside them. Francis, using his limited Spanish, was able to establish that these Villarreal supporters had got into the game free.

The day before the game, in Valencia, Francis had had his wallet nicked, with all the hassle and inconvenience that involved, including cancelling credit cards. Then he had to stand and watch his team get comprehensively defeated. After the match the official party were rushed away without much opportunity for communication with the locals. On the plane on the way home, Francis was just starting a very hot cup of coffee when the plane hit a patch of severe turbulence. The coffee went all over him, and his documents including his passport went flying down the plane. All the above would have been enough grief to ensure that Francis did not rate the Villarreal trip as his most positive European experience. But there was a further more painful dimension to his unhappiness. It can be exclusively revealed here that some of Francis's extra pain was caused by the knowledge that he had contributed directly to the defeat of his team. The defeat wasn't just due to the fact that Villarreal had the better players, playing tactically more advanced and astute football. It was aided by the fact that the referee and far side linesman gave several dubious offside decisions against Celtic caused by Francis and Martin sitting at the side of the pitch in their hoops jerseys. The Villarreal officials noticed this was happening and eventually brought bibs to them both to cover the Celtic jerseys, but by then the harm was done.

Francis was so annoyed by the whole cumulative set of disappointments that he wrote a stiff letter of complaint to Celtic Park on behalf of the four of them and received in return a letter of apology from the Head of Security Ronnie Hawthorn, and a refund of the ticket costs. He did not mention in the letter his contribution to their defeat. With such a bad start, it is to Francis's credit that he has subsequently become one of the most positive contributors to the relationship between Celtic supporters and the Villarreal Celtic Submari.

Most of the Celtic supporters comprising the invasion force were battle hardened veterans for whom the Villarreal trip was "Just another away game", at least until they arrived in the town. But for Linda Orr, it was a first initiation into foreign invasion, at least on football business. Linda had been born 49 years earlier into a football mad family of Celtic supporters, her father and brothers all being fanatics. As a young girl she had gone to a few games, in the old Jungle days, but had found the noise, the crush and the pressure too much, indeed frightening, and had abandoned the notion of becoming a regular attender. It was only a few years previous to the Villarreal trip, with Celtic Park converted into an all seater safe haven, that she had resumed the habit after a 25 year gap, reintroduced gently by her friend Patrick Higgins. She found this second wave experience so exciting, and so rewarding emotionally, that she signed up the next season for a season ticket, and started going to all the games along with her brother Tam and her colleague Tosh McLaughlin.

Linda early discovered a natural affinity for languages while at St Patrick's High School, Coatbridge, and went onto the Strathclyde University to take a degree in languages including Spanish, French and Russian. She became a language teacher and soon worked her way up the school hierarchies to become Principal Teacher of Modern Languages at John Ogilvie High in Hamilton.

Spanish has always been her favourite language and a trip to Vila-real seemed as good a place to start her European football travel career as anywhere. She found the whole experience of the 14th April 2004 overwhelming and finds it hard to remember specific detail. She does remember the fantastic atmosphere of the day and the wonderful sights of so many Celtic supporters on the streets, mixing freely with the locals. She remembers the general sense of excitement, and togetherness. She remembers the specifics of the mutual singing, and the two sets of fans applauding each other, both within the stadium and outside afterwards. She did not really get much opportunity to use her Spanish. The one interaction she did have with a local resident, was on the walk back from the Stadium after the game. An old Spanish man said to her and Tosh, "Your team did not play well tonight, you must be disappointed", and she had agreed with him, in perfect Spanish.

Linda Orr in some ways is the very essence of what this book is all about. A good woman, shy, withdrawn not self-seeking. From a trip to Vila-real and a related offer to be an interpreter, has grown a relationship in which she has become a full member of a Vila-real family and will end up making her home there after retirement. As well as gaining a family, she has made many friends in the Spanish community. She has acted as host and enabler to a whole string of Vila-real visitors to Scotland over the past 5 years. In the meantime, with quiet professional efficiency and dedication, she has improved the lives of hundreds of young people in both communities by enabling them to learn to appreciate each others culture as well as improve their own ability to speak the others' language.

Tosh McLaughlin who had accompanied Linda on the trip and shared that conversation with the old Spanish man, was a much more seasoned traveller on the European football scene. A lifelong native of Hamilton, he has taught for 25 years as a languages teacher at the local John Ogilvie High School and is now also Principal Teacher of Pastoral Care (Guidance). His first European game was as long ago as 1963-64 against Leixoes in the then Inter-Fairs Cities Cup. He has been a regular attender at all Celtic games, home away and in Europe, since 1965-1966. To his great lifelong regret, he was "too young and too skint" to go to Lisbon in 1967, but was at Milan and Seville. He had never heard of Villarreal before the 2004 draw and it was "just another away game" to him at the time. Tosh whose harsh features, harsh voice, harsh demeanour and shaven head give off a mistaken aura of a harsh man, when really he is a wonderfully friendly, caring and humorous person, had been very impressed with the atmosphere of the day and the behaviour of both sets of fans "I have never seen anything like it anywhere else before or since." But while he thought the experience had been marvellous, like most Celtic supporters he thought that was the end of the matter, an unforgettable day, great memories of friendliness and togetherness, but still nothing more tangible than happy recollections. As he says now "Boy, how things have changed."

If Pepe Mansilla has become a legend with Celtic supporters, through his ability to outdrink them all night long while singing, dancing and being friendly in exuberant style, the nearest Celtic equivalent has been Thomas O'Hare, known in Celtic circles as Tam and in Vila-real legend as El Abuelo (the grandfather). Since his first visit in 2004, Tam has become a frequent visitor to Vila-real, coming over several times a year, generally around Fiestas times. He is well known in just about every Vila-real bar, and for a town of 50,000 there are many. His drinking capacity, seemingly unlimited, is part of the legend. Tam is one of that peculiar breed of Scottish drinker who seems half drunk after his first pint, but then does not seem to deteriorate further no matter how many more disappear down the throat. He has taught Vila-real people the meaning of the phrase, 'hollow legs', unknown to them until then, but only a partial explanation of where he puts it all (they are pretty scrawny after all). Tam hobbles about the town in that slow gait of his, encountering that dream problem for any Scottish drinker, no bar is prepared to take his money, but they are all honoured to ply him with drink.

Tam was born and brought up in Lanarkshire, has lived for over 30 years in Coatdyke and earned his living as a plater in steel works until the industry disappeared around him. Three of his siblings including sister Linda became teachers, but Tam says, "They might have got the brains, but I got the common sense." Tam grew up with a strong identity as a Celtic supporter, inherited from his father and shared with his brothers. He vividly remembers at 10 years of age, being taken to Parkhead to see the Celtic team, straight back from Lisbon, being driven around the stadium on the back of an open decked lorry.

Ever since that dramatic and fantastic post-Lisbon night, Tam's main identity has been as Celtic supporter. He has watched them all his life and been a season ticket holder for many years. Both his sister Linda and her pal Tosh, have season tickets seats in the same row as Tam. Tam was in Seville in 2003 and had been a regular traveller to away games, often with Tosh, before Celtic drew Villarreal in 2004. Tam had never heard of Villarreal before the draw and had no idea where in Spain they came from. He nearly missed out on going to the game, with the effects of long term unemployment beginning to seriously impact on his life style, but his brother Kevin and sister Linda insisted he go with them, assisting him financially to do so. Tam is very glad they insisted "Otherwise I would have missed out on the best moment of my life, when the Villarreal supporters lined up in the street after the game and clapped us all the way down the road." Tam has been a full part of the phenomenon ever since. "I have never met better people in my life than the Celtic Submari members". He has a particular admiration for Ernesto, "a special man, a brilliant man". "They have all made me so welcome. I come out here whenever I can. I can't praise the people highly enough, they are so friendly, so welcoming." He knows of his reputation and legend as the "Abuelo" and has a pride in that identity.

How many Celtic supporters actually were in Vila-real on the 14th April 2004? Some accounts put it as high as 15,000. Most contemporary Scottish accounts settle for around 12,000. The Spanish newspapers estimated it variously as between 8,000 and 10,000. There is no way of getting an accurate figure. Taking everything into account, newspapers reports, police reports, eyewitness accounts, I reckon that the actual number was probably somewhere between 9,000 to 11,000, with the lower end of that estimate more likely than the top end, so I have used the round number 10,000 throughout this chapter.

Chapter Thirteen   April 14th 2004   The Villarreal view

Vila-real is not one of the prettier small towns in Spain. In truth it lacks even the charm and attraction of the likes of Coatbridge. It does have one or two interesting older buildings, all religious, but it has no known tourist attractions and does not attract visitors from the outside world, either for sightseeing or holidaying. Vila-real is not on any known tourist trail and its population decreases rather than increases in the summer months, as even its own residents seek to escape to somewhere more pleasant and enjoyable. The twice yearly Vila-real Fiestas, while very important to the town's population, are not the kind of events that have ever attracted outside visitors. With the Spanish disinclination to go to away games, even its few years in La Liga did not lead to any influx of more than the thousand or so fans that Barcelona brought to the its first few league games at the Madrigal.

So in April 2004 when Villarreal drew Glasgow Celtic in the Quarter Final Round of the UEFA Cup, Vila-real realised something unprecedented was about to happen around the second leg game at home. Authorities and the people began to panic, as early estimates emerged that suggested perhaps as many as 15,000 drunken British football hooligans might invade their town.

Saul Ramos remembers being less worried beforehand about the coming Scottish invasion than some were. He knew about the UEFA and FIFA Fair Play and Good Behaviour prizes. His main memory of the day is how "they made me laugh a lot. It was a hilarious day." He found the level of friendliness and interaction unbelievable, as was the amount of beer the Celtic supporters could drink. He remembers supporters of both sides wishing each other luck before the game, and thinking how refreshing that was. He found the noise and atmosphere in the stadium for the game reminded him more of one of his trips to a British stadium than the normally rather genteel Madrigal. At the end of the game, Saul swopped his Villarreal scarf with a Celtic supporter sitting near him, and proudly put on the Celtic one he got in return.

"Outside the ground I met up with several of my friends in the usual congregating place. It was just where the main mass of Celtic supporters were exiting from the stadium. Simultaneously each group of spectators began applauding the other. As we lined up on one side to applaud the Celtic supporters out, I noticed Javi Salas (now a well known Celtic Submari member) and some of his friends on the other side doing the same, which created a sort of corridor down which the Celtic supporters passed. Other Villarreal supporters saw what was happening and spontaneously extended the corridor so that Celtic supporters were applauded all down a route with clapping Villarreal supporters on either side."

Once every one was out the stadium the partying began. Saul remembers in particular his group of friends being joined by a young Celtic fan in his early twenties who couldn't speak Spanish but was excitedly communicating with all Saul's non-English speaking mates. Their new friend accompanied them to several bars until eventually they noticed all the other Celtic supporters had disappeared and that that the last train to Valencia where their new friend's hotel was, had left. Saul later heard one of his friends had put the young man up in his own house and put him on the first train the next morning.

Luis Broch the banker describes the 14th April 2005 as "My happiest moments as a football fan". He said "I had thought the notion of a Paella Party for all the Celtic fans was a crazy one, but I was amazed by how well it had gone, and how very excited and very friendly everyone was." He had two particular memories from a wonderful happy day. One was when "a young man Celtic fan had fallen down, drunk, and cut open his head quite badly, with a lot of bleeding. I talked to him in English but he refused to go to hospital as he did not want to miss the game. I was only able to persuade him to do so, when I gave him an absolute guarantee that one of my friends would take him in his car and have him back at the ground before kick-off time."

The other was the only bit of physical trouble he saw the whole day, a fight between two drunken Celtic fans. It was quickly stopped by other Celtic supporters who had explained to a bemused Luis and his pals, that it was a father and son, and they were always like that when drunk and it didn't mean anything. And sure enough they had gone off with their arms round each other.

Estrella has very happy memories of the 14th April, what she can remember of it anyway. She could remember the Celtic supporters vividly, but not the score of the game. She describes the Celtic fans as "behaving great. I had expected them to be like the English, nasty and aggressive, but they were all very friendly and very nice, even though they were all drunk. I was particularly surprised, and very pleased, at how great and friendly they were with our children, playing with them, giving them sweets and other presents." Estrella, who has a natural gift for engaging with people, reckoned she made many friends in the few hours before the game. She danced, as she always does, almost non stop and was delighted that many Celtic supporters at least tried to dance with her, though none could keep up. Estrella loved all the Celtic supporters wearing skirts/kilts, especially those not wearing anything under them.

There is a Castellon variation of the "Yard of Ale" challenge which involves a traditional goatskin flask, with a long neck, filled to the brim with wine. Estrella remembers one young Celtic supporter who took her up on the challenge and lay prostrate of the bar floor as she tilted the flask down his throat, while the other Celtic supporters in the bar cheered furiously. "He failed but at least he died trying, with a smile on his face" she recounted with that unique smile of hers.

She was impressed after the game with the way the Celtic supporters responded to all the Villarreal supporters clapping them. They made a passageway on two sides, funnelled the Celtic supporters down it, clapping them all the way. "It was good to see, that despite having been beaten, they were nice and happy and still friendly, and when we clapped them furiously, they returned the clapping." She ended up with a Celtic top and a Celtic scarf having swopped her own Villarreal ones. Her daughter and all her pals did the same. That was very special, and is her favourite single memory, all the clothes swapping.

The 14th April 2004 had been amazing day for Vicente Arneu, despite knowing a little what to expect after his trip to Parkhead the week before. "All the

Villarreal bars ran out of beer" he assured me, "Not myth but fact. We had never seen so many people drink so much, so quickly". It was incredible seeing "so many people on the streets of our town. It boosted the population to the highest it had ever been". Vicente pointed out that as well as the normal 50,000 and the 10,000 Celtic supporters, there were also the 10,000 Villarreal season ticket holders who live outside Vila-real, boosting the normal population by 20,000 or 40%. "That day all you could see was green and white, a sea of it everywhere. Everyone came out of their houses to see the Celtic people. Many had the same initial idea I had started with the week before, that Celtic supporters were British and therefore likely to be hooligans, and that it might be dangerous to be around them, but they were all so friendly they quickly realised that was not the case and soon they were all talking to each other." Vicente reckoned "It was well received by the people of Vila-real that a fair number of Celtic supporters went to the main Church, St Pasqual's, not something they were used to visiting supporters doing."

Vicente reckoned that about half the Celtic supporters did not get into the game but others have said the percentage was much lower than that. He had heard some stories of some Villarreal supporters selling or even giving their tickets to Celtic supporters, but also knew that his sister-in-law had been offered a ticket by a Celtic supporter outside the ground just before the game was due to start. He had pointed to his friend lying drunk on the ground and said "It's his, but there is no way he will be using it, you might as well have it." Vicente had marvelled at someone travelling 1800 kilometres to fall asleep outside the ground.

Vicente accepted that Celtic supporters, although in the clear minority, had made by far the more noise. He was impressed by the communal singing of the Celtic supporters, all singing the same songs. This was a concept unknown to Villarreal, where the only noise they ever made was the 'Villarreal, Villarreal' chant. Other than the unsingable club hymn, there was no song belonging to Villarreal supporters that they all knew and sang. Vicente reckons that the subsequent adoption by Villarreal supporters of the "Violeta" song owes a great deal to how impressed they all had been by the Celtic supporters repertoire and wanted at least one of their own. "At the end of the game, all the Villarreal supporters stood and applauded the Celtic supporters. In turn despite having been beaten, all the Celtic supporters sang "You'll never walk alone" and kept singing happily, all the time they were made to wait before they were allowed to leave the ground. Once Celtic supporters had exited the stadium they were clapped all the way down to the town centre by rows of Villarreal supporters. They did this because they were amazed at the positive behaviour of the Celtic supporters, supporting their team so well even in defeat. The Villarreal supporters had never seen anything like that before, or since."

Pepe Mansilla had to work in his shop on the day of the first Celtic game. Ernesto had come to his shop on the day of the game and said, "You must come out and see what is happening" but he could not leave the shop. Later Ernesto told him about going up Avenida Allemana and he and Jose Manuel watching the fans. It was his first time out since the death of his son. Ernesto told him "They drunk the bar dry. They are giving their tops away, these are good people." Pepe did manage to get to the actual game and see the truth of that remark for himself.

The invasion of the Celtic fans in 2004 had an enormous impact on Angel. He said "The town had never seen so many strangers in it, ever before. We were all amazed how well behaved they were". Angel had watched the game from the Fundo Norte only two rows down from where most of the Celtic fans were located. He was impressed by how friendly, open and positive they were. One incident that stood out for him was when one Celtic fan threw a plastic glass, all the other Celtic fans turned on him angrily, even though it could not have harmed anyone.

Ximo has very happy memories of the 14th April 2004. He went to the Plaza Llabrador with his wife and son before the game, and was delighted with the interaction with all the Celtic supporters. He and his wife were given free beer by Celtic fans and his son was treated very well. He remembers a group of Celtic supporters getting off a bus, including a priest who, in the magical way such people have of knowing who are true believers, came over to Ximo and wished him and his team well, which impressed Ximo greatly. Ximo was clear "These are good people". Ximo and his family were among the Villarreal fans who chanted "Celtic, Celtic" at the end of the game, in recognition of the good sportsmanship and behaviour of the visiting supporters. He was pleased after the game, that Celtic fans applauded the Villarreal supporters in turn.

Ioan had arrived an hour before the game in the Plaza Llabrador and was blown away by the numbers of Celtic supporters already there, and the friendly atmosphere. Ioan knew about Seville and the UEFA and FIFA Awards so he was not expecting hooligans, but the degree of friendliness was way beyond his expectations. Within minutes of arriving he had swapped his Villarreal scarf for a large tricolour which he still has today. Ioan took many photos and a video film which captures well the amazing atmosphere of the day. What he remembers is after the game the Villarreal supporters clapping the Celtic fans. He was so impressed that even though the Celtic had been beaten, their fans were still so loyal to their team. "It was obvious that they were good people who live and breathe football."

Domingo called it "One of the most significant days in my life, the day Celtic came to Vila-real. It was obvious that they were all fans that knew how to behave, how to interact, that had a passion for football but were orderly and well behaved." Domingo was one of the thousand or so Villarreal fans that attended the Paella parties with thousands of the Celtic fans.

The above are just a selection from some of the many comments I received from Villarreal supporters about that day. It seems every single resident of Vila-real has a positive memory of that unforgettable day, and a colourful story to tell about it.

The next morning the local Spanish papers were full of reports of the off-pitch activities of both sets of supporters as well as details of the actual game. The main headline in El Periodico Mediterraneo was "The Celtic Tide invades Vila-real in a day of festival celebrations, and without any negative incidents". The paper reported the great success of the Paella Party which it had helped sponsor. The paper also reported on the Supporters game, which it described as having helped positively warm the relationship between the two sets of supporters. The paper commented on the excellent comportment of the Celtic supporters who they said definitely lived up to their wonderful reputation gained in Sevilla and other places. It praised the way both sets of supporters had mingled happily, posing for photographs together and exchanging scarves. It commented positively on the wonderful singing ability of the Celtic supporters and concluded that these wonderful supporters had definitely left a favourable impression on Vila-real. Elsewhere in the paper, it was quietly noted that Villarreal had played Celtic off the park, with only Larrson showing the quality expected from a team that had beaten Barcelona in the previous round.

Fernando Roig, the Villarreal President, with his usual prescience drew a slightly different conclusion from the events of that wonderful day. He did pay lavish praise to the excellent behaviour of the Celtic supporters whom he described, "As always, having behaved excellently", but he went on to give even more praise to his own supporters. He described the Villarreal support as having come of age on the 14th April. He gave them 10.5 out of 10 for their behaviour and their great contribution to a true festival of football. He described himself as euphorically proud of the behaviour of the Villarreal supporters. He used, as did many others, the word "incredible" to describe the events of the day.

Chapter Fourteen   Ernesto's day 14 April 2004

None of us who have not been there can completely comprehend what the death of a young child does to a devoted parent. The pain can be numbing, all-embracing and eternal. Ernesto Boixader took the death of his son on 24th March 2004 extremely hard. He felt numb, vacant, depressed, empty and many more emotions he could not then, and still cannot now, put into words. He withdrew into himself and would not leave the house. He became obsessed with housework, something he normally left to Maria Dolores. He did not seek or take anti-depressants, though any doctor would have offered him them.

Even football, a refuge for men in emotional pain and distress, offered him no relief. He couldn't go to the home game against Atletico, one of the big games of the season which took place in the week or so after his son's death. He ignored the following game the next week, away against Barcelona. He was only vaguely aware that some of his friends went to Glasgow in early April to see Villarreal's UEFA Cup Quarter Final away leg against Celtic. By the 11th April he still had not come out the house, missing his second home game in a row. He told his family he was not going to go to the Celtic game, due the following Wednesday. His brothers, Jose Manuel and Julio in particular, were very worried about him, and tried desperately to re-engage him in the world. Julio had played a large part in arranging the friendly game between Villarreal and Celtic supporters to take place on the afternoon of the 14th, before the second leg home game at the Madrigal. Jose Manuel had signed up to play in that game and along with Julio he put incessant pressure on Ernesto to agree to take part, emphasising how much they needed his professional skills against the wild Scotsmen. Eventually they wore him down and he reluctantly agreed. He would do his duty and play, but he would not go to the game at night.

Ernesto has subsequently admitted that he knew very little if anything about Glasgow Celtic before the 14th April 2004. He had no real interest in football outside Spain, and like many Spaniards, was only vaguely aware of Scotland as somehow a part of England. He had known that Celtic supporters had distinguished themselves in Sevilla the previous summer, but still saw them as English supporters, with all the negative connotations that phrase had in civilised Europe.

On the afternoon of 14th April, Ernesto turned up, boots in hand, expecting to do his duty and retreat home. Instead something happened to him over the next few hours that transformed not only his life, but that of many other people. The game itself was a stroll in the park, for a half-fit ex-professional of 40 years of age. Half the Celtic team were somewhat the worse for drink. They had an assortment of tops, mostly Celtic ones, but very few shorts. Two or three of them did not even have proper footwear, having been press ganged into action from a nearby pub. But Ernesto loved them all, loved being part of a friendly football experience. "These are good people" was what he thought of the players and their many excited supporters.

Ernesto began to get affected by the camaraderie, certainly enough to be persuaded to go for a beer after the game. The pub near the Plaza del Labrador he went to with his brother was, like most of them that day, full of happy noisy Celtic supporters. Jose Manuel, who had been the goalkeeper for the Villarreal supporters team, ordered two beers but before he could pay for them, some large Celtic supporter plonked his money on the counter and insisted on paying for their drink.

The Celtic supporters sang some of their songs, then challenged Ernesto, Jose Manuel and the few other Spaniards in the Bar to sing a Villarreal song or two. At that time they didn't have one. Finally out of pure shame and embarrassment, Ernesto agreed to sing them a local Valenciano song, "Mantelcoy", a song nothing to do with football. The Celtic supporters applauded enthusiastically and the party notched up a gear or two. By coincidence Ernesto was to meet one of these songsters years later, as the husband of the contact he made at Yorkhill Children's Hospital when making the arrangements to hand over thousands of pounds raised by the Celtic Submari.

Up to that day, Ernesto had had a mind set that football was about rival sets of supporters. He saw, at the game, in the streets and in the bar, that in fact football could be about camaraderie, about a celebration of universal friendship, about something more than football. He felt he wanted to be part of this. Suddenly in a quiet part of his head, Ernesto had a notion of his young son saying to him, "Papa, go with these people to the game, please". His mind blown away with the friendliness and generosity of the Celtic supporters, he agreed.

When I asked Ernesto what was his greatest memory of the actual game, his reply was about what he clocked on his walk to the ground, the numbers of fathers and sons going to the game together. On the Celtic side there seemed to be more than normal, partly due to a Sevilla compensation factor. "OK, you were not allowed to go to Seville, but you can come this next trip to Spain." On the Villarreal side, every game is for the family, fathers go with their sons, and daughters, and mothers rather than as in Glasgow primarily with their mates. But Ernesto saw these sights as happy ones if tinged with regret, rather than desperately sad ones. After the game he vividly remembers coming across one sad wee Scots boy, sitting on a short wall weeping his heart out, while his father tried unsuccessfully to console him.

His other memories of the game are also incidental to the football. The predominant memory is of the noise made by the Celtic supporters, and his pride that the Villarreal supporters, normally exceptionally quiet, made a real effort not to be outdone, banging any receptacle capable of making a noise. Although Celtic fans were in the minority, Ernesto admitted they won the noise war but he was proud that it was not a walk-over. The other memory that struck him forcibly was how the Celtic supporters were spread out throughout the Stadium, but everywhere the interaction was warm and friendly, not the slightest hint of anger or aggression anywhere.

But it was the events after the game that perhaps made the greatest lasting impression on Ernesto. Celtic supporters had come to Vila-real hoping, indeed expecting, to win. Who were Villarreal anyway, compared to the mighty Celtic, last season's finalists? On the night their team was comprehensively outplayed by a Villarreal side managed by Paquito, who fully deserved their 2-0 victory. Yet despite the crushing disappointment of this defeat, and the realisation that there would not after all be another Sevilla in Gothenburg, the losing supporters were as wonderful in defeat as they had been in anticipation of victory. They were generous to their victorious hosts, both verbally and physically. In what Ernesto described as a veritable orgy of shirt swapping, Celtic fans gave away many of their possessions. Sometimes they took Villarreal goods in exchange, but many a time they just gave, to children and adults, without any expectation of return. Each set of fans kept applauding the other, victors and vanquished all equally positive. There was no anger or downheartedness. Ernesto watched this generosity of spirit in defeat and knew he was watching something special, something unique in his experience. He saw true camaraderie of spirit made possible through football. He saw genuine friendship exercised even in defeat. In the magnanimity of the losers, he saw something worth preserving.

Later over the next few days, recollecting these emotions in tranquillity, he saw and sensed the contribution of his son in guiding him. He determined that his son's contribution would not end there but would push him into finding a way of recreating these marvellous acts of friendship, solidarity and togetherness. When he heard from his brother Julio about the cash collection the Celtic supporters had made, and how they had insisted on the money be given to a local good cause, the final elements of the small jigsaw clicked together and he saw a full picture. He saw how these feelings could be translated into something tangible, something ongoing and something that would benefit others.

Recollecting these feelings years later, he told me "It was a beautiful thing I beheld that day and I was determined it would not just fade into a distant memory. I realised that football was not just about kicking a ball. I realised for the first time football was not about hating your opponents. I understood that with that sense of camaraderie, football could be a force for good."

The Sunday after the game, as every other Sunday, there was a Boixader family lunch. Ernesto spoke about what he had seen and what it had meant to him, and how he would like to find a way to recreate and prolong the phenomenon. Julio and Jose Manuel saw in him greater animation than for a long time, and the first stirrings of real feelings from the numbness of weeks past, and so they supported him. All present became excited at the possibilities being discussed, and over the course of the afternoon a definite plan took shape. They would form a Villarreal Penya (Supporters Club) dedicated to Glasgow Celtic, committed to demonstrating the Celtic virtues of friendship, respect and care for others. They would make regular trips to Glasgow and they would invite Celtic supporters back to Vila-real. It was at that first family lunch that the name, the 'Celtic Submari' was first launched. Julio contributed the information that the Penya to which he belonged, the Penya Grocs, had just collapsed through disinterest and disunity, and that the premises they used, the basement below Lluiso's restaurant in one of the main streets of Vila-real, would be available. And so the Celtic Submari was launched.

It was never explicitly stated, but Ernesto knew, and Maria Dolores knew, and Uncles Julio and Jose Manuel knew, and the whole family knew, that this venture would be a living memorial to young Ernest. They recognised that somehow he had helped direct his father into a role that would begin to fill the huge hole in his heart. They all sensed that the many benefits and positive experiences to come would be a continuing homage to the memory of the beautiful young boy who had been denied the opportunity to experience for himself the many positive virtues and vicissitudes associated with the best that football can offer.

Chapter Fifteen   The Villarreal Celtic Submari Penya forms

Things happened very quickly after that Boixader family lunch. Ernesto says "I went around town, mentioning the ideas, sounding out the people I thought might be interested. The feedback to the notion was very good. Most people seemed to have had the same feelings about what we saw that day as I did. I did not want to create just another small 'family and a few friends' Penya. I wanted something much more open and inclusive." Ernesto had by then a clear vision of what he wanted the Celtic Submari to be about, and what he wanted it to achieve. "I wanted the Penya to help Villarreal supporters become the kind of supporters Celtic fans had proved themselves to be by their behaviour on 14th April. 2004. That was the model I wanted to emulate. I particularly wanted the Penya to be about friendliness rather than hostility to opposing fans, not just in Europe but at home too. And I wanted it to be about learning magnanimity in defeat." Very important for Ernesto was the strand of using the Penya to raise money for people in need. He saw Aspanion, the Spanish Association for the support of families with children with cancer, as a natural first recipient, but from the beginning he wanted a range of charities and causes to benefit. One of his first priorities for action was to take people from Vila-real over to Glasgow to see and learn from the Celtic support, to mingle with these great people.

Over the many social gatherings for the May Fiestas that year, Ernesto began to firm up the idea and start to sign up the initial group he had chosen to help him. The first ten on board apart from himself, were his brothers Jose Manuel, Javi and Julio, and his close friends Jose Luis Broch, Vicente Andreu, Saul Ramos, Vicente Llop, Luis Broch, Enrique Navarro and Pepe Mansilla. Agreement was reached with the owners that the new Penya could take over the lease on the premises below Lluisos, previously rented by the Penya Groc. Maria Dolores designed a logo for the new Penya, honouring Celtic with its conning tower hints of a pint of beer. The design was an inspirational flash of genius integrating perfectly the Celtic essence. Fellow member Javi Salas took her notion, and using the latest technology and software, refined it into the logo still in use today.

On the 27th of May 2004 the new Penya, the Celtic Submari, was formally founded with a written constitution. Shortly thereafter it was admitted to membership of the Agrupacion of Penyas of Villarreal CF. Ernesto Boixader was declared the first President and Jose Luis Broch took on the role of Secretary. The initial supporting Committee was formed by Saul Ramos, Vicente Llop and Enrique Navarro. Over the next 7 or 8 months a great deal of hard work went into creating the new Penya. Much physical work was required to transform the premises into something suitable, but there was no shortage of skilled volunteers. A Celtic theme was of course predominant in the decoration of the premises. Much work was done to continue the process of recruitment and from fairly early on preparations began for the first trip of Penya members to Glasgow, which was fixed for April 2005. Through Gerry Martin, arrangements were made for the Celtic Submari to have a formal link with Glasgow Celtic

Football Club. Derek Rush of the Celtic Supporters Association proved helpful with this and official recognition was received by November 2004.

Ernesto was delighted in October 2004 when the invitation came from Hope Wightman and Pat McGorry to send two members to Scotland to be guests of the Carfin CSC. At first he thought of sending Gerry Martin, but eventually it was decided that Jesus Del Amo Bort and Jesus Uno Vilanova would go.

Ernesto recognised that some of the early members of the Celtic Submari saw it as "A bolt hole from the missus", but he was adamant that it was to be family orientated, for all members of the family, from young children to grandparents, and he ensured this was reflected in both the growth of membership and the signing up for the first trip to Glasgow.

There was an official opening of the Penya in February 2005 and membership began to grow. At the end of 2004 there were about 30 members but by April 2005 the number had swollen to well over fifty, most of whom signed up for the trip to Glasgow. In the end 105 people went with that first Celtic Submari trip to Glasgow. Those who were not members of the Penya, all joined on their return. After the trip, when word about how wonderful it had been and how well they had been received spread through Vila-real, membership continued to grow.

Vicente believes that the credit for transforming the 'good day' experience into on ongoing phenomenon lies on Ernesto's shoulders completely. "Ernesto was not at his best moment. Normally he is a very positive man, but then he was depressed, in a very bad state. He had lost enthusiasm for everything, even football which he had always loved." He knows Ernesto saw the good things that day, the exchanging of scarves, the friendly talking, the intermingling, the good behaviour, the magnanimity in defeat. Vicente thinks Ernesto felt moved to harness the power of football to achieve good things, rather than the enmity he had always associated with football until then. Ernesto saw the possibility of using football as a way of making friends rather than enemies, and his many friends all were happy to support him. Partly for the ideas themselves, partly because they thought it would do Ernesto good. Ernesto and Maria Dolores had come to Vicente's house for dinner one night and they had talked about it at length, what some of the options might be, the possibilities of a Penya. Later Ernesto took Vicente with him to meet with the owner of the premises below Lluisos, and they both agreed they would be very suitable as the premises of the new Penya.

"If Ernesto had not promoted the Penya, we would not have taken part, or joined any other Penya." Vicente, Jose Luis, Saul and the others fully agreed with the values and objectives Ernesto was outlining for the new Penya. Essentially it was a club to foster friendship. Ernesto took the initiative and they followed him.

For Vicente, the Celtic Submari has been an opportunity for a generation of friends, all born in the 1960s, who grew up together very close but who, in their 20s and 30s grew apart as they married and started families, to get together again, with their families and not only spend time together but more importantly do things together. They have had fun, travelled together, made holiday trips together, organised many events and most importantly raised a great deal of money for charities like Aspanion and SMARA, a refugee charity.

Saul knows that the Celtic Submari owes it's existence to Ernesto and his suffering around his son's death. Saul described Ernest's death as "The spark that lit the whole fire." A few days after the game, Ernesto had talked to Saul at school about how he wanted to build on the remarkable events of that day and not allow the goodness demonstrated to be lost. Ernesto had said to Saul "We must do something to continue this" and Saul knew he would definitely respond to his friend's request. Saul used a phrase similar to one used in the same context by Luis Broch and others. I am sure that there is no collusion but merely a strongly similar sense of shared feeling. He said "If Ernesto had asked me to go to Afghanistan with him, I would have gone, gladly." so a request to help form the Celtic Submari was a minor thing in comparison. With his natural inclination to take on responsibility, Saul helped considerably at the beginning with things like constitutions and mission statements and letters of intent, and has continued to be an active member of the inner group ever since. Saul recognised that the Celtic Submari "was partly about offering Ernesto an escape from his situation of extreme sadness" and welcomed that part of its role, but he also fully signed up to the more explicit goals about friendship, learning from others and using football to help other people. Saul remembers sensing from the beginning that the Celtic Submari would become something big. He claims to have told Ernesto early on "We cannot control this. We don't know where we are going or where it will take us" so he has not been too surprised by the subsequent growth in size and scale. "It is unlike any other Villarreal Penya in that it is not just a football Penya" "Indeed" he told me laughing, "some of the members don't even like football. Imagine that, a football supporters club where some of the members don't like football!"

One of the most important things Saul believes the Celtic Submari has learned from Celtic supporters is the importance of the charity aspect of the club, the raising of money to help others. While the original focus inevitably was on Aspanion, it has spread to cover a number of local Vila-real charities. Saul is particularly proud of the Christmas Parties to which many children, including cancer sufferers, are invited. Saul is proud that the Villarreal club always supply players to dress up as the Three Kings (the Spanish equivalent of Santa) "To see so many excited children waiting for the players to come, as if they were gods is wonderful." He added wryly "to see some of the players think they are gods is not so wonderful" but quickly qualifies that as a general comment about modern footballers, not a reference to those who gladly and freely gave their time to help the Celtic Submari help children.

Luis Broch had been friends with Ernesto for a very long time. He saw joining the Submari as supporting a good friend in a bad moment. Luis who thought the Celtic supporters had been "Crazy but fantastic" was not totally sure about the learning from them aspect, but liked the other parts and signed up readily. Luis had been excited about the charitable aspect, that the new Penya would raise funds for good causes. Luis, with his professional connections within the club, was the one who mentioned that Fernando Roig had been a bit suspicious about this new Penya at first. "What are they glorifying Celtic for, rather than Villarreal?" had been the apparent gist of his concerns, but according to Luis, he soon realised they were all committed Villarreal supporters and soon got the sense that they were offering something rare, positive and excellent to the image of his club. As Luis put it, "Roig gets it now."

Pepe Mansilla remembers that three days after the Celtic match Ernesto started telling him about his ideas of starting the Penya. Pepe remembers saying to Ernesto "That's a cracking idea, but make sure you are surrounded by good friends, life long friends". Pepe was happy to support him, and was delighted to see him so involved in something positive. Pepe explained that until then, and even now, most Villarreal Penyas are small inward looking groups of friends, closed to outsiders. "But Ernesto made it clear from the start that the new Penya would be different. It would be about camaraderie and brotherhood and be open to anyone who shared its values. It would not be a closed clique". Pepe looks back at the difficult days then, and the poor state Ernesto and Maria Dolores were in, and the stature Ernesto has now, the person he has become. And says "Ernesto Boixader is my team, my idol is Ernesto" a sentiment shared by many of the Celtic Submari members, original and subsequent.

Jose Luis Broch also knew that his involvement in the Penya was about his commitment to Ernesto. His friend was suffering but seemed animated about this new venture, so Jose Luis had no hesitation about agreeing to back him all the way. He willingly signed up to be Secretary, and like the workhorse he is, took much of the initial work on his own capable shoulders.

Jose Luis is one of the Penya members who most realises the value of Gerry Martin. "Gerry is funny by himself. With some members of the Penya he is sometimes a criticised character, but I know he is a necessary person and has done many important things. He has very good links with Glasgow which have helped the Penya a lot. He is a terrible organiser, there are always problems with buses and cars. But somehow he gets there, and gets us there. He is a very generous person with a big heart, who does an incredible amount of hard work, at his own expense. He taught us the importance of charity and its place within football".

Enrique Navarro was one of the small group who went to Celtic Park in early April 2004 for the first leg game of the UEFA Cup Quarter-Final, so he got an early appreciation of how friendly Celtic supporters could be and was one of the few who knew roughly what to expect the following week. He enjoyed the 14th April immensely so when Ernesto told him about his idea for the new club, including a planned visit to Glasgow, he was amongst the first to sign up. He is one of the 5 signatories on the initial Constitution where he is described as one of the three committee members. He saw the Penya as a meeting point, where he could bring his children, and be guaranteed to meet really nice people. He saw the Celtic Submari members as honest people, just like the Celtic supporters.

Ximo was also keen to join up with the new Celtic Submari, when Ernesto suggested it to him. He knew an important part was about Ernesto's grief reaction to his son, but Ximo also liked the notions of sharing values and attitudes, and the charitable side. Ximo was quite insightful about how important the Celtic Submari has become as a social force in what was always a cautious, socially conservative and self contained village. Like several other Submari members, he acknowledged that as well as the international dimension, the Penya has helped him meet and become friendly with many people in his own village he would not otherwise have got to know. He felt part of the reason for its success has been in the people who have become members, all decent down to earth people. Ximo has also valued the ability generated through the Penya to make a close and two way relationship with Celtic supporters. But probably the most important aspect for Ximo has been the ability of the Penya to help people, through its charitable work.

Ximo gave as an example of the essence of the Celtic Submari Penya, the joy he gets every time fans of opposing teams come to the Penya and are always welcomed warmly. This is just such an alien concept in Spain, but Ximo feels good every time it happens. He feels that "Yes, thanks to the Submari, Villarreal fans have learned the main lesson from Celtic fans, about camaraderie and togetherness".

Angel had not been one of the original founding members, even though he had been very impressed by the conduct of the Celtic supporters before during and after the game. At that time Angel, as he had been for years, was President of another Penya, the Pilar Groc (Yellow Virgin). But he found that Penya rather stagnant despite his presidency, there wasn't really much point or purpose to it. It was dying a natural death. The more he heard about the new Penya, the Celtic Submari, the more impressed he became. "It seemed to suit my frame of mind better. It offered me something new and exciting, a sense of purpose and direction. I resigned my presidency and membership of the Yellow Virgin and signed up with the Celtic Submari, happy just to be an ordinary member, glad to serve under Ernesto". He joined just in time to take part in the planning for the first Celtic Submari trip to Glasgow

Jesus del Amo Bort is a journalist by trade and feels passionately about the value of the Celtic Submari Penya. "To me, being part of this group is very important, special. We are a group of extraordinary people who, in the spirit of Celtic, are trying to help those in need using football as an excuse. In a short time, we have become known in much of the world, and all for good things. Above all, as part of helping, we try to show that football is just a sport, which instead of dividing supporters, can help to unite fans of all teams. Celtic gave us a lesson that we try to implement at all times.

Thanks to the Celtic Submarí, I have met wonderful people, both in the city of Vila-real, and from various parts of the world. One anecdote that I remember fondly was not long ago. I was doing a course in corporate communications at Disneyland in Orlando, Florida. I also worked in the park of Disney's Hollywood Studios as a Park Attendant. There I talked with many Celtic fans who came to the park. They were pleasantly surprised when I told them that I was a fan of Celtic. There was one man who told me he had been in Vila-real the two times when both teams had played each other, and had kept a great memory of his two visits. He even knew of the existence of the Penya. So far from home, it's nice that people who do not know you, speak so highly of your town and your Penya."

Estrella joined the Penya early on in December 2005, through her brother Pablo who is an old friend of Ernesto and his brother Jose Manuel. She likes the Penya because it is a community, not necessarily just about football. It is a place, indeed probably the only place, where she and her 24 year old daughter can go together, and age is not a problem.

Ioan's boss Pasqual was an early member of the Celtic Submari and introduced Ioan to Ernesto and the Penya. He became a member and now comes to the Penya every Friday night and whenever it is open before Villarreal games. He particularly likes it when supporters of opposing teams are brought to the Penya and always makes a point of talking to them, either in Spanish or, if they are from the UK, in his quite good English.

Domingo tells of how the Submari always looks to receive visiting fans, from around Spain and abroad. Indeed he is one of the ones who goes out on the streets looking for them, to drag them into the Penya. He particularly remembers a very good time with Nastic supporters, the one season they were in La Liga. Nastic fans, from Tarragona, traditionally have a bad relationship with Castellon supporters, but they developed very good relationships with Villarreal.

The Penya is entered by descending a flight of dimly lit stairs leading from ground level to the basement of Lluiso's Restaurant on the main street. A single door opens out into a large barn like room, with kitchen and toilets off one side. The whole of the left hand wall is devoted to a pictorial history of the Celtic Submari and in particular their various trips to Glasgow The other walls are a mass of football memorabilia, most of them commemorating Glasgow Celtic but also every other team Villarreal have ever encountered, including Glasgow Rangers. Most of these memorabilia have their own story to tell. The cumulative effect is wonderful, particularly for the many Celtic supporters who find their way to the Penya and are delighted to see how their club is so celebrated in a small Spanish town.

The Celtic Submari Penya is not like a bar. It is not open every night. It does not employ staff and, when open, drinks are served by a rota of volunteers. It is open every Friday night during the season which is the main social occasion for most of the 700 or so members. Friday nights, other things being equal, members head for the Penya to meet friends and have a quiet drink. Ernesto succeeded in his aim and it is truly a family affair, with everything from babies through toddlers, children, young people, right up to grandparents. It also tends to be open on the weekend evening, either Saturday or Sunday, that Villarreal are playing. If the Yellow Submarine are at home, it will be open for an hour or two before the game, then everyone migrates the half mile up the road to El Madrigal. If Villarreal are playing away the game is shown in the Penya on the big screen at the far end. Celtic games are also regularly shown live when available.

Every year there is an End of Season Dinner Dance, which tends to take place outwith the Penya premises. And every year there is the Penya Christmas Party to which many children are invited, over and above those of members. Players tend to be roped in as "The Three Kings" who distribute presents to all the children. The Celtic Submari Penya comes to full-time life twice a year, for the Vila-real Fiestas in mid May and mid-September, when there are events organised day and night.

These are the fixed activities. In addition the Penya runs a whole series of special events during the course of a season, almost all of them linked to raising money for one or other of their charities. Maybe once a month there will be an event or special dinner. Near the start of every season, new players will be invited to meet with the Celtic Submari. At the end of every season any loyal player released or transferred will be invited along and thanked for their contribution.

The charitable focus has remained a crucial part of the Celtic Submari. Over the first four years, an amazing amount was raised by the Penya and presented to Aspanion and other local charities. A copy of every cheque presented is kept on show in the Penya. It is a source of pride to all the key Celtic Submari people that they learned this lesson from the Celtic tradition, and their Penya has been able to help so many others through their incessant efforts.

The Question of Credit

Most Celtic supporters who know about the phenomenon of the Celtic Submari assume, perhaps not totally unnaturally, that the credit and explanation for this wonderful story lies in the excellence of the Celtic support. But there is a logical fallacy here, involving old reliables like 'necessary' and 'sufficient' conditions. Celtic supporters all seem to believe, with to be fair a degree of hard evidence to back their view, Celtic supporters are universally wonderful everywhere they go. However if the credit for the Villarreal Celtic Submari were down to them, there should have been a succession of similar phenomena everywhere the green and white hordes have been, been seen and conquered. But it is only in the small town of Vila-real that a club of 700 members dedicated to honouring the name and concept and principles of Glasgow Celtic has been formed and flourished.

So the explanation and credit for the phenomenon of the Celtic Submari has to lie in Vila-real with the people who made it happen, brought it to life and have lived its principles in such an effective and convincing manner. Though of course the positive behaviour of the Celtic invaders of 14th April 2004 was a necessary precondition.

From the start of his reign as President, Fernando Roig has always been at great pains to publicly lay the credit for the success of his Project with the citizens of Vila-real, claiming that they are exceptional people. This is not just diplomatic froth on his part created for the purpose of selling yet more season tickets, but something he not only fully believes, but something that he is correct to believe. The people of Vila-real are different, hence the record percentage of the population as season ticket holders, hence the record percentage of female season tickets holders, hence the 7,000 members of the Yellow Groguet youth section. And the Celtic Submari has a phenomenal percentage of very good and decent people within its ranks. Why should that be so? The best I can offer is the thought that exposure to someone so blatantly good and caring as Ernesto Boixader rubs off on those in close contact with him, creating a ripple effect of imitation. In a closed community like Vila-real such ripples can flow backwards and forwards without escape, enhancing everything in their repeated path. But Ernesto would be embarrassed and offended by the mistaken view that he is the single source of the goodness around. His family, his friends, his narrower and wider social circles, all contain people whose essential goodness and decency is an inherent quality rather than something derived solely from contact with him. But the combination of events and people described in this book have undoubtedly had a reinforcing impact on each other, and on the sum total of goodness and decency. And all Celtic supporters should be rightly proud of their contribution in enabling such a community of good as the Villarreal Celtic Submari to be formed.

Chapter Sixteen   Gerry Martin and the launch of the Celtic Submari

A few days after the Villarreal-Celtic game, Gerry got a phone call from Julio Boixader. The gist of it was that the people of Vila-real were still amazed at the visit of the Celtic supporters. They were very positive about the way Celtic supporters had behaved themselves before, during and after the game, and their character in defeat. Julio told Gerry it would be hard to overestimate the effect it has had on people in Vila-real. "My brother and I have talking about it and we have decided to start a club in Vila-real to honour the Celtic Supporters and to keep the relationship with them alive". He asked if Gerry could come up to Vila-real and advice them on how they might go about making formal links. A couple of weeks later, Gerry went up to Vila-real to talk with Julio, who introduced him to his brother Ernesto. Ernesto had actually played in the Supporters game and met Gerry then in the passing. But faces and names are not areas of strength with Gerry and he did not make the connection. Ernesto had remembered Gerry from the 14th April, and had been very impressed with his energy and evident generosity of spirit. It would be a further few weeks before they talked to each other seriously, about meaningful things, including the death of Ernesto's son and the impact of all that on his motivation in committing to this new venture.

At that first meeting after the game, Ernesto told Gerry "Your people are absolutely amazing. I want Villarreal supporters to learn how to be like them". Ernesto and Julio said the new organisation, which would be called the Celtic Submari, was already well on the way to becoming registered as a new Villarreal Supporters Club, but they would like to become registered as a Celtic Supporters Club too. Gerry agreed that he could probably help with that. Ernesto said that the new organisation would like to organise a trip to Glasgow early in the next year, and Gerry knew that was something he would very much like to help with.

So Gerry got involved with the building up of the Penya and the preparation of its new premises and over the next few months travelled regularly to Vila-real from his Betera home. He also kept the Huddleboard fully informed of the progress of this new venture, which in the main the Huddleboard members regarded very positively and wished to support. Many promised to help or at least socialise when they came to Glasgow. The Huddleboard has played a crucial and important role in relation to the Celtic Submari Penya, centrally in the early years 2004 and 2005, but also in the years since then.

For Gerry "Huddleboard.net is the Wild West of Celtic Forums and is definitely not for the faint of heart or those with an aversion to robust venacular. If the Celtic Board, certain players, politicians and other periodic targets of its ire want an explanation for the ear-burning sensation they sometimes feel, then they need look no further for the source. However it is also a good place for anarchic and eclectic debate. That's one of its charms. You can go from arguing the toss about the transfer window to the status of Jaffa Cakes to the intricacies of Quantum Theory (sometimes within the same thread!).You may vigorously disagree with and be taken aback by some of the views expressed on there, but it is populated by some of the kindest hearted people you could meet. The response to many Huddleboard instigated fund raising initiatives has always been fantastic. They have collectively raised many thousands of pounds for, amongst many others; the Vila-Real Children's Xmas Party, the establishing of a Room To Read Library for people in developing countries, Children's Education in Thailand, and Yorkhill Childrens Hospital. All great causes but the one that sticks with me was when forum member Ciaran Garry, whose username was Toffeebhoy, lost his battle with Hodgkins Lymphoma aged only 27. The humanity, sincerity and kindness that people on the Huddleboard responded with was life-affirming. Thousands of pounds were raised to help his family with funeral and other costs. R.I.P Ciaran. Huddleboard.net is not everyone's cup of tea, especially if you prefer your tea with sugar, but behind the seemingly incorrigible, mischievous online personas beat massive hearts."

In the course of researching and writing the book I have visited the Huddleboard on many occasions. Several Huddleboard members gave me considerable assistance very willingly, talking to me in person about their involvement in the relationship between Celtic, Villarreal and the Submari. So I know well what he means about the goodness and decency of the people involved, and their love of a good argument.

On 23rd January 2005 Gerry was present in Vila-real for the first real event held by the Celtic Submari for visitors, an event when the Benidorm CSC, composed mainly of Scottish and Irish ex-pats, came to Vila-real to party and to watch Villarreal play Valencia. In a thrilling game of high quality football, Villarreal won, 3-1, with superstar Riquelme getting a hat-trick, two of them penalties. Ah, the little ironies of life.

Over those months preparing the Submari for its formal launch and its first trip to Scotland, Gerry grew very close to Ernesto and became impressed with the quality of the man. "He's such a really worthwhile human being, it is just something he gives off." Gerry was a regular visitor to his house and they compared views on many matters, spiritual and political. Gerry learned how Ernesto believes his son's hand was involved in guiding him into the Celtic Submari, and that Ernest somehow knew what he was doing and approved of it. From these discussions Gerry also learned how Ernesto had seen how football can be used for good. Gerry claims he came up with an original phrase to sum up what the Submari was all about, "The polar opposite of hooliganism - doing good through football". Through his Huddleboard link with Derek Rush, Gerry made official contact with the Celtic Supporters Association. Derek helped him with the relevant paperwork and a month later the Villarreal Celtic Submari were officially a Celtic Supporters Club.

Gerry put an enormous amount of time, energy and ingenuity into organising the first Celtic Submari trip to Glasgow, finally fixed for early April 2005. The nearer it got, the greater the excitement in the Penya and its surrounds grew, and the more people signed up, causing further headaches for the uncomplaining organiser. In the end 105 signed up for the trip. Gerry organised the accommodation for them in Glasgow, all in the one city centre hotel. He worked with Derek Rush and another Huddleboard member, Damien Kane, on the detailed programme for the Saturday and Sunday and once the whole programme was set, Gerry organised the transport arrangements for the whole four days. Gerry flew to Glasgow in January 2005 to ensure all the arrangements were in place and workable. He did all the hundreds of hours this organisation took, in his own time and at his own expense. In his words "I had to do a lot of ducking and diving. It tested my negotiation skills to the limit." Gerry is entitled to a massive amount of credit for the overall success of the trip. He does not have the great memory and attention to detail of natural born organisers like Derek Rush, Saul Ramos or Jose Luis Broch. But he has vision, integrity and a high degree of lateral thinking and problem solving skills. Okay, some mistakes were made. Okay, some of the transport arrangements were defective, the buses provided were not the most modern and had some mechanical problems. But hey, it all came home within the small budget provided, and they all got everywhere they were meant to go. Overall the plans succeeded, the programme was fully implemented, and the trip and the later ones proved a resounding success. Even the more harping members of the Penya will agree that the debt of gratitude owed by the Celtic Submari to Gerry Martin as an organiser, is an enormous one, one that will never be repaid by any amount of free drink. Finally, by the end of March 2005, even Gerry felt he had all the pieces in place, and the Celtic Submari Penya were ready to invade Scotland.

Without Gerry Martin there would have been no Celtic Submari.

There are two elements to this definitive conclusion. It was Gerry Martin that gave birth to the concept, took the initiative and made the arrangements to ensure a game of football took place between supporters of Villarreal and Supporters of Celtic. If that game had not been arranged, then it is quite probable that Ernesto Boixader would never have left his house that day. It is quite certain without the initial experience of playing in the game, and seeing first hand what good people both the players and the Celtic spectators were, he would not have been emboldened to carry on into town and integrate with the greater mass of Celtic supporters there. Without those cumulative experiences he would not have gone to the game and experienced the further wonders he saw during and after the game, including the magnificent magnanimity of Celtic supporters in defeat.

The second crucial concept, to which Gerry Martin both gave birth and brought screaming into the Vila-real world, was the notion of a collection by football supporters for a good local cause. When Ernesto heard all about this development from his brother Julio, the final part of the jigsaw in his mind fitted into place and he could see how something good and positive involving help to others could be created out of the experiences he had witnessed.

Even if Gerry achieves nothing else, that is not a bad legacy for a wee boy from Shettleston.

Chapter Seventeen   Jesus comes to Carfin

Hope Wightman is one of the key figures in this story and, for reasons that will become more apparent in a later part of the book, she has taken on a symbolic dimension in the relationship between the two sets of supporters.

Hope was born in 1942, in East Whitburn, a traditional mining community. She was one of two daughters and 4 sons born to Thomas and Mary McCabe. Football was always a very important part of what was a happy family background. Her father was a strong Celtic supporter and the whole family grew up in that tradition. Hope remembers that although times were hard, her father always ensured that the brothers had a proper leather football. On the few occasions the brothers were not outside playing with it, other people would come to the door and ask "Can we borrow your ball?" Sometimes in that era, owning a ball was the only way for a poor player to get a game, but none of her brothers needed to resort to that tactic. One of her brothers played professional football for Aberdeen and another for Airdrie, but while the family were proud of them, it did not alter their basic affiliation to the Hoops.

After a conventional education in Blackburn and St Mary's Bathgate, Hope left school and learned a trade, as an upholsterer. She was very good at this, and was something of a perfectionist. She married William Wightman, known to all as Willie, and moved to Bathgate. They have one son, Paul, who inherited both parents' love of Glasgow Celtic. Hope has been a Celtic season ticket holder from as far back as she can remember, and has lived through all the developments of the club, both in terms of the team and the Stadium, for well over 50 years now. By the early years of the 21st century, both Hope and Willie were showing their age and having problems with mobility which required, particularly for Hope, special assistance for disability. Partly because of this Hope and her sister had season tickets in a different part of the ground, the North Stand, to Willie and their Carfin friends in the Jock Stein Stand.

Hope looks like a softer, slightly older version of Ma' Broon, an identikit portrait of everyone's favourite granny. Willie is quieter, slimmer, less forward but with dignity and depth. For a long time, Hope and Willie have been members of Carfin 1948 CSC which is where they met Francis and Pat McGorry, and Martin Kane.

Pat McGorry is an Englishwoman who has lived in Scotland for nearly 20 years. Brought up by a football loving father, she supported Arsenal as a young girl and still has residual loyalties there. In 1980 she took a temporary 6 month contract within the NHS and has worked for it ever since. She has qualifications in HR and Business strategy and is a highly efficient administrator. She met and fell for a Health Board accountant Francis McGorry, moved back to Scotland with him, and married him. Francis has been a Celtic fanatic all his life and his wife and daughter have been happy to share this obsession with him.

Francis and Martin Kane are soulmates, accountants and Celtic supporters. They were both born in 1967, a further link to that magical number. Martin came to work with Francis and has become firm friends with both Francis and Pat. Francis has been involved with Celtic Supporters clubs all his life. He brought his accounting skills to the role of Treasurer for Carfin CSC, for whom Hope was a Committee member and Pat a regular volunteer "to get jobs done".

The five of them became very close friends, and began to travel to European away games together. They were all in Seville together in 2003, so when Celtic were drawn against Villarreal in 2004 it was "just another away game for us", with the bonus of a return to Spain igniting happy Seville memories. Hope and Willie have much happier memories of the 2004 trip than Francis. They were not terribly impressed by having to sit on a wooden bench "but at least we got a ringside seat right next to the action." However at half time they were moved into the crowd, beside very friendly Villarreal supporters, and had a great time. "We really appreciated their kindness and affection".

Pat McGorry always regrets that she did not make the original 2004 trip to Villarreal. She watched it on TV with her Celtic mad daughter Francesca. At previous games they had watched together, it had become something of a running joke that Pat would say "There's your father!" and Francesca would be dubious and unconvinced. But this time even Francesca was in no doubt. Every time the ball went into that corner of the pitch, there he was, Celtic top and all, sitting on a bench at the very edge of the pitch.

A Scottish Sun reporter Antonio Carlo heard of the setting up of the Celtic Submari in Vila-real, and ran a small story on it in late October 2005. The story said "The Spanish townsfolk were so taken by the Hoops and their fans during the UEFA cup clash with Villarreal that 670 people are already lining up to join the new club. Spokesman Jesus del Amo said "We have decided to create a new fans association in honour of Celtic. So many of us had a fantastic time when they were in our town, and that day will stay in our memory for a long time. The Celtic fans showed us the right way to be a fan and enjoy a football party. They behaved fantastically; even after the game and their team had lost they were still talking about them. They are the best fans in the world and we want to be part of it."

Hope Wightman read the article and felt very proud. She felt this was a wonderful thing to happen, a magnificent response to a magnificent occasion, and she decided she wanted to do something to foster this new relationship. She discussed it with her friend Pat McGorry.

Hope and Pat decided that they would like to invite two members of this new club over to Scotland to be the guests of Carfin Celtic Supporters Club of which they were both members. Francis, the Treasurer of the Carfin CSC, put the notion to the Committee, of which Hope was also a member, and after some humming and hawing it was decided, yes they would invite two members over. Carfin CSC would pay for the air fares and Pat and Hope would sort out free accommodation for them. Hope and Pat then turned detective and tried to track down someone from the Celtic Submari to share this good news with. Hope finally ended up phoning the Villarreal CF offices in Vila-real and eventually was given a telephone phone number for Jesus del Amo Bort, the Celtic Submari member mentioned in the article. Although neither Hope nor Pat spoke any

Spanish they managed to communicate with Jesus, who speaks some English, and the invitation was made, and gratefully accepted.

Ernesto Boixader as President finally decided that the two representatives should be Jesus del Amo Bort and Jesus Uso Vilanova. The nomination of Jesus del Amo Bort was particularly appropriate since it had been due to him that Antonio Carlo had written the story that appeared in the Sun. Jesus was born in Vila-real in 1980. He has a degree in journalism and has worked in press, radio and TV for a variety of local and national media sources. He covered the Villarreal Celtic game for a local radio station Ona Activa. In the course of his duties he linked up with a visiting journalist, Antonio Carlo, of Spanish origin, but working in a Scottish newspaper, the Scottish Sun. They spent several days talking, and exchanged e-mail addresses.

Jesus sent the information to Antonio Carlo about the formation of the Celtic Submari, in case he might want to use it professionally. He was surprised that one outcome of his action was the invitation to Carfin. "The truth is that we were surprised because we never knew that we had such an impact in Scotland." But he was delighted to accept the invitation.

Pat McGorry is a natural efficient organiser, in her work but also in her own life. She took on the task of organising all aspects of the visit of the two Jesuses to Carfin, including liaising with officials at Celtic Park, who were delighted to co-operate. Pat picked the two Jesuses up from Prestwick Airport on the 5th November and took them back to their hotel, where a social meeting had been organised with the whole Carfin CSC Committee. It turned out to be a good night. The two Jesuses spoke very little English and none of the Carfin crew spoke Spanish but they somehow managed to communicate well all evening. The two Spaniards found Pat easiest to communicate with, with her being English, and none of the rest of the Carfin group speaking anything approximating closely to English. The next day Pat took them a carefully planned and constructed tour of Glasgow, with the highlight being delivering on her promise that they would end up in Paradise, which they did, at Parkhead. They were given free tickets to the game on that day, against Kilmarnock, which Celtic won 2-1. The two Jesuses were made part of the Celtic Pools Paradise draw and introduced to the Parkhead crowd. That was the first indication most Celtic supporters were given that their trip to Vila-real had resulted in a club being formed there in their honour.

That night the 6th November there was a dinner dance, the first official Scottish function at which members of the Celtic Submari were represented. The dinner was a great success. The President of Carfin CSC could not resist the making the obvious joke "I hadn't quite expected to meet Jesus so soon in my life, but now" and in the best broad Scottish-Irish accent "we have Jesus, be Jesus, two Jesuses." Pat remembers watching the local parish priest, Father Miller, guardian of the famous Grotto, flinch.

The President presented the visiting Spaniards with a framed Celtic Supporters Club Rosette. In his words of thanks Jesus del Amo Bort said, "I am in a dream, I can not believe the friendship and generosity I have encountered since we have arrived in Scotland and I never want to wake up from this dream." Two Celtic players Ross Wallace and John Kennedy attended the Dance, and everyone present was enthralled with the stories of the main guest, Lisbon Lion John Fallon. After the speeches, the two Jesuses had an opportunity to have their photographs taken with the SPL Champions Trophy and Scottish Cup.

Jesus del Amo has nothing but wonderful memories of his few days in Carfin. "Finally we went, another member of the Penya and me. I was very nervous about the trip. First, because we were going to represent our supporters club, which at the time had about 80 members. And then, it was going to be my first plane ride. I hadn't flown before and I had the typical first-time traveler's nerves. The next day they took us to visit the Carfin Grotto, a very nice and beautiful place."

He really enjoyed the Celtic match. "We entered the VIP Box of Celtic Park, we were treated like real celebrities. We saw the match and after the game, we returned to the country club, which hosted the dinner. We were the guests of honor and we spoke with Celtic players, including John Fallon, one of Lisbon's Lions."

"The trip was one of the most beautiful of my life. I met wonderful people who were at first unknown to me, but they would later become an important part of my family. It was the first time I met Hope and Willie, Pat and Francis, and Martin. Since that time, they visit us every year and have become a part of my family. Thanks to Celtic, I have now a second family."

The whole experience confirmed for Jesus that proceeding with the Celtic Submari was the right thing to do, and he went back to Vila-real and spread the word about how welcoming Celtic supporters were, and how well they would all be treated when they finally made it over. When the two Jesus ambassadors left Carfin, it was not yet known when the full Submari party were coming over to Glasgow, but early in 2005 Pat got an excited text "Fantastic News – We are coming". That was the signal for the next phase of the process to begin.

Chapter Eighteen   The Celtic Submari comes to Scotland

It was always one of the key aims that Ernesto Boixader envisaged for the Celtic Submari that they would make regular trips to Scotland, to see Celtic FC but even more importantly, to reunite with the supporters who had inspired the creation of the Penya. So almost from the very first meeting, always high on the agenda was the planning of the first trip, provisionally scheduled for Spring 2005.

The planning group were clear that there would be 5 main elements to their trip.

1. Central would be a visit to Celtic Park to see Glasgow Celtic and meet the 60,000 supporters likely to be congregated there. Celtic Football Club were pleased to cooperate and supplied 120 free tickets for the Saturday game against Hearts.

2. It was also agreed that another game between the supporters of the two clubs would be held and the Huddleboard agreed to organise the Celtic end of this. Derek Rush called in an old favour or three and was given the use of the pitch and facilities in the Gallowgate. Arrangements were made for a trophy to be prepared, a Friendship Cup, to be awarded to the winning team, with medals for all players of both sides.

3. Socialising was a key aim of the trip with every opportunity to be taken to bond with as many Celtic fans as possible. Two major dinners were arranged, one for the Saturday night, in Celtic Park, and one for the Sunday in a city centre hotel.

4. The opportunity was to be taken to get a flavour of Scotland and another Huddleboard member, Balloch Boy Damien Kane, agreed to organise a trip to Loch Lomond linked to a visit to a local Celtic Supporters Club.

5. Ernesto determined that raising money for a good cause would be an integral part of the trip, and that this time a Scottish charity should benefit. After discussion with Gerry Martin it was agreed that all monies raised would go the Yorkhill Hospital for Sick Children.

I have subsequently spoken to many of the Celtic Submari who made that initial trip to Glasgow in April 2005 and, without exception, they all describe it as one of the great experiences of their life. I have seen the various video films made of that trip and have become so involved in the images and memories that I have occasionally to remind myself that I was not actually there at the time.

Ernesto describes the trip to Glasgow as "the best journey of my life". The unforgettable moments began right from the time the buses left Vila-real to go to the airport. Everyone on the buses sang Celtic songs from the song-sheets in English that Saul and Gerry Martin had helped provide. A CD of Celtic songs was played, and they all tried to sing along with it. For weeks prior to the trip there had been practice sessions in the Penya in songs like "Hail, Hail, the Celts are here" and other similar terracing classics. At least once the politically correct Submari members were assured that "Hail, Hail" was not a Nazi drinking song!

The tone of the Glasgow end of the trip was set right from the arrival on Scottish soil. The Submari members had anticipated a quiet landing and a solitary drive to their hotel for a quiet night before the hard socialising began on the following day, the Saturday. They were flabbergasted, stunned and delighted beyond words, to be welcomed at the airport by a large gang of Celtic wellwishers, as well as several journalists. The partying started immediately and didn't let up until the buses left for the airport on the return journey.

When the convoy fleet of cars and buses arrived at the chosen hotel, the visitors made it clear they wanted to do it "the Scottish way," and if that meant drinking pints of beer rather than the more sensible smaller glasses they were used to, so be it.

It was perhaps not quite the best preparation for a game of football the next morning, but none of the potential players were going to be left behind in the socialising stakes. Incredibly by midmorning the next day, there they were, at the Gallowgate, stripped and ready for action, before a fair sized crowd. The football match turned out to be a quite hilarious affair. Scott McCorry, an original game survivor, had arranged for the Huddleboard team, which was on the verge of joining a proper competitive League, to take on the Villarreal supporters. The first half was fairly serious with a young Huddleboard team organised on the pitch by Scott McCorry, overwhelming the all-night revellers, who included Saul wearing his glasses, a slightly portly Pepe, and more than a few tired Spaniards feeling their age. The team did not include ex-professional player Ernesto Boixader, which was to prove a bit of a selection mistake in hindsight. Only the heroics of Jose Manuel Boixader in goal kept the score vaguely respectable, but eventually the Celtic Submari in their yellow strips were overwhelmed 5-1 by the younger bhoys in green and white. It was at that point they brought on the cavalry, in the form of a dozen or more youngsters from 3 years of age upwards. Inspired by the enthusiasm of these youthful players, and the active support of an unbiased referee, the Submari fought back. The Celtic goalkeeper was "arrested", frogmarched off, and the resultant penalty was rolled home by a 5 year old who was then carried aloft around the ground in triumph. So 5-2 is the official final score.

Ernesto's funniest memory from the whole trip was without a doubt this football match against the Huddleboard team. After the game and the presentation of trophies and medals, the whole group, players and spectators of both sides, headed for the London Road Celtic Supporters Club for food and drink. Amid the fun, the happiness and the laughter as the groups of Spaniards and Scots started the process of getting to know each other without the benefit of a shared language, there was a moment of solemn seriousness that has remained an abiding and powerful memory for many of those present. Through the Huddleboard Gerry Martin had given an artist contact a photograph of young Ernest and asked him to create a portrait of the beautiful child he had been. Without any forewarning, this framed portrait was presented to an unsuspecting Ernesto, who made a short and extremely moving speech in response. There was not a dry eye in the house. Ernesto later described that as the single most powerful and emotional memory of his whole time with the Celtic Submari, indeed of his whole life. Ernesto cried, he felt great pain, but he also felt great warmth and affection from everyone around him. He was only sorry that Maria

Dolores was not there, having stayed at the hotel. It was a wonderful recognition of the sad reality that lay behind the formation of the Celtic Submari, but at the same time a very positive affirmation that a powerful process of friendship and understanding had emerged that would provide an appropriate memorial.

Then there was a stop in a pub in the Gallowgate, where Angel demonstrated the value of the hard work put in preparing for the trip. Angel had told Gerry he wanted to speak like him, not English but Glaswegian. So Gerry carefully taught him how to order a drink. Well-prepared and well-rehearsed, Angel was definitely ready to demonstrate he was a good learner. Watched apprehensively by the whole party, Angel made his way alone up to the bar and uttered the immortal words "Gonniegiesapintolager, Jimmy". The old barman was so delighted, he handed it over and refused to take Angel's money. The whole group burst into spontaneous applause and the party began.

From there it was onto Celtic Park where the 105 Submari members received a wonderful reception from the crowd. Just before the match Ernesto recollects, "I remember standing outside Celtic Park when this guy came up to me and said 'I'm the person who sent you the CD of Celtic songs.' It was one of the people I had met on the 14th April 2004. We had exchanged addresses as you do, and I instantly lost his, and then one day not much later, before the Penya was even up and running, this CD, which is still behind the Bar in the Penya, came through the post, an unsolicited act of generosity."

At half time Ernesto and the Alcalde (Provost or Mayor) of Vila-real, Manuel Vilanova, were taken onto the pitch for the Alcalde to give a presentation of a Villarreal Ceramic Plate to the then Celtic Chairman Brian Quinn. There was a great deal of discontent around amongst the Celtic support at that time, directed against the Board. The discontent was caused by the Board's recently stated determination to live within their means, and not to spend more than they could generate in income. As a result of this new policy, Quinn as Chairman was booed by a significant number of the crowd as he carried out what should have been a pleasant duty, welcoming the representatives of a large group of visitors captivated by the Celtic phenomenon. It was probably part of the problem that the team were 2-0 down at half time. Describing this process later, Brian Quinn expressed his disgust at the discourtesy involved, not to himself but to the visitors. He worried that they had not received a typical Celtic welcome.

There is no need for him to worry. Ernesto and the Alcalde, the wily politician Manuel Vilanova, knew exactly what was happening. Their group had been massively applauded by the whole crowd when their presence was announced. They were warmly applauded all the way out to the centre of the park. They were warmly applauded all the way back off the pitch. They knew the boos were for the Chairman not for them. Ernesto did find it a memorable experience, being on the pitch before 60,000 of the people he wished to emulate. "I'll never forget being applauded by that wonderful support."

The game itself could have been a let down. Celtic lost 2-0 to Hearts. But just being there, and being part of such a great crowd, was happiness enough for the Villarreal Celtic Submari people who had sung and chanted along with the rest of the crowd the whole game. They loved the whole experience and felt they had been a part of the Celtic family in the Celtic home.

That night, the Saturday, was the centre piece of the whole trip, the dinner at Celtic Park. 600 people were present, 120 from the Celtic Submari connection and 480 Celtic supporters keen to offer friendship to their visitors. Given that very few of the Submari group spoke English, it was a brave decision taken by Derek Rush, the organiser, to mix up all the guests rather than allow them to sit segregated in their language blocks. Brave it might have been, but inspired it definitely was. People refused to let the language difficulties get in the way of establishing relationships and friendships. Many friendships were created that evening that have lasted and are likely to endure forever. The night was a tremendous success and is still talked about warmly by all of those present interviewed for this book.

Ernesto made a speech that night mainly in Spanish but some of it in English, explaining the principles behind the Submari and the desire for friendship and a long term relationship between the two sets of supporters. It was very well-received by the whole audience, almost all of whom by then had been told privately the sad personal story that lay behind the more positive aspects of the formation of the Penya. Domingo's main memory from the evening was of his daughter being involved in the charity collection with another girl. The two got a very good reaction from the Scots present. Domingo saw it as a form of collective conscience, like a universal brotherhood in action, and was very moved.

Sunday morning

Most of the party recovered in time to make it to Loch Lomond the next morning, cold, hungover but definitely impressed. Ernesto's mother and father loved the beauty of the Loch and its surrounds, and the boat trip was a definite success. After some shopping at the Loch Lomond Shores it was on to Dumbarton Harp CSC where a great time was had by all. They had such a ball that it was hard for the organisers to get them out back to hotel for the second if smaller formal Dinner in a row.

Pepe has good memories of the trip to Loch Lomond and the subsequent party in the Dumbarton CSC. Rab Douglas the Celtic and Scotland goalkeeper turned up, which had been much appreciated. There they had raffled Forlan's boots which raised lots of money which all went to the Submari collection for Yorkhill Hospital.

The second dinner party, the Sunday night

Jose Luis Broch talks with awe of the Sunday evening dinner at the City Centre hotel. Since it was originally due to be a do for only the Celtic Submari members, the dinner had been booked for 100 people only. Over the first couple of days they met so many new friends, specials friends, that they had ended up, as you do, inviting about another 150 people. Gerry was supposed to have cleared this with the hotel but when Jose Luis and Gerry turned up at the hotel an hour before the dinner was due to start, they discovered only 100 places were laid, and they knew 250 people were coming and expecting to be fed. Gerry didn't panic, well not much, but ran around begging and cajoling. An hour later, there were 250 places set for dinner and somehow everyone who turned up got fed. Jose Luis was impressed at this ability to muddle through while staying on your feet.

There was a comic highlight that evening caused by cultural differences creating confusion. It was mentioned by several but best described by Ximo. "Us Spaniards are used to fruit being prominently displayed on tables at meal time, as a preferred healthy alternative to heavier deserts and puddings. And all around us, on the walls of the room, were parcels of fruits, part of elaborate decorative presentations. Assuming this was part of some strange Scottish tradition, one brave person in our company took the initiative and grabbed an apple from the centre of one such decorative ornament on the wall beside him. The rest got the message and like a plague of locusts we all simultaneously descended and devoured the art work, stripping the walls bare." Thank goodness it was not November and that the organisers had creatively used real fruit in abundance rather than wax models.

It was at this dinner the Espumita Dance was launched in Glasgow, to great effect. This dance, the 'little froth' dance, is Pepe's speciality. He gets everybody to stand up and join the dance. At the start, every body is up, the beer froth on top of the glass, but as the beer gets drunk, the froth goes down, and the dancers have to wiggle down with it. More beer comes, the froth goes up, and the dancers wiggle back up. And then back down as the froth goes down, then back up, and on and on until everyone gets the pattern and wiggles up and down in tuneful unison. Several hundred people ducking up and down, Celtic supporters couldn't understand a word but got the pattern, the flow, the sequence and by the end a couple of hundred had joined in, all bobbing up and down to Pepe's instructions.

The Celtic Submari donate to a Scottish charity

Another happy, and proud, memory from the trip for Ernesto was presenting people from Yorkhill Children's Hospital with a cheque for 10,000 euros, then worth around £6,000, which had been raised by the Celtic Submari members and their new friends over the 3 days and several events of their visit. On a later visit to Glasgow, Ernesto went back to Yorkhill and was very moved to see that a plaque had been put on one of the Yorkhill machines, dedicated to young Ernesto Boixader, as a token of gratitude for that first large donation.

Ernesto has no real sad memories about his trips to Glasgow but he remembers being depressed by the environment around Parkhead. Vila-real is no beauty spot, but Ernesto was surprised by the evidence of deprivation, decay and poverty he saw travelling to and from Celtic Park. He summed it up in one English word, "Grim". His other sadness was that on two trips to Parkhead he never saw Celtic win. He worried that he might be a Jonas. He was impressed with the number of Celtic supporters who came up to the Celtic Submari people and apologised that they had not seen a better performance from the team.

Ernesto has met many hundreds, indeed thousands of Celtic supporters on his several trips to Glasgow but the two that have made the greatest and most lasting impression on him have been the two teachers, Linda Orr and Tosh McLaughlin. They first turned up at the Barrowfield grounds for the April 2005 game between the two sets of supporters, offering as Spanish Teachers and Celtic supporters to help the party with translating skills. They went everywhere with them that first trip and have become very close friends ever since. Both have been adopted as part of the Boixader family. Linda tends to stay with Ernesto and Maria Dolores on her trips to Vila-real, and Tosh is often put up by Ernesto's parents or by his brother Jose Manuel.

Saul Ramos has many happy memories of the first Celtic Submari trip to Glasgow. The first of them was surprise at the number of journalists that were waiting for them at the airport, something he, correctly, put down to Gerry Martin's extensive network of contacts. Saul also played in the football match at Barrowfield, wearing his glasses. Saul enjoyed the game and was delighted to learn that his performance had been captured on DVD, although he acknowledged he was not expecting a call from Garrido, the new Villarreal manager, any day soon. Saul made many new friends at the dinner that night, most of whom he has met many times since.

One of the Submari who has the happiest memories of Glasgow is Pepe Mansilla. "When I went to Glasgow in 2005, I had no English but I surprised a lot of the Submari people with my ability to communicate. Everyone is deaf and dumb unless they want to understand. Language is only half of communication. It is simple to communicate if the desire is there." He has a large range of universal sign language gestures. He did have happy memories of the CSC in London Road, after the football game, which he played in, a good drinking session and then subsequent visits to most of the pubs in the Gallowgate, all packed with friendly Celtic supporters for him to introduce himself to.

Pepe had two specific memories of that first Glasgow trip that made him laugh again just describing them. He told how he and the rest of the Submari members at first appreciated that Glasgow Police were walking around with yellow jackets on, thinking they were showing their support for the Yellow Submarine! Pepe being Pepe had insisted on telling them all how much he appreciated it. Most of Glasgow's finest played along well, in good humour. The other memory that produced a broad smile was about the Gallowgate Pub where he was welcomed behind the bar and allowed to take it over, as if he was the owner. He ended up on the bar top, conducting the whole ensemble in raucous song.

Pepe acknowledged there would be bound to be cultural differences, with Vila-real being a village and Glasgow a city, but in many ways they were very similar particularly when it came to the love of football. The big difference which he never quite came to terms with was the fact that in Glasgow women got drunk in public, which never happens in Vila-real. "Glasgow is how I thought people should be when I was a child, friendly, drinking beer, good with children, liking everyone". On hearing this description of his own city, Gerry Martin made a mental note to take Pepe a tour of Easterhouse on a Saturday night on their next visit.

Ximo and his family have been involved in several trips to Glasgow. He describes them as marvellous occasions. The first time they went to Parkhead he was so impressed with the Celtic Superstore he went and bought a large suitcase, filled it completely with souvenirs for family and friends, and on the return journey paid willingly to put it through customs as an extra piece of luggage.

Angel talks of that first trip, in April 2005 as "an indescribable memory, one that will stay with me all my life." His most powerful memory was at the end, as the bus left the hotel, the friends they had made being upset. Angel's only regret about the 2005 trip was one echoed by many of the other Submari travellers I spoke to. "That first trip was so good, so memorable, so outstanding, that there was the danger that nothing thereafter could ever replicate it, compete with it".

Later Trips
Glasgow March 2006
The 2006 trip was really more a working trip for the Champions League first leg game against Rangers at Ibrox rather than a social expedition. For some Celtic Submari members this was used as an opportunity to make a return trip to meet with the many friends they had made on their social trip the year before. For others like Luis, it was a more straightforward trip to an away game, quickly in and out.

Because it was a midweek game during a working and school week, the mothers and children did not come and the Celtic Submari party of over 50 that did come, much more closely represented the normal profile of male travellers than the 2005 group had done.

The trip started well, building on the 2005 one. During the first trip the bus driver got to know Pepe well, becoming as everyone does, his friend. When the 2006 bus pulled up at the airport, it was the same driver, who screamed "Pepe!!!" followed much greeting of each other like long lost brothers. When his old friend presented Pepe with rosary beads, as a lovely gesture, the bus was full of people all in tears.

Luis did not enjoy the experience of the Ibrox trip, at least not the three or four hours around the game itself. He felt the police were unnecessarily controlling with the Villarreal supporters, shepherding them together. He felt the general atmosphere to be an unfriendly even hostile one, and at one point he felt a little frightened for his own safety. In the ground, Stewards were quite aggressive about making them take down and fold up a Penya banner because it had a Celtic crest on it and the words Celtic Submari. They were taunted by some of the neighbouring Rangers supporters but in the end there was no actual trouble. As Luis said "It takes two to make a fight, and we were not interested in that." He was amazed at the contrast with the behaviour of Celtic supporters, both in Glasgow and in Villarreal.

Javi went over the first time in 2006 to see the Rangers game. He has a vivid memory of being on the bus going to Ibrox with 50 Villarreal supporters and 10 Celtic supporters all singing Celtic songs loudly. And Gerry Martin getting more and more nervous and warning that they were definitely not to sing any of these songs once they got off the bus. On the way into the ground, Javi found the

Rangers supporters to be friendly, "talking to us with the only Spanish word they seemed to know 'Si', and we would go 'Si, Si' back. One or two of the party were asked to exchange scarves which they did willingly. Javi remembers "I was disappointed the Rangers stewards would not let us stand, or wave our scarves and banners, but otherwise the game passed peacefully, except for the eviction of some of our Celtic friends. And afterwards there was no trouble at all". The other highlight was when, after the Rangers game, Gerry Martin had taken the whole party to Arta, in the Merchant City. Javi had found the venue very impressive and the night very memorable, with lots of Celtic supporters joining them.

Vicente's main memory of the match against Rangers was "We were told not to wear Celtic colours. One of us put a yellow t-shirt on top of his Hoops jersey. Later he insisted a photo be taken of him with two police, in their yellow jackets. But as the photo was being taken he lifted his t-shirt, and nearly got us all arrested." Vicente has still got the photo.

Ximo and his son had attended the Champions League Knockout Stage first leg game at Ibrox, between Rangers and Villarreal. After the game he hailed a taxi which picked them up and began taking them to their hotel. When they had hailed the taxi, his son had been holding a Rangers programme, but when they settled into the cab, he took out some of his Celtic related memorabilia. The taxi driver noticed what he was doing, screeched to a halt and ordered them out of his cab, muttering something along the lines of he was not having any fucking fenian bastards in his cab. Unfortunately Ximo had not known enough to note his cab number, so the furious people to whom he later related this adventure were not able to follow it up with a complaint. The driver had presumably, and sadly correctly, assumed he could get away with that kind of behaviour with foreigners.

Glasgow April 2007

For the April 2007 visit it was back to a bigger social expedition, with whole families over for the full social and cultural experience as well as the football. Organised activities included another Supporters Match, a first team game at Parkhead, a Dinner Dance at Celtic Park, a social in a Hibernian CSC and an evening in the Oran Mor. All this interspersed with day time trips to Stirling and Edinburgh to absorb some Scottish history, culture and politics.

The main highlight was probably the Dinner Dance at Parkhead when once again many hundreds of Celtic supporters signed up to join their visitors. Peter Lawwell, the Celtic Chief Executive, made a speech of welcome to the Celtic Submari members at the start of the Dinner. He spoke of how delighted the Club were that people in far-off Spain had responded so positively to meeting Celtic supporters, that they had become Celtic supporters themselves in turn. The thrust of his remarks were that Celtic supporters were the greatest supporters in the world and the presence of so many Spaniards supporting Celtic was proof of that. He said how delighted he was to welcome them all to the bosom of the Celtic family. He spoke of the developing links between Celtic Football Club and Villarreal CF, and of his pride that football could lead to such friendship.

One of the highlights of the trip, for both visiting Spaniards and open-mouthed Scots, was when Pascual Broch and Domingo dressed up to go to the game at Celtic Park. Domingo went to the game in a bright red Toreador costume, while Pascual dressed in traditional Valenciano outfit. They both have very special memories of the extremely positive response, including much applause they received from delighted Celtic supporters. There was one slight problem though. It had been a bright warm morning and it seemed fine for Domingo to wear the very thin Toreador clothes but he had underestimated the capacity of the Scottish day to grow much colder after midday. Poor Domingo, a warm blooded man at the best of times, nearly froze to death. After the game while most of his compatriots headed for pubs, he dashed back to the hotel for a reviving hot shower and proper clothes. Pascual, whose outfit had more layers, made it to the pubs.

As for the game itself, once again Celtic tried to spoil the party by losing but once again even defeat didn't dampen the enthusiasm of the Celtic Submari at being back in their new spiritual home, where they had once more been applauded by the whole crowd. Ernesto took what satisfaction he could. "Three times I've seen Celtic play, three times they have been beaten. But each time the crowd has been wonderful. Maybe I am not meant to see them victorious!"

The 2007 Supporters game again took place at Barrowfield, followed by another social event in the London Road CSC. Ernesto who had opted out of the 2005 game, played this time and the rest of team turned up in a better state than they had been in in 2005. Scott McCorry by now slightly less fit than he had been at the time of the first game, and also struggling with a beer belly and a dodgy groin, graduated to manager of the Celtic Supporters team. The game ended up 6-3 to the younger fitter home team but that was no disgrace, with the bulk of Scott's team playing regular competitive football. One young Celtic supporter I met in the toilet at Celtic Park who had been at the game, told me what a good player Ernesto still was. Ernesto himself told me he had struggled, feeling his age but still enjoying the experience.

Gerry Martin always tells a story about Antonia Mansilla in Glasgow 2007. The first two nights had followed the usual pattern, of Pepe leading Gerry astray into serious all night drinking while his wife stayed in the hotel room with their young daughter. Gerry and Pepe were sitting in the hotel bar the third evening, just warming up for another of the same, when Antonia stormed into bar. "You, upstairs now" she roared, nodding in the direction of her quaking husband. Then to both Pepe's and Gerry's astonishment, she added "I am taking your place drinking with Gerry tonight."

As Gerry reported later "She is almost as good a drinker as her husband, and much better, and better looking, company. I struggled to keep up with her."

Ernesto went back to Yorkhill at the end of the 2007 trip with another large cheque of funds raised by the Celtic Submari on their Scottish travels. This time Yorkhill were not the only recipients, as Ernesto agreed with Pat McGorry that some of the monies raised should go to another children's charity, one with a Lourdes connection.

Chapter Nineteen   Villarreal comes to Scotland - the Scotland end

The main credit for organising the official parts of the Celtic Submari trip to Glasgow in 2005 belongs with Derek Rush. Derek is one of those solid dependable guys without whom the world does not go round. In some ways he is the Scottish equivalent of a mixture of Saul Ramos and Jose Luis Broch, the two men who have been Secretary of the Celtic Submari over its existence. If you want something done, ask Derek to do it, and you can then relax, knowing it will be done well and to a high standard. Derek has considerable skills in all matters around new technology, which helps with his work in the city centre as a Pensions Technician. Derek is a true son of the East End of Glasgow, having lived in various parts of it all his 33 years, making him one of the minority of Old Firm supporters who supports his local team. After spells in Carlton, Tollcross and the Gallowgate, Derek has ended up back in Tollcross, with his wife and young son. Derek is the product of that not unusual Glasgow institution, a mixed marriage, with his father a Rangers supporter and his mother from Celtic stock. The usual battle raged over Derek's soul but it was won by her mother's side, by the time Derek was 7 years old, largely due to the efforts of his maternal grandfather who induced him into the Celtic ethos and the Celtic ranks. The sister was captured for Celtic too, but the beaten father learnt a lesson though, and won the battle for the younger brother, leaving Derek and his sister on the opposite side of the great divide from their brother.

As a young boy Derek would go to Celtic games with his grandfather but his granddad died when Derek was 12, and he went thereafter with his uncle. As he got older, about 15, he started to go with his mates, most of whom joined the Dennistoun No 1 CSC, and he began to go to away games with them. He began to go to trips to Europe with Celtic in the 1990's, Paris being the first at the age of 18. He went to Seville in 2003 but found it a big anticlimax. He has happier memories of the semi-final away leg against Boavista, where Celtic and Porto fans celebrated together.

That same year Derek was 'encouraged' by Eddie Toner to get involved with the Celtic Supporters Association Committee where his natural organising abilities were soon well appreciated. He left two years later, with too many other things going on in his life.

Derek with his long time interest in Spanish football was one of the few Celtic supporters who had heard of Villarreal and knew they were no mugs, especially with Riquelme running their midfield. Derek, to his great regret now, did not go to the Villarreal away game in 2004, but soon heard all the tales from returning Celtic supporters about what a great time they all had had, and how friendly and welcoming the natives had been. Derek was used to bar owners welcoming Celtic supporters, but this was the first time he had heard of a whole population doing so. Derek made the point that Celtic fans were then in 2004 probably behaving themselves even better than usual, boosted by the two recent awards from UEFA and FIFA. They had an image to live up to.

Derek is one of the original members of the Huddleboard, known as Delbhoy, and first heard about the plans to set up the Celtic Submari via that forum. When

Gerry Martin started asking about formally registering as a CSC and also organising a trip over, Derek knew he could help him with these matters better wearing his Celtic Supporters Association hat, and got formally involved in that capacity. Arrangements were made to register the Celtic Submari as a CSC. Derek agreed to take on organising the Dinner in Celtic Park, the arrangements for the friendly supporters match and the related lunch.

The Celtic Submari party arrived on the Friday and Derek was part of the large welcoming Committee. The first thing that struck the welcoming committee was the composition of the group. Initially Derek had been expecting 100 Spanish guys "When the St Pauli lot came they were all men, the Scandinavians had been all male, the regular Irish visitors tended all to be men. I was expecting the same this time." His jaw had dropped when Gerry had told him the full diversity of the travelling party with toddlers, young children, adolescents, women and the elderly, leaving the anticipated macho middle aged males as a minority. It had dropped even further when Gerry assured him all of them would want tickets for the game, not just the men. "It was when I relayed that extraordinary information to the officials at Celtic Park that I got the impression they began to realise that something extraordinary was happening here." It wasn't until they all trotted through the airport exit gates though, that Derek fully realised Gerry had not been exaggerating. "It was a total shock, I tell you. We wondered if we would have to rethink all the arrangements, especially the drinking ones."

For the Saturday morning, Derek had "pulled a few favours" to get the Barrowfield facilities for the game and the London Road CSA club for the lunch. Derek watched the game standing amongst a group of the Spanish women and was impressed with their obvious knowledge of, and appreciation for, the game. Derek had taken his then fiancée, now wife, to Sevilla, for a holiday rather than the football, and told me the story of how, as extra time began, she had said to him, "Is there much longer to go now?" It was on the Saturday morning that Derek first properly met Ernesto. "It was quite a humbling experience really. I had heard the story but I hadn't expected such a nice guy. It was obvious just meeting him that he was special. You could tell that too from the way people were round about him, looking to him, trying to impress him."

Derek had been worried before the dinner, particularly after Celtic lost 2-0. "You know what Celtic fans are like after a defeat, bad tempered, not wanting to socialise. All these people had been desperate to see Celtic and they got beat. And all the Celtic supporters will be depressed too. But I need not have worried, it turned out well, the best night ever." As the organiser of the dinner on the Saturday night, with about 600 people present, Derek had after much thought and agonising decided to mix everyone up rather than sit in blocks by nationality. He had drawn up a seating plan to ensure integration, with some Spaniards at every table, spread equitable among the greater number of locals. After a quiet start his gamble paid off big style with everyone making a real effort to communicate despite very little shared language. Derek had worked hard soliciting prizes to ensure several raffles and auctions could be held during the night but he was amazed by the determination of everybody, from both camps, that as much money as possible be raised. In the end over just over two days, about £6,000 was raised all of which was given to Yorkhill Children's Hospital as planned. Derek had also worried at the end of the night whether any of them would be fit and sober enough to go to Loch Lomond the next day. "They had started off drinking beer in small glasses but most of them, even the women, soon moved onto pints, washed down with whiskies and vodkas. They were determined to do it the Scottish way". But they all made to Loch Lomond and all of them made it to the Sunday night dinner for a smaller but still robust evening.

When I asked Derek for his most powerful memory of that whole first visit, he narrowed the time to precisely 2.15 am on the Sunday morning. "We had ushered the reluctant Spaniards out the door, after a great night, with much drink consumed, and there waiting for them were the two buses arranged through one of Gerry's crazy contacts. And one of the buses would not start and the driver had given up trying to sort it and left to get help. And I thought, here we are all standing outside a multi-million pound stadium, where earlier 60,000 people had watched players, some paid as much as £60,000 a week, and here we are with a bus that will not start. But the Spaniards were unfazed. Two of the Submari party were mechanics and fiddled about with the engine, another 50 of them started pushing the bus. Amongst that 50 were women, children, Spaniards, Glaswegians, all in their best party gear, pushing a bloody bus and lo and behold, they got it started. I knew then this relationship would last for ever."

Derek was left feeling that all his hard work over the previous months had been well worth while. "I felt an enormous pride that I contributed to something so wonderful, that I had played a part in making it all happen."

Damien Kane

Damien was born in Balloch in 1978 and stayed there most of his life until moving 4 years ago to Glasgow, where he lives round the corner from Hampden Park, with his fiancée. He did an engineering degree at Strathclyde University and is currently a Consultant Engineer. Damien has been a Celtic fan all his life, helped perhaps by the fact that ex Parkhead hero Charlie Gallagher was his godfather, and his father was a staunch supporter all his life, an early traveller to European away games including Lisbon in 1967. Damien saw his first game aged 7, against Falkirk, and was hooked for life. He became a member of the Renton CSC and regularly travelled with them to both home and away games. He has been a season ticket holder for many years and currently has a seat in the North Stand. He progressed onto European games and his list of favoured destinations includes Milan, Barcelona and Seville. He did not go to the away Villarreal game in 2004, but his friend Scott came back full of excited tales about a mad football game between supporters, and a collection that had raised over 400 euros for a local charity.

Damien followed the subsequent discussions about the 2004 experience on the Huddleboard, and was intrigued when he heard that "real Spaniards, not expats" were talking about forming a Celtic Supporters Club in Spain. He read on the

Huddleboard that this new club were organising a trip to Glasgow and decided to respond to the request for suggestions for activities. The suggestion on the Huddleboard had been that maybe the Sunday should be for history or culture, so Damien responded suggesting a trip to Loch Lomond on a Sunday morning might be just the thing for hungover Spaniards. His own CSC, Renton did not really have the facilities to cater for a party of over 100 travellers so Damien arranged that after the boat trip and time at Loch Lomond Shores Visitor Centre, the whole party would go on to Dumbarton and have lunch at the Dumbarton Harp CSC. Damien took Gerry to meet John and Margaret Mulvenna, the key people at the Harp CSC. While they were keen to help, they had worries at first that a very enthusiastic Gerry might be getting ahead of himself. However after full discussion, they happily agreed to cooperate and in the end Gerry had underestimated the scale and numbers rather than the reverse.

Damien met Ernesto for the first time at the Supporters game. Damien has a powerful memory of the presentation made in the London Road CSC to Ernesto of a framed portrait of his son. "A very special moment. We all felt that. We could see Ernesto was really moved, but we all were too, yes definitely a very special moment, for everyone there." Damien admits to having a tear in his eye. It was at that point for Damien that "something clicked and I realised this was not just a normal set of relationships but something very very special".

Then Damien went with them all to Parkhead to the Hearts game, which Celtic lost. He remembers feeling very disappointed that they had come all that way, to see Celtic, and been let down by a poor performance but it didn't seem to depress them.

That night Damien attended the big dinner within Celtic Park. "It was such a big party. Good friendships were formed that night, all over the place. Nobody let the language barrier stop them interacting." Damien remembers lots of joint singing of Celtic songs, and many raffles, with everyone knowing that all the cash would be going to Yorkhill, to the Schaehallion Unit.

It was obvious the next morning that many of the Spaniards had spent the previous night drinking more, and at a faster pace, than they were normally used to doing. And were suffering, paying the price for having tried to keep up. Except for the legendary Pepe who was already boldly leading the way into a third day of celebration. "There were some definitely the worse for wear. That was their first exposure to the Scottish way, heavy drinking. But I must say they have proved quick learners and have made up for it over time. They can drink with the best of us now."

At Balloch, Ernesto's mother made a point of popping into the local Church and speaking to the Parish priest, with some translating help from Linda Orr. Ernesto's mother gifted the delighted priest a Spanish prayer book, so that some small bit of Spain would stay represented there. Most of the party went on the boat with Damien but a few, especially the more queasy ones, opted out, and went shopping in the Lomond Shores centre instead. It was a typical Scottish April day, bracing but not particularly cold. But in a good example of cultural dissonance, while all the Spaniards were well wrapped up in many layers,

Damien had his jacket off and commanded the boat in his shirt sleeves, to the amazement of the party who thought he was incredibly brave, or stupid. To this day, they refer to him as the "the man with no jacket."

Then it was to the Harp CSC for more cultural differences. The local members had expected the normal, a group of beer drinking males, and were amazed to discover women, children, even babies as well as males of all ages. A buffet was put on and some of the local women had prepared traditional Scottish food, including a plentiful supply of home made shortbread, to meet Gerry's request that the visitors get a good sense of Scottish culture. Gerry remembers the exceptional generosity of the Dumbarton CSC people, buying up all the scarves the Celtic Submari had brought, donating fortunes into buckets. The CSC made a presentation of a Celtic jersey signed by the first team squad. It was arranged that the Alcalde would receive it on behalf of the whole delegation. There was much embarrassment when he immediately took it and put it on, beaming proudly at his new acquisition. He had to be taken aside and politely told "Actually it is not really for you alone, and it's not supposed to be worn. It is supposed to be framed." Sheepishly, the normally astute politician took it off and handed it over to Jose Luis. Now it sits proudly on the far wall of the Penya in Vila-real, safely behind a glass frame, available to all.

"My abiding memory was the way everybody just intermingled. At one point everybody was on the dance floor, in a big circle, almost a big Huddle, and all the kids were dancing happily. Standing there watching everyone enjoy themselves was something special." Damien experienced the kind of problem that is probably the best reward an organiser can get for their hard work. All the Spaniards wanted to stay on, they were having such a great time. But eventually everyone was reluctantly packed back onto the buses and headed back to the city.

Damien felt proud that he had been able to contribute such a good experience to such good people. It made the hard work of months well worth while. Many of the Celtic Submari members have talked fondly to me, of their day on Loch Lomond and the party that followed. Damien knows of lots of friendships formed that day that have continued ever since.

The whole Carfin crew went to the big dinner at Celtic Park. Pat McGorry was delighted that the Celtic Submari had given a formal invitation to the Carfin CSC President and his wife and put them at the top table, in recognition of the hospitality given that November to the two Jesuses. That night was the first time Hope, Willie, Pat, Francis and Martin met Ernesto, and they were, as everyone always is, blown away by the niceness and decency of the man. "He was so shy, very humble, very likeable, and totally friendly. He treated us as if we had just become members of his family." They made a friendship that night with Saul Ramos that has continued ever since.

Gerry Martin's memories

At the best of times, Gerry Martin's otherwise fine mind struggles with dates, names and sequences. When you add to that natural weakness, the dual pressures of being the main organiser, and trying desperately to keep up with the non-stop

24 hour a day drinking of Pepe Mansilla, it is no great surprise that much of Gerry's recollections of the three trips, 2005, 2006 and 2007 is a vast blur, with no absolute certainty about what event happened when, where and in what order. But his head is full of vivid unforgettable memories, and two conclusions about which he is absolutely certain. All three trips were a great success enjoyed in full by all Celtic Submari members present. And Gerry Martin had three of the greatest times of his life.

By 2005 Gerry had not lived in Glasgow full time for almost 30 years. He found the three trips an opportunity to reacquaint himself with the city of his childhood, but also to see it afresh through Spanish eyes. Amongst his many standout memories are two culture clashes. The day after the Celtic Hearts match, he came across three of the Penya men sitting in the foyer of their hotel, cutting jamon off the leg of ham they had brought all the way from Vila-real, contentedly eating it with their fingers, oblivious of the bemusement of hotel staff. Another of the days it had been a sunny 14 degrees in Glasgow, the warmest of the year so far, and half of Glasgow seized the opportunity and began walking about half naked. Meanwhile the Vila-real contingent were sitting huddled together, double wrapped in jumpers and coats, complaining about the cold, and marvelling at the bravery of their scantily dressed hosts.

Gerry saw many examples of the generous nature of Celtic supporters. On the way to the game, the Villarreal party, which contained many children, attracted much friendly attention. "Celtic supporters were giving weans scarves, giving them the shirts of their back, literally. They were so generous."

At the Dinner at Parkhead, Gerry acted as MC and communal translator. One of the items donated for raffle was a Henrik Larsson painting. The bidding for it was the most frenzied of the night and eventually it went to a £1000 offer by a business man. Gerry, not normally a fan of businessmen, remembers being very impressed when the man walked over with his new expensive purchase and donated it to Ernesto, to thunderous applause. It currently is in pride of place in the Penya premises in Vila-real. Gerry was proud of Celtic that night. The Dinner was well presented and Celtic paid for the band "Spirit of 67". Celtic also put on Irish dancing which went down well. Gerry remembers some of the Submari members furtively listening to the Villarreal game in Spain on a radio, and an outbreak of white hankies being waved when Villarreal scored. When Gerry explained to the main body what that was about, everyone cheered furiously and demanded regular updates. Villarreal made up for Celtic's defeat by winning. Gerry feels his finest hour was after the raffle, he was quietly told and then had to announce to the whole gathering that the Pope had died earlier that evening. Gerry suggested they should use the evening to celebrate his life rather than mourning his death. Gerry felt relieved the night was such a great success. Gerry who had literally spent months planning the whole trip, had felt very stressed, desperately wanting it all to go well, and was so relieved when it did, beyond all expectation.

Gerry had an unexpected family bonus. For the first time for many years, many of the Martin family were together at Celtic Park that evening. "My Uncle

Tommy was there with my Aunty Betty. He hadn't spoken to me for years. Tommy started greetin', "I'm so proud of you, son" he told me. I was surprised how much that meant to me".

The Teacher who reached out and found a new world

It can sometimes be quite frightening to realise what an enormous impact on your whole life apparently minor decisions turn out to have. Linda Orr offers a striking example of the phenomenon. Linda had gone to Villarreal in 2004 and had enjoyed the trip, but had assumed that the good experience of the day was the end of the matter. One day at the end of March 2005, she was casually reading the latest edition of the Celtic View when she came across a small item saying that a party of Spaniards from Vila-real had formed a Celtic Supporters Club, were coming to Glasgow in April and as part of the trip would be playing a charity match on the Saturday morning at Barrowfield against a Celtic Supporters XI. Linda mentioned it to her colleague Tosh, and suggested that maybe they should offer their services as translators to both Celtic and the Villarreal people. Tosh agreed it was a good idea and might be a pleasant enough way of spending a Saturday morning, exercising their Spanish. Linda swithered about it, but eventually decided, 'Yes, why not', picked up her phone and called Derek Rush of the Celtic Supporters Association. It is no exaggeration to say that that simple act of making one phone call transformed Linda's life. That simple act also transformed, and improved, the lives of many hundreds of others, in two separate communities.

Derek Rush accepted Linda's offer with alacrity, the bite mark can still be seen on her arm, and so Linda and Tosh turned up at Barrowfield, quite unaware how soon both their lives would change for ever. One of the first things that happened that morning was that Tosh gave his Celtic scarf to a Spanish woman who had admired it. Linda got involved in the transaction. Once the woman realised Linda spoke perfect Spanish, she started talking to her, and instantly the whole story spilled out. How the Celtic Submari had started. How her son had been devastated by the tragic death of his son, her beloved grandson. How the friendliness, kindness and camaraderie of the Celtic supporters had reawakened her son's love of football and people. How the collection for a local charity had so impressed people. How in the aftermath of these wonderful experiences, the decision had been taken to hang onto these memories and create an organisation that would keep these values alive. Linda listened entranced, responded warmly and with enthusiasm, and both women soon knew they had found a friend for life. As this conversation developed, Tosh started talking to the woman's husband. Very quickly each could see the recognition dawning on the other; they had met and talked before. Tosh realised this was the same old man who had commiserated with him and Linda after the game in Vila-real about how weak Celtic had been. This man was also Ernesto's father. The coincidences involved in these two encounters are staggering. The consequences of these coincidences were benign and massive. Linda and Tosh were instantly co-opted into the Celtic Submari party, and invited to all subsequent events on the itinerary. They went with the group to London Road CSC, then onto the Celtic Hearts game with them, before attending the big Dinner that night in Celtic Park. The next morning it was off to Loch Lomond, then Dumbarton, followed by the evening Dinner in the City Centre Hotel.

Linda, like everyone else who has ever met him, was very taken with Ernesto Boixader. Linda also gets on very well with Maria Dolores and has become very friendly too with a couple of Maria Dolores' female relatives. By the end of the trip, Linda had arranged with Ernesto's mother that when Linda was in Salou in June, with a school trip, she and all the pupils would come down to Vila-real for the day and between Ernesto and his mother, a full day's programme of activities would be arranged. They delivered on that plan, to a perfection and level of detail that amazed and delighted Linda. By the end of that June day, Linda had been invited to stay with the Boixader family that summer, which she did for a week in July 2005. That first visit she stayed with Ernesto's mother and father. On all her subsequent, and frequent, visits she has stayed with Ernesto, Maria Dolores and wee Maria. Linda Orr is now indisputably an important member of the Boixader family, and they have become her primary family. She has stayed with them both in their houses in Vila-real and in the family summer holiday home in Benicassim. It is her intention to move to Vila-real to be beside her new family when she retires from teaching in a few years time. Linda has made many close friends in Vila-real. She has become well known and highly respected within Vila-real. She cannot walk the less than a mile straight line from Ernesto's house to the Penya, without being stopped by at least a dozen people keen to speak with her.

The day trip from Salou and its great success was the foundation from which Linda has been able to build, with the active support of Tosh, a whole structure of regular exchange visits between pupils from John Ogilvie High in Hamilton and Francesc Tarrega School in Vila-real. The parents of both communities have responded magnificently, ensuring family accommodation is willingly proved for all visiting young people. The young people of both communities have responded even more magnificently, showing a great willingness to embrace each others language and culture. These exchanges, which grew out of a shared love of football, have extended well beyond a narrow focus on the game, and broadened out to ensure that the integration between the two communities will continue for many generations to come, regardless of what happens to their football teams. But football still remains a key part of the whole experience, with every trip having as its highlight a trip to either Celtic Park or El Madrigal to see a game, as honoured guests of the home club.

Ernesto's brother, Julio, also a teacher, has become involved in the Hamilton school spending two spells working there.

The Submari go to Ibrox   2006

When Villarreal were drawn against Glasgow Rangers in the first Knockout Round of the 2005-2006 Champions League, the Submari knew this was a god sent opportunity for another visit to Glasgow. Gerry Martin did most of the Glasgow end organising for the 2006 trip, including accommodation and transport. Derek Rush helped with the bits around Celtic Park and the organisation of the social highlight, a party at Arta after the game at Ibrox. For Derek, the 2006 visit had been much more like he had originally anticipated, with it being largely men over, briefly, for the Rangers game rather than a social visit by the whole Penya. In March 2006 Derek got the message "We are coming over, just for the game, does anyone want to come with us?" Derek was one of the first to sign up. He got some negative reaction from a minority of Celtic fans. 'Why are you giving Rangers £42, and not even to support your own team?' "I tried to explain to them it was not about football, it was about supporting our friends."

The afternoon of the game the Celtic Submari group visited Edinburgh, then went onto Celtic Park for a meal and a tour, and for shopping at the Celtic Superstore. According to Derek "Sky Sports news did a wee feature along the lines 'Villarreal are in Glasgow today to play Rangers, and where are their fans? They're all at Celtic Park' which put a few cats among the pigeons, I tell you". After that Derek had arranged for them to visit a pub in the Gallowgate owned by a friend of his. In that pub there were, as usual, many Celtic fans and as they got to know the Villarreal people, more and more of them asked if they could get a ticket for the game, to come and support them. The two buses that left the Gallowgate to go to Ibrox were rocking as everyone, Spaniards and Celtic supporters, were raucously singing Celtic songs at full blast, while a frazzled Gerry Martin was desperately trying to tell them to stop that singing as they got close to the ground.

Gerry asked the bus driver to pull into a lay-by while he addressed the bus and told them all the rules, "All Celtic colours to be hidden and no Celtic songs as we get nearer to Ibrox". To his relief, for once his words were heeded, but he knew it was a fragile line between safety and disaster. He observed many Rangers supporters looking at the bus and thought "You could almost see them thinking 'these don't look very Spanish'."As they got nearer the ground, he gave the Celtic contingent a crash course in how to appear Spanish. "Don't say anything if you can get away with it, just shrug your shoulders". He taught them the three Spanish phrases they would need in an emergency, "No" "No Comprendo" and "que?", all to be spoken in as near a Spanish accent as they could manage. They would pass groups of Rangers supporters, most of whom waved at the bus in a friendly manner. The Villarreal contingent would wave back in an equally friendly manner. Gerry Martin loves telling the story of how some of the Celtic supporters on the bus, disguised as Villarreal fans, would return the friendly waves with v signs, and bemused Rangers supporters would stand there, obviously wondering why so many Spaniards giving them the Vickie were pasty faced.

They got safely into the ground 30 minutes before kickoff, before most of the Rangers supporters arrived. Derek tells the story of how one of the Celtic supporters amongst them spotted a neighbour of his in the section of ground next to their segregated one, and waved to him. The neighbour came down to the dividing fence and Derek's pal went over to him and they chatted for a few minutes. Derek's pal is quite dark-skinned and could easily pass for a Spaniard.

When the conversation was over, the Rangers neighbour went back up to his section, and was applauded by the mass of Rangers supporters for his ability to communicate with the opposition. Unfortunately the neighbour spoiled his moment of glory be saying in a loud voice, "He's no' a Spaniard, he's a wee Tim fra' Lenzie" at which point the applauders turned nasty, started booing and demanded that the stewards evict the wee Tim.

At that point Derek decided that for the sake of peace, at least until the game started, he and the other Celtic supporters should go down into the concourse out of sight. Still dressed as Villarreal supporters, some of them decided to put a bet on the game, and approached the Ladbrooke's window. The poor betting clerk, seeing 'Spaniards' standing before him, started explaining in broken English how to put a bet on, to 6 hardened Glaswegians punters. When it came to Derek's turn, he spoke his bet in perfect English. He was overheard by a steward who proceeded to evict him, on the grounds that he was Scottish. Derek managed to clarify with the stewards that that was indeed the grounds on which he was being evicted. "Since when is being Scottish an offence?" he protested to no avail. "This area is for Spaniards only" was the line. So 5 minutes before the match started, Derek was out on his ear. Several of his colleagues were similarly evicted. One Steward heard Gerry Martin talking Glaswegian, trying to calm things down, and started to evict him too, but Gerry switched into a torrent of excellent Spanish and the bemused Steward let him go.

After the match Derek still felt indignant at this racist treatment and wrote a letter of complaint to Rangers FC. In this letter he made the point that he was a personal guest of the Mayor of Vila-real, who had indeed been present earlier and insisted Derek come to the game with them. Derek threatened to go to the press if he didn't get satisfaction. Derek also demanded that the price of his ticket, £42, be donated to his favourite Catholic charity. He got a polite reply offering an apology, and an assurance that a cheque had been sent to the required place.

Derek had retreated back to the Gallowgate pub to watch the match on TV, and then made his way to Arta to reunite with the main group for the after match party. It was there that Pepe Mansilla attained legendary status with more of his "Espumita" dancing for the whole bar amongst other delights. Derek describes Pepe Mansilla that night as truly the stuff of legends. "He was right up for it, cheerleading everyone along, involving everyone, leading by example. Despite having no English, he was communicating by every means possible, arms, legs, gestures whatever. He became an absolute legend on the Huddleboard after all the amazing photos from that night were posted on it".

Derek made the point that he felt the publicity around the Villarreal supporters trip to Glasgow, and the publicising of their links with Celtic, their wearing of the hoops, their trips to Celtic Park before the game, was a contributory factor in the bad behaviour of the Rangers fans two weeks later in Vila-real, when some of them stoned the Villarreal team bus and many were hostile to the natives.

Damien Kane like many of the Spaniards found the subsequent visits a bit of a memory blur, what was 2006 and what was 2007 is sometimes difficult to distinguish. He does recall the sense that these times he was meeting friends rather than new acquaintances. "It was good to reinforce the relationships made in the 2005 encounters".

Damien recalls the trip to Ibrox in 2006 was hilarious, sitting in the away end. Some of his friends refused to go, wouldn't give money to the Ibrox club but "For me it was a show of solidarity and friendship to our friends". Damien was on the buses from the Gallowgate and remembers being a little apprehensive as they disembarked and walked to the ground. After all, despite his Villarreal disguise, he was a Celtic supporter in hostile territory. Some of the Rangers supporters outside Ibrox were trying to swap scarves. "I was wearing a Villarreal scarf and of course I did not want to swap it for a Rangers one. I put on a fake Spanish accent, saying no politely, but one of my friends was less sensible and after the third Rangers fan said to him "Swap scarves?" growled "Naw. Fuck off" to the utter astonishment of the poor Rangers supporter. At one point some of us started a chant, "The Rangers are shite", and you could see some of the Rangers supporters beginning to twig. Then after the game, it was onto Arta, for a great night, with much intermingling between Celtic supporters and the people from Villarreal".

2007 Visit

Derek Rush was involved too in the arrangements for the 2007 visit. He felt some more undue guilt and responsibility when once again Celtic lost at Parkhead in front of their Spanish visitors. Derek had enjoyed the big Dinner that trip at Parkhead.

Derek Rush remembers Ernesto's speech that night, more so than the more bland one by the Celtic Chief Executive, Peter Lawwell. He noted Ernesto's English had improved considerably since 2005. Many of the new audience that night had heard of him but never met him. "Ernesto made a real effort to reach out and explain what the Celtic Submari was all about. He expounded great values, and a great concept, derived from himself and his own experience, without personalising himself". Derek remembers being very proud that night, that he knew Ernesto, that he was part of something so good and so positive.

Damien Kane was also present at the 2007 Celtic Park dinner and has a strong abiding memory of the tireless performance by wee Maria Boixader. "She was dancing all night, the star of the show."

The Carfin Crew particularly remember the Celtic Submari 2007 trip, and the great party that was organised, mainly by them, in the Torridon CSC Hibernian Club. They gave an example of the whole atmosphere in that when their friends in the catering company, Abercrombie Catering, whom they were fully intending to pay, learned what the Celtic Submari were all about, they refused to take any money for the buffet, and snapped up extra tickets for themselves and their friends. That is just one typical example of the waves of generosity that have emitted outward from the example of the Celtic Submari.

That night with the Celtic Submari at the Hibernian Club, £1600 was raised for charity. With Ernesto's enthusiastic blessing, Pat organised that some of that money was given to a local Hospice Charity, to take children with cancer to

Lourdes. The amount raised was helped by the raffle of yet another pair of Forlan's boots. Perhaps that was the reason Forlan left Villarreal a few months later, he had no boots left to play in!

Chapter Twenty   Scotland comes to Villarreal

It was part of Ernesto's grand design from the very beginning that Celtic fans would always be welcome in the Penya. In the emotional euphoria of the first Celtic Submari visit to Glasgow, many promises were made by tired and emotional Glaswegians to return the favour and come back to Vila-real. It was agreed that the best time to do so would be in September, when the Vila-real Fiesta would be in full flow. A surprising number of those promises were kept.

The Expeditionary Force that sought to reinvade Vila-real in September 2005 was far smaller than the original Armada of 2004. But at around 200 strong, it was far from negligible, and already comprised many veteran socialisers with Submari people. Unlike the Celtic Submari party to Glasgow, this force was largely adult and travelled in many small groups rather than one large one. Accommodation was sorted out all over the town. When the few hotels, and the many boarding houses, ran out of rooms. the Vila-real Council gave the Celtic Submari Penya access to rooms in the Council run local hostel, the Albergia.

Six of the 67 Carfin crew came over for the trip and had had a great time. Right from the airport, where they were surprised but delighted to be met by a large reception committee who ferried them all up the road to Vila-real in a fleet of private cars, they were taken aback by the generous hospitality of the whole town. As Francis said "We got to meet people, see the town, learn a bit about it". The local Vila-real people tried very hard to communicate, and persisted until they were successful. The first port of call for all travellers was to be introduced to the Celtic Submari Penya rooms under Lluisos. Many were able and very willing to donate Celtic souvenirs to add to the already impressive collection on every wall. Most of the travellers definitely appreciated the main rule of the house, 'Celtic supporters can't pay for their drink.'

Pepe Mansilla still talks of the time the 200 Celtic fans came to Villareal for the September 2005 Fiestas as something magical, another 200 friends to add to his collection. He had set up his own small penya for them in a ground floor garage space and had expected about 8-12 people. The visitors were supposed to split into many small groups so that none of these impromptu penyas the Submari had planned would be over run, but somehow many of the groups had ended up at his. Pepe had coped well until the food and drink ran out, then had shepherded them off into various side streets to find other parties.

Vicente like indeed every Submari member has strong and happy memories of the visit of 200 Celtic fans for the September 2005 Fiestas. He was proud of the way the whole town, not just Submari members, pitched in to entertain their guests, and the way so many temporary penyas were opened up to include them all. Vicente as a rational man had been worried about the dangers of the Bull run. "They just couldn't seem to grasp or realise that wild angry bulls were roaming the streets. However fortunately the barriers worked and no-one was harmed." Like most locals, Pepe and Vicente were impressed by the numbers of the visitors who went to the Basilica and the St Pascual church to quietly pay their respects.

This time Francis McGorry and Martin Kane got to play for the Huddleboard team rather than just watch, along with Hope's son Paul. They found it a hard experience, given the heat and the drink they had consumed the night before, but coped, like the troopers they are. For the Carfin crew that trip was the start of a process of regular visiting. As Willie put it "We just keep coming back because we love it, and they love us."

Pat McGorry wrote a contemporary account of this 2005 trip which I have included in large part since it conveys so well the atmosphere of those happy days.

"Over 150 Celtic supporters made a return trip to Vila-real last week to visit Celtic Submari CSC and attend the city's Fiesta. This was a special trip for members of the Carfin CSC as they had forged a friendship with the Submari CSC last year, when they brought two Submari members over to attend their Annual Dinner Dance.

It's hard to describe and put into words the events over the last few days, and the kindness and hospitality shown to us by the people of Vila-real, but here goes.

The five day event kicked off on Thursday with dinner at a restaurant and then down to a night of entertainment at the Celtic Submari's supporters club. This gave the visitors an opportunity to meet and greet past friends and make new friends from across the globe, as Celtic fans had travelled from Germany, Switzerland, Sweden, America, England and from Paradise itself. The Celtic Submari club is a great wee place, with all sorts of Celtic and Villarreal memorabilia on the walls.

Vila-real is a small town with a population of 50,000 and ceramics looks to be its main industry. Friday the travelling fans were guests of the President of Villarreal CF. He invited them to his Ceramic's factory (Pamesa Ceramics) to see how tiles were produced, an impressive process. On leaving the factory the travelling fans were given gifts from the President. In return Gerry Martin presented the President with a rosette from Carfin CSC.

The day continued with complimentary paella from the Vila-real town council in the Maison de Vino. In the evening the travelling fans and locals joined in a dinner dance as a part of the Casals De Festes. Entertainment came from a local rock band, La Penya de Lenya, and Irish Dancing from Celtic Caos Dance Troupe followed by an impromptu Ceilidh. Then to round off the evening, on came the Mourne Mountain Ramblers to belt out some of the songs we all know and love.

Saturday morning started later than planned, as the Submari guys had forgotten that the Scots would drink them under the table and still be ready for a game of football in the morning. The Submari challenged the Huddleboard to a re-match of the Friendship Cup won by Celtic Supporters at Barrowfield in April 2005. The game was good humoured and entertaining, there were girls, boys, children and even ex-professional footballers (Ernesto Boixader former Villarreal player and President of the Celtic Submari CSC) playing. The final score was 3–3. After the game everyone was presented with a medal from the mayor of Vila-real, the president of the Sports Council and Willie from Carfin.

The cup was collected by Mikey on behalf of Huddleboard FC. After the game we returned to the venue from the night before to watch the Celtic Aberdeen game, projected onto the wall of the building. In the evening the travelling fans were allocated to different Penyas (social clubs) where they were treated like royalty. Our Carfin crew were taken into the home of Jesus Del Amo Bort and sat down to dinner with his parents and extended family. Despite the language barrier, the two groups struck up a friendship that will last forever.

After dinner we were taken to the "Bulls of Fire", this is a bull run with a difference; it's a larger bull than any of the previous bull runs we had seen and there are two torches set alight and attached to the bull's horns and set free amongst the streets as the crowds follow the bull around the street.

Sunday was a day of relaxation at Burriana Playa Arenal beaches, the sun was splitting the trees. The local council of Burriana erected a stage alongside the beach where again we were treated to some more live music from the Mourne Mountain Ramblers. After the beach the travelling fans were taken to watch the Villarreal v Seville game. This was amazing, the locals were not sure who they were playing as there was almost more Celtic Supporters than Seville fans. Before the game the Celtic Supporters sang long and loud and, to top it off, before kick off Villarreal played "You'll never walk alone" as a tribute to the travelling fans. With the game played the travelling fans returned to Celtic Submari to make their farewells and to drink the bar dry. For those travelling fans that were left, Monday gave them a further opportunity to say farewell to the people of Vila-real and to thank them for their hospitality.

There were too many people involved to thank them all by name. However Ernesto Boixader and Gerard Martin Co-Presidents of the Celtic Submari CSC, we salute you and all in the Penya. Jesus Del Amo Bort and his family, we thank you for the welcome you gave us and for sharing your food and drink, allowing us to celebrate in your culture. To the people of Vila-real 'respect'. All the local people made us feel extremely welcome. Finally to all other travelling fans, thank you for making our visit to Vila-real a memorable, as this is what it's all about, and why we love and support Celtic. 'Amarillo, Submarino es; Amarillo es, Submarino es!!' "

One funny memory from that trip was during the family meal in the ground floor with the whole Del Amo family, the main course was an elaborate chicken dish. All the visitors were served first, with generous portions, except for Martin whose plate, for no apparent reason, remained bare. One of the Del Amo family intervened and said something to Carmen, the mother and chief Cook, which seemed to cause some consternation. When Pat asked, "What did you say?" the immortal answer came back in English "Martin has no cock". Amidst much mutual hilarity, the different meanings of this were explained all round and Martin took a long time for his reputation to recover. After the meal Pat and Francis were given a full conducted tour of the Del Amo residence, during the course of which Pat was given a picture of the wall to keep and Francis was given a beautiful ceramic Villarreal CF crest plate. As Pat said, "We turned up with wine and chocolates and left with family treasures."

Tosh McLaughlin was a good source of many funny stories around that first trip to Villarreal. His mate John Donegan will probably not appreciate Tosh sharing with a wide audience the one about John and the Farmacia. In 2005 at the September fiestas. it was so hot that John developed a rash at the top of his legs. He went to the local Farmacia(chemist). John does not speak any Spanish and tried to communicate as best he could the nature of the problem, and eventually the slightly bemused pharmacist gave him something, which John profusely applied at the first opportunity. It later transpired that he had been given a cream for THRUSH! But it worked, so what the heck. The same John Donegan earned himself a further claim to fame by wandering through the town centre on the first day, noticing all the metal bars and grids on the windows and doorways, and thinking "Hey, this is a rough place!" Unfortunately he shared that thought with his pals, who all knew, as he did not, that the barriers were purely temporary ones, for the bull running due that night!

John Donegan also got separated from the main group on a trip to the Cuidad Deportiva but eventually turned up there under the safe shepherding of what John described as "some big blond guy" but others recognised as none other than Diego Forlan!

"Again with Dougie in a penya. A guy comes in like an ice cream salesman. White hat and uniform. No ice cream however. His cart was full of beer! No sooner does he leave, when a guy with a Hoops top comes in. We get talking to him and discover he is from Transylvania. DRACULA C.S.C! Later I became very friendly with him, Ioan, a lovely generous man who does not bite."

After his experiences in April 2005, Damien Kane had been determined that he would take up their offer to return the hospitality and he willingly signed up to attend the September 2005 Fiesta in Villarreal. Damien wrote an account of that experience at the time for the Huddleboard. I have included much of it here, because it gives a slightly different, but still very positive, flavour of what was obviously a fabulous few days, than does Pat's account.

"Myself, my mate Danny Neil, Lurkerghirl, Mikey, ElGrecoLoco, Paulo67 and Roper03 arrived back in Glasgow last night after four memorable days in Vila-real. It's hard to put into words and describe the events over the last few days and the kindness and hospitality shown to us by the people of Vila-real. Chuck kept saying to me on Saturday night – "How do you explain this to folk when you get back?" Well hopefully this will!

Thursday (Day 1) - Arrive around 2pm on Thursday from Alicante. First man we met was our very own Valencia Bhoy, running around like a madman trying to organise things and make sure everything was going according to plan! The first night was spent mainly in the Celtic Submari club (or 'penya' as they are known) with plenty of cervezas consumed and songs sung. The Celtic Submari club is a great wee place, bedecked out in Celtic and Villareal colours, with all sorts of Celtic and Villarreal memorabilia on the walls.

Friday (Day 2) - Started for some of us with a tour of a local tile factory. The reason we went on this tour was because we were invited to it by Fernando Roig, President of Villareal FC who owns the company. After the tour he came out to meet us and we had our picture taken with him. Following the tour it was then on to Maison de Vino. This is a wee area on town with lots of open air bars. And we were treated to some free local paella.

Later in the evening a few of us (myself, Danny and the Kettering boys and their family) watched the bull ('El Toro') run from the safety of one of the wee stands/terracings. Some of the Swiss Bhoys and Mikeybhoy were a wee bit braver standing close to the fence goading the bull. The Swiss CSC 'El Presidente' was resplendent in his Obelix style green wig (complete with ponytails) and it was hilarious watching him roar at the bull as it looked at him as if he was mad!

Here's a wee story that sums up the way we were treated by the Vila-real people – we were walking around the side streets outwith the bull run area, we passed by a Penya where the room to the back appeared to be the family's kitchen. They were all sitting eating. They saw us hovering about outside and called us in and gave us beers. Like the Penya we were in the previous night the people would not take money off us. The Penya's are small social clubs consisting of family and friends and are like small garages or rooms at ground level within their apartment blocks. They all have their own 'uniform' or 'kit' – either t-shirts or polo shirts in their colours with their Penya's name/logo. Some even have mad coloured trousers to match. Anyway – we were finishing our beers in this Penya and the family were about to leave to go to the bull run. We were also going to leave but they told us to stay – 'We leave our Penya open for you. Help yourself to beer and food'. Absolutely crazy, we couldn't get over it!

That evening at 10pm was the Celtic Dinner/Concert in Casals De Festes. This was like a big aircraft hanger but we were told it was used for playing basketball in. The place was set out into big rows of tables to seat over 400 people. We were treated to a traditional Spanish buffet meal and the place was bedecked out in Celtic flags. The Huddleboard flag proved to be popular amongst the people with loads of folk queuing up to get their photies taken in front of it. We partied on into the wee small hours with Vila-real well and truly aware that 'Hail! Hail! The Celts are Here'.

Saturday (Day 3) – There was more than a few folks looking a bit worse for wear the next day when we arrived at the Vila-real training complex to play the return game against a Villareal supporters team. So all credit to the guys who managed to turn up and play that day playing in high temperature with hangovers. The game ended up 3-3 with the highlight being a goal from HBFC's Mikey with a lovely run in behind the defence, one on one with the keeper, he chipped it over him and into the net. There was also one moment of sublime skill by Ernesto Boixader when a smart turn sold the HBFC a dummy! The Villarreal training complex really puts Barrowfield to shame. 3 or 4 full size astro grass pitches, several 5 and 7-a-side pitches and two full size grass pitches. One of the grass pitches has a small terracing/stand along the touchline and there are several buildings with changing facilities, showers etc. After the game everyone was presented with a medal from the mayor of Vila-real and his wife. Then Mikey walked up to pick up the cup on behalf of HBFC from the mayor.

We then wandered back down the road back to Casal de Festes where we would watch the live coverage of Celtic v Aberdeen. The council of Vila-real paid the entrance fee for all Celtic fans and put on a typical Valencian Paella for everyone to enjoy before the game began. Amongst the speeches at the Casal de Festes was a moving tribute from Ernesto to the Celtic supporters. "You taught us how to support a football team, and even more importantly, you taught us that supporting a team is about more than football". Before the Jock Stein tribute, Valencia Bhoy explained to the locals what it was all about and who Jock Stein was and what he meant to us – the hall then whipped up into a crescendo of noise with clapping and whistling honouring our greatest ever manager! Then onto the game – a great result, a cracking Zurawski goal and a very assured looking performance as the Bhoys passed the ball about with ease. And what a cheer that went up when we heard Falkirk had equalised! After the game finished, a local banned played us into the town. The band was made up of young kids playing trombones, trumpets, saxophones, base drums and symbols. The Spanish boy at the front had his hoops and 'See you jimmy' hat on. So we all followed behind the band for a 20 minute march into town – and what a reception we got. People were coming out their houses to cheers us on, the cars were sounding their horns, young kids shouting 'Celtic, Celtic!' Unbelievable!

Later that evening we headed back to the Submari CSC where we were all split into groups and assigned to a small Penya for the evening. We'd be their guests for the evening where we'd be fed and watered to our hearts content! Myself and my fellow huddlers, including C'mon the Hoops and his lovely wife who we'd met over there, had the honour and privilege to be guests of Pepe Mansilla's Penya where we were treated like kings! We were served up a lovely bull stew which raised much hilarity. The latecomers walked into chants of 'Eat the bull, Eat the bull, Eat the bull!' and couldn't sit down for a beer till they'd eaten a bit! The food and drink just kept coming and I think its fair to say this was the best meal we had all eaten so far on the trip! It was a very humbling experience for me – we walked into Pepe's Penya where it was packed with his own family and friends and all the young kids sitting round their own table. Seeing these kids faces light up and join in the celebrations was a joy to watch. We also had the pleasure of having the band, the Mourne Mountain Ramblers, join us at the Penya and after the meal had finished, out came the guitars and sound system as we enjoyed some more tunes, dancing, and partying. This night and the hospitality we enjoyed will live with me forever.

Sunday (Day 4) – Up again at 11am to find the Sevilla players wandering around our hotel reception. A few of the bhoys took the opportunity to get their photos taken with the likes of Saviola and Kanoute. One of the lads asked Saviola if he'd sign for the hoops to which he politely replied – 'Maybe some day'. Sunday was a day of relaxation at Burriana Playa Arenal beaches. A perfect way to clear the head and recover from yet another hangover. Sadly at 4pm we had to depart for our flight back to Glasgow with a 2.5 hour drive to Alicante ahead of us. But we departed with memories of a great trip that will live with us for the rest of our lives.

Ernest was a beautiful child whose life was sadly far too short.
But in the Celtic Submari he has a legacy that will endure.

Ernesto the footballer (2ⁿᵈ right back row).
And Ernesto the supporter; with iconic scarf, and with Angel

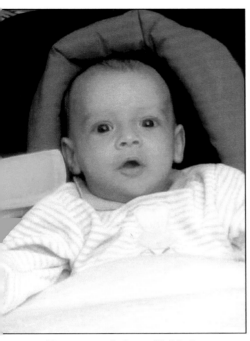

Ernest a truly beautiful baby

Ernesto and Maria Dolores were left devasted by his death

Now a happy family of four, three down here and one up there

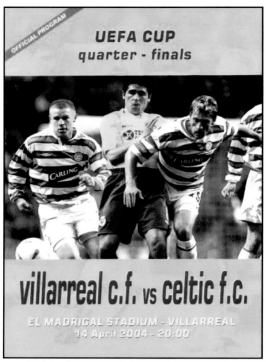

Lennon and Riquelme, strong men who attract strong feelings

A valuable souvenir of the tie that started it all

Celtic fans behaving wonderfully in Villarreal 2004

Forlan scores

Rangers fans attack Villarreal Team bus

Villarreal knock Rangers out

Rangers scarf has place of pride on the Penya wall

Any time Villarreal are on TV look to the right side of the right hand goal for the CS banner

Estrella,(far left) leads the Celtic Submari at a game

Matteo's Arsenal knock out
Ernesto's Villarreal

Domingo(the toreador) and Pasqual dress
traditionally for Celtic Park

Celtic Submari donate to their main Scottish charity, Yorkhill Hospital again

Tosh with pupils from John Ogilivy High and Franscesc Tarrega schools on one of their regular a school exchanges

Gerry Martin on behalf of visiting Celtic supporters exchanges gifts with
Fernando Roig President of Villarreal CF at his Pamesa factory

Huddleboard team maintain unbeaten record in Europe

Action from 2008 Champions League Clash

Respect in symmetry,
2008 style

The 2008 Paella Party inside the Hall

Paella Party Outside the Hall

Four Faces of the legendary Pepe Mansilla

Pepe thinks Strathclyde's finest wear yellow to support Villarreal

Pepe leads the singing

Pepe leads a humble prayer, with Domingo and Gerry behind him

A Spanish Cock, of the walk, among Scottish Hens

A Collage of good times

The happy Celtic Submari crowd on any Friday night

The uncensored cake of shame

Scottish Minister in bomb scare

Ernesto and Saul Ramos with Pat McGorry,
an adopted member of the Celtic Submari

Ernesto and Pepe before the shock of
the Old Firm game 2011

Three exceptional men, Ernesto Boixader, Neil Lennon and Gerry Martin

Scenes from the Celtic Submari Children's Christmas Party

In the words of Ernesto "There is Faith, Hope and Charity, and the Greatest of these is Hope"

Another Christmas Party, another cheque for charity, Linda Orr with Marchena and Borja Valero 2010

I'll end this by paying tribute firstly to Ernesto Boixader and the Celtic Submari CSC. It's hard to explain the emotions of the last weekend, but when you find yourself in a small town in Spain in a Celtic supporters club that consists mainly of native Spaniards, I found myself sitting there saying to myself 'This is what its all about, this is why I love and support Celtic!' So I can't thank the Villareal Celtic Submari enough for their generosity and goodwill over the last few memorable days – you can't buy what we all experienced.

Secondly to the people of Vila-real – outwith the Celtic Submari itself, all the local people made us feel extremely welcome. They literally welcomed us into their homes, shared their food and drink, allowed us to celebrate their culture with them – and for that reason I salute you, the people of Vila-real.

Lastly and certainly by no means least – there's one other thank you. The whole weekend's events were down to the help of a number of people, particularly the Celtic Submari, the local council and people nearer to home – but the large proportion of the organization was down to one man, our very own Valencia Bhoy. You done us proud yet again. To say what he has taken on, not just over the last weekend but also the Submari's trip to Scotland, is massive, is an understatement. The man and his actions sum up what it means to be a Celtic supporter. What he has done is 'above and beyond the call of duty' and I am eternally grateful to him and his fellow Celtic Submari members for giving me the opportunity to experience their culture and meet some new friends, something I would not have had the opportunity to do had I not supported Celtic Football Club. God bless you all!"

Gerry Martin had been quite worried about the possible dangers of exposing Celtic supporters to the local bull-run. Gerry was well aware how unexpectedly fast these bulls could be, and how dangerous. Every year in small towns throughout Spain, several people are killed during bullruns of the kind organised in Vila-real. Gerry knew the key Risk Indicators which warned that the two groups most at risk were people very drunk and foreigners. So most Celtic supporters were guaranteed to be in both Risk Categories, significantly increasing the odds of disaster. So Gerry spent the early evening loudly spelling out the dangers to as many visitors as possible, then spoiled it slightly by spending the late evening creeping up behind Scots loudly bellowing "Bull, Bull, run, run!" Quite a few wished they had been wearing their brown trousers.

The emphasis of raising money for good causes was maintained during this second Scottish invasion and the course of the long weekend another considerable sum, of several thousand euros, was raised, which Ernesto determined should mainly go to Aspanion.

Ernesto had felt very pleased that the second Scottish invasion, while much smaller, had gone very well and enhanced the process of permanent links and relationships being made between the two sets of supporters. He encouraged Gerry to publicise on all the relevant supporters forums and internet sites that all Celtic supporters would be very welcome in Vila-real every Fiesta time, May and September. And sure enough ever since that first mini invasion in September 2005, every subsequent Fiesta has seen parties of Celtic supporters arriving to celebrate the Fiestas with their Submari friends. As well as these larger expeditions, there has also been an incessant stream of individual visits from Celtic supporters, not just from Scotland, but Ireland, England America, Australia. All have been overwhelmed with the great welcome and wonderful hospitality shown to them. None have ever been able to pay for their own drinks in the Penya.

The shared responsibility of organising both 2005 expeditions brought Gerry and Ernesto even closer together. "He is a genuine altruist, who makes altruism seem effortless by his hard work. He is the very essence of what being a good person is all about. It is very easy to love him." And then in a wave of emotion and public affection that runs counter to the whole West of Scotland male ethos which Gerry usually inhabits, he went on to add unashamedly, "Indeed I do love him."

Gerry has a strong awareness of his own many defects, and knows that while he is generally popular, he may also not be everyone's cup of tea. But he knows that "Ernesto sees me better than other people do." That New Year, coming into 2006, Ernesto sent Gerry a text message at midnight "Don't you dare ever change" which Gerry knows is probably the nicest thing anyone has ever said to him, made all the more meaningful by being said by the best man he knows.

Chapter Twenty One   The Celtic Submari in Europe

The first real European expedition for the Celtic Submari was in the Champions League, to the play-off game against Everton in Liverpool in August 2005.

Billy Spencer is a lifelong Evertonian living in Liverpool. Through the course of an active life Billy has picked up some grasp of Spanish and when the draw for the knock-out round was made, he remembers thinking two things. The first thought was "Great, a small Spanish club, it could have been much worse, Everton should definitely make the Group Stages now." This confidence of Billy's was shared almost without exception by not only the Everton people but by the whole English football community, and by the bookies who gave odds on such things. Billy's second thought, since he is by nature a very sociable fellow, was "Great, I should be able to get some Spanish conversation with the Villarreal supporters."

Billy knew what pubs visiting supporters were most likely to frequent and made a point of visiting them the night before the game to see if he could implement his second wish. "The first thing that struck me, as distinctly weird, was the large number of Celtic tops being worn in the relevant pubs. What was even more weird was that some of them were being worn by Villarreal supporters!" It didn't take a man of Billy's social skills and grasp of Spanish, long to work out what was going on. All of the English speaking wearers of Celtic jerseys were Celtic supporters. About half of them had come down from Glasgow and its environs to meet up with their Villarreal mates and support them, against his team. The other half, were Celtic supporters living locally and from further afield in England who had signed up to do the same. Billy was even more intrigued by the explanation given to him by the Spanish speaking wearers of the Hoops, which involved the whole story; Ernesto and his son, the April 2004 invasion, the April 2005 aftermath. Billy was enormously affected by the story and its obvious positive manifestation in the friendly relationships all around them. There and then he signed up to visit Vila-real and come to the Celtic Submari Penya. When Villarreal almost broke his heart by outclassing his team and defeating them 2-1 at Goodison, he took some consolation from the fact that he had met some remarkable people and would be soon be enjoying their hospitality. He held onto that major consolation during the process of the second leg where Villarreal administered another football lesson to his team in ensuring their own qualification for the Group Stages.

Luis Broch has been a regular traveller to Villarreal away games in Europe, especially in the Champions League. He went to Merseyside for the first leg game, against Everton and both he and Jose Luis Broch remember linking up with Billy Spencer who has by now, many visits to Vila-real later, become a good friend of theirs, and many others of the Celtic Submari.

Billy made such good links and friendships with the Submari people that he had no hesitation, in November 2005, in linking up with them all again when they came over for the Group Stage game in Manchester against the famous United. He proved very friendly and accommodating during that trip, acting as a host, facilitator and translator. The one thing he drew the line at, was to accompany them inside Anfield. Some of them had expressed a desire to visit this ground, linked in their mind to their new shared Anthem, "You'll Never Walk Alone", as part of their cultural activities for that trip. Billy agreed to drive them to the ground but on principled grounds refused to enter inside with them for the tour, much to their bewilderment. Although it helped some of them, later in the tournament, make sense of their similar bewilderment at the Celtic fans in 2006 who would not, quoting the same perverted principle, accompany them to Ibrox

Manchester November 2005

Spaniards call Old Trafford La Teatro de Suenos (The Theatre of Dreams). Around 150 of the Celtic Submari signed up for the trip for the Group Stage game against the legendary Manchester United. Gerry Martin took responsibility for organising entertainment and other aspects at the Manchester end and someone, who shall be nameless, organised the travel and accommodation arrangements from the Villarreal end. The first slight snag was encountered at Reus Airport when the Celtic Submari party turned up for their flight but there turned out not to be any plane scheduled, due to heavy fog. After a succession of frantic phone calls, the best that could be cobbled together was that 50 of the party were to go on up to Barcelona and get a plane from there direct to Manchester, while the remaining 100 took part in a frantic several hours bus convey to Zaragossa, where a flight to London Stansted would be followed by another up to Manchester. The Barcelona connection did not work out too badly and the 50 intrepid travellers eventually made in to Manchester the morning of the game, and were able to link up with the small party including Gerry Martin already in Manchester. However the party routed via Zaragossa were not so lucky and encountered one minor disaster after another. Luis Broch, the bank manager, outlined the various stages of catastrophic confusion and delay in a process which eventually ended up with most, but not all, of the party arriving at Old Trafford halfway through the second half. As Luis put it wryly, "At least we didn't miss any of the goals." After the game was over, the whole party sought consolation in drink. Since no hotel accommodation was available for them, they drank the night away until leaving for the airport via a trip to Liverpool.

For different reasons Gerry Martin has unhappy memories of that 2005 trip to Manchester. Through the Celtic Supporters Association, he had been given a contact in Manchester to link up with to provide hospitality and entertainment for the Celtic Submari people the night before the game. Gerry had wanted it to follow the normal simple formula; some music, much drink and enough space for the Spanish visitors to circulate with the well-wishers that had come down from Scotland and across from other parts of the UK to support the people from the Yellow Submarine. A collection would be taken at the night to continue the Celtic Submari tradition of raising money for a good cause. In principle it was not too difficult a remit, given his previous successes for the Submari in Glasgow and other places. Gerry had wanted to organise an event that would be free, at least for the Spanish travellers. But he came under severe pressure from the people at the Manchester connection end to have a particular band present.

Gerry was assured that this band was so good, and so popular, that word they were performing would attract loads of football people from all around, and that enough money would be made from the small entry fee required to cover the band's costs of some £900, and that there would be sufficient profit to add to the Celtic Submari collection for charity. Gerry's initial reaction was to resist this notion, and insist on a free event, but eventually, much against his better judgement, he was pushed into agreeing that £5 a head would be charged for admission. "You know how, against your better judgement, you sometimes eventually agree to do something you are not sure is right. You immediately regret it, but having agreed you are stuck with it."

Due to the travel cock-ups very few Spaniards from Villarreal were around, and the supposed sure fire draw effect of the band on the Merseyside/Manchester football fraternity proved to be grossly exaggerated. The organisers took these events personally, and with much aggressive posturing made it clear to Gerry that they held him personally responsible and would extract their money from him one way or a more painful other. Of course no donation to the Celtic Submari Charity collection was forthcoming from them after the event. Not even members of the Manchester CSC, this group had clearly spotted an opportunity to make some money and were not pleased these plans had fallen flat.

Damien Kane's friend Danny, who had been in Villarreal with him in September 2005, had travelled down from Glasgow along with some one hundred other Celtic supporters. They had gone not so much to support Villarreal, though they did that gladly, but to link up again with the people from the Celtic Submari and to support the friends they had made in the September trip to Vila-real. Danny, and other Huddleboard members present, were disgusted with the cynical exploitative attitude of the people from Manchester and the way they treated Gerry. Danny confirmed that these people were not only trying to rip off the Celtic Submari visitors but were quite happy to also exploit the local Manchester CSC members.

Gerry, in his 'ValenciaBhoy' role, shared these unhappy events including the collection failure, fully with the Celtic Huddleboard Forum, and the response of many of the Huddleboard members was generous and positive. Huddleboard members organised various whip rounds and through their efforts almost £1200 was raised which Gerry made sure was handed over in full to Ernesto and the Celtic Submari to add to the amount they had raised by their own donations. The money was put towards helping organise the New Year party for children, including Aspanion members, held early in January 2006.

So on some levels the trip to Manchester was not the greatest success known by the Celtic Submari. However they had seen their wee team, from its small town, live in easy equality with one of the giants of World Football. Two games against United, no goals lost. Villarreal finished top of the Group, and some of the Celtic Submari began thinking of Paris and the Final to come there in May 2006.

For the knockout stages of the Champions League there were three trips to be made in early 2006. The first was to Glasgow for the game at Ibrox against Glasgow Rangers which has already been described in an earlier chapter.

Milan

Then there was the trip to Milan, to play Inter Milan the very rich Italian club who had spent 100s of millions of pounds trying to buy European success. Now the sophisticated Italian city played hosts to country cousins from a small town in Spain.

Luis was one of the relatively much smaller group of Celtic Submari members who made the trip to Milan and the famous San Siro stadium. He described that as a much happier trip than the one to Ibrox.

A surprising highlight of the trip for the Submari members was coming across their Abuelo friend from Scotland, Tam O'Hare, drunk in the main Milan square, waiting for them. I don't know if they were more surprised that he was drunk than surprised he was there, because they had seen him drink all night before, but never to any great effect. Tam himself blamed the Italian beer and the anxiety that he might miss out on meeting up with his Spanish friends. Jose Luis in particular was delighted to see him. They enjoyed Milan, as a city. And they enjoyed Milan as a football experience. Their team lost, 2-1, but most of the travellers returned home happy, in the belief that they would overturn that score in the return leg, and they had the advantage of that away goal.

London trip April 2006

Then it was onto the even greater city of London, for the semi-final first leg of the Champions League. Gerry Martin did most of the organising of the London end of this trip. He still had a flat in London and used this as the base from which to organise the trip. He made sure the Celtic Submari visitors got the full Cultural tourist experience, Big Ben, the Houses of Parliament, the Tower, the lot.

But for Gerry the highlight of that trip was introducing his son Matteo to Ernesto. The night of the game, Gerry organised access to a pub near Highbury for both before and after the game.

Although they lost 1-0 few of the Celtic Submari voyagers were depressed. They returned home confident they would overcome the Arsenal in the second leg, then it would be off to Paris. Villarreal were one game away from the European Cup Final!

Villarreal invade Paris for the Champions League Final

In the confidence generated by the first leg trip to Highbury a fair number of the Celtic Submari went ahead and booked flights to, and accommodation in, Paris, for the Final. Despite the bitter disappointment generated by the Riquelme penalty miss and their undeserved elimination by Arsenal, a fair number of the Celtic Submari including Ernesto and Maria Dolores, Saul Ramos and Pepe Mansilla decided to go to Paris anyway, so in that sense at least some part of Villarreal CF did make it to Paris. They did not pay inflated prices for tickets but happily settled for watching the match in Paris bars where they mixed happily with both sets of supporters, in the best Celtic Submari style.

St Petersburg

There was no separate Celtic Submari trip organised for the St Petersburg first leg tie but some of the Submari members like Jose Luis and Luis Broch signed up to accompany the official team party plane. The main memories of that trip were about the frio rather than the football. "Cold, very cold, very very cold." But they did like what they saw of St Peterburg, and said enough about the football to convey that Villarreal were a better team than the Russians. In Luis's view, "We should have beaten them over the two legs, would have done so but for bad luck and worse refereeing, and if we had, I genuinely believe it would have been us and not Zenit who would have gone on to win the UEFA Cup".

It is quite a thought what Manchester might have been like if Rangers had been facing a team with a close affinity with Celtic rather than just some 'dirty commies'.

Chapter Twenty Two   A strange case of Paranoia, a shared link between Villarreal and Celtic

There was one aftermath of the Champions League campaign that demonstrated a less positive similarity between Celtic and at least some in Villarreal. Villarreal are a very religious club. There is always a close tie between their celebrations as a local football club and the celebrations in the local religious community. There is no hint of sectarianism, in its ugly Scottish sense. No intolerance, or dismissal of other religions. Just a close identity between club and church. There have been a succession of local priests that have doubled up as the club priests. The latest in this honourable line is Mosson Guillermo, a most unusual priest. A rebel and a workers' friend, the bane of his bishop but adored and admired within Villarreal and its football club. Mosson Guillermo always refused to take credit for Villarreal's success. When asked, as he was daily in the good times, "Did you ask God to look after us last night, tonight, tomorrow?" he would piously reply that God had more important things to do than ensure football success. But then smile sweetly and know his audience would still attribute the success to a degree of divine intervention. Surely the same god that had supported them, had not capriciously denied them their due place in Paradise or at least Paris?

As it happens Mosson Guillermo had a more earthy explanation for Villarreal's failure to make the 2006 Champions League final than capricious or disinterested deity. He patiently explained to me in complete seriousness, that it was all down to the powers that be in UEFA. After the Inter Milan result, they were dismayed to realise that an all Spanish Final was a very real prospect, with one of the teams being very unglamorous. That was definitely not what they wanted on both economic and aesthetic grounds, and they took the necessary steps to ensure that glamorous Arsenal not dowdy Villarreal would make the final. Hence the refereeing travesty enacted at Highbury. When I asked him how that thesis coped with the last minute award of penalty to Villarreal in the second leg, which would almost certainly have ensured their qualification, he smiled the most sublime beatific smile and outlined the enormous subtlety involved in that act. Riquelme was in on the plot. Mosson Guillermo (from his seat in the Directors Box on the halfway line) had looked into Riquelme's face just before he took the penalty, and knew that he would miss it and would not care about doing so.

An interesting pattern developed when I tested Mosson Guillermo's theory out on a range of Villarreall supporters, at all levels from senior directors to ordinary supporters. No-one else bought it outright in the full terms it had been created. But not one dismissed it as arrant nonsense, the ravings of a paranoid mind. That is maybe something else Villarreal supporters have in common with Celtic supporters, an inbred certainty that the rest of the world is inherently against them. As late as the 1950s there were small-minded nasty bigoted men around the upper reaches of Scottish football who would gladly have harmed the 'Irish' club if they could. The serious attempt in 1952 to throw Celtic out the Scottish League for their refusal to stop flying the Irish Flag at Parkhead was perhaps the last serious manifestation of 50 years of bigoted anti-Celtic, anti-Catholic prejudice. But a further 50 years on, whole successive generations of Celtic fans (most of them not even born in 1952), otherwise intelligent people, still act and believe as if that level of prejudice against them still exists.

All Villarreal supporters consulted believed there was something not quite right around the Arsenal games. The less sophisticated muttered about how the powers that be would do anything necessary to stop a small club spoiling their show. The more sophisticated talked of something more subtle than an explicit plot. They related it to the power of "senses". It was clear to them that senior UEFA officials would have been worried that their showcase Final would be devalued by the appearance of a small unglamorous club, particularly if it made it an all Spanish Final. There was no doubt UEFA would prefer English glamour and English money. This 'sense' emanating from the high and mighty was absorbed by others without necessarily any conscious exposition, resulting in different outcomes than if the 'sense' had not been so powerful. It was part of the price paid for being small and unglamorous, the need to fight the power elite as well as the opposition. And it had cost Villarreal what should have been their god-given right, derived from the date of the Champions League Final coinciding with the fiesta day of their local saint. But in the end, God's will had proved less strong than the European football hierarchy's sense of need. So Mossen Guillermo exhibited a paranoia worthy of the Celtic connection. Most of the Submari were amused by their priest's theories but refused to dismiss them as entirely groundless. However, generally, Ernesto and the rest of Celtic Submari do not believe the world is against them and that Spanish football authorities and referees conspire to do them down, in the way too many Celtic supporters feel about the Scottish powers that be.

Chapter TwentyThree   The Ran(gers) in Spain falls mainly on the plain, but also on the righteous and the ungodly alike.   Part One

The 7th March 2006, the day Glasgow Rangers came to town, definitely has a place in the history of Vila-real. But in a rather different and less positive way than the visit of Glasgow Celtic in April 2004 had done.

It was with a mixed range of emotions that Celtic Submari supporters prepared for the visit of Rangers supporters in March 2006. There was a degree of fear or at least trepidation, stoked in part by the warnings and predictions of their Celtic friends and contacts. But basically they were prepared to be friendly and hoped to recreate to at least a degree, the atmosphere of togetherness generated at the Celtic visit two years earlier.

The Celtic Submari members who had visited Glasgow for the first leg game at Ibrox had come back with a range of stories, but none had had a bad experience which might lead to an expectation of serious trouble.

They had been warned that the very title of their Penya, the Celtic Submari, might act as a trigger point for negative emotions and even negative actions. And Pepe Mansilla had taken some persuasion that leaving Celtic strips highly visible in his sports shop window might lead to it being attacked, and that it would be politic for him to remove them from sight. But eventually he was persuaded to do so. There had been some discussion of whether the board outside the Penya club room, with its Celtic Submari name and green and white conning tower, would in itself represent a provocation and should be removed temporarily or covered up. In the end it was decided that that was unnecessary, that the sign should remain, and the Penya should be open to welcome the Rangers visitors, just as it had been for all other visiting supporters. So overall the general desire was to welcome this next wave of Scottish visitors and to offer them the same courtesies and acts of friendship as always.

There was a heavy riot police presence near the stadium, the match having been classified High Risk. Part of the reason for this was a fear that many more Rangers supporters were coming than the 3,000 tickets that had been reserved for them. The events of the previous two years, including the runs to the semi-finals and then quarter-finals of the UEFA Cup, and the qualification from the Group Stages of the Champions League, meant that the Vila-real police were much more prepared and experienced in the handling of foreign invasions than they had been in early 2004 when Celtic represented the first major influx of foreign football supporters. By 2006 the system had been developed and refined whereby visiting supporters were to stay in Valencia until several hours before the match, then come to Vila-real by train and be escorted from the station to the main square outside the ground. After the game they were to remain in the stadium for 15 minutes, then again be escorted en mass back to the station.

So the kind of lunchtime events that had been organised for Celtic in 2004 were no longer really feasible. However the other main act of togetherness, the creation of half and half scarves, was continued and the Celtic Submari invested in many of them for themselves and their visitors to show willing and togetherness.

Some Villarreal supporters did report pleasant exchanges on the day with the Glasgow Rangers visitors, with some friendly swapping of scarves and, in a couple of cases, tops. But the general experience was of a sullen hostility displayed by the visitors, who at best resisted invitations to talk, and at worst responded with invitations to their 'fenian bastard' hosts to go and multiply amongst themselves. Some of the closest pubs around the Plaza Llabrador were shut on police advice, but in the wider circle of open bars there was none of the happy intermingling of 2004. In the main, the visitors kept to themselves and made it clear that was the way they wanted it to be.

Domingo had been to the Rangers game in Glasgow and enjoyed most of his 3 days in Glasgow. He had no real problems with the behaviour of the Rangers fans that night in Glasgow. However he recollects that when the Glasgow Rangers fans came to Villarreal the next week, they weren't friendly and some of the visitors appeared to be actively looking for trouble, inviting it. But the Villarreal people were not looking for aggravation, so they didn't get any response. His negative experience was shared by many of the Celtic Submarine.

Jose Luis Broch, a calm and gentle man, was shaken by the hostility he saw displayed by the Rangers fans. He acknowledged that the bus attack was the only physical aggression displayed, but he was surprised, alarmed and disappointed at the degree of verbal aggression he witnessed, the rebuffing of all attempts by the locals to be friendly, and a general sense of hostility and antipathy.

Because of his negative experiences in Glasgow, Luis Broch the banker had not expected the return visit of Rangers supporters to be anything like the positive experience of 14th April 2004. Even so, he had not expected things to be as negative as they were, with Rangers supporters on the streets of Vila-real actually being hostile and aggressive, verbally at least. Being a good English speaker, he could make out some phrases like "Catholic bastards". He struggled to make sense of others, but did not miss their hostile tone. He saw none of the fraternisation and top swapping of the 2004 invasion. Luis was clear about one point. There was no negativity from Villarreal people towards Rangers supporters before their visit. While people knew about the Rangers Celtic rivalry and Rangers' Protestant origins, Luis was clear that Rangers supporters were very welcome, and many people had been hoping and expecting that something like the atmosphere of April 2004 would be recreated on their streets. Along with many of his friends, Luis had been disappointed that the reality was so different, very different. These invaders made no attempts to integrate, mix or mingle, and were at best surly, if not rude and aggressive.

The attack on the Villarreal team bus by Rangers supporters

There was one major incident before the game, what has gone down in history as "the attack on the Villarreal Team Bus by Rangers supporters". The streets of Vila-real leading up to the stadium are narrow, have room only for traffic one way, and any traffic has to drive slowly, brushing against pedestrians. The Villarreal Team Bus heading to the stadium turned into one of these streets, in which there happened to be a fair number of Rangers supporters. Some, but by no means all, of the Rangers supporters converged on the bus in a hostile manner, banging aggressively on the sides of the bus, much to the alarm of the Villarreal players and staff in it. Some Rangers supporters threw bottles, others stones and bricks lying around. In a classic example of innate behaviour, some Ranger supporters even threw plastic glasses full of beer at the bus. One supporter somehow managed to smash one of the side windows of the bus. Fortunately no-one inside the bus was hurt by the shattering glass. The Spanish onlookers were stunned, literally, by the openness of the hate and hostility displayed, and by the ferocity of the physical assaults on the bus. They did not attempt to defend their team or its bus, which quickly forged away from the trouble, so there was no mass brawl, as there probably would have been in any other city or location. It would seem that around 40 Rangers supporters were involved in the hostile mobbing of the bus. Some of them pursued the bus towards the stadium and continued banging on the sides but at the Stadium doors the Riot Police established control and set up a cordon to enable the players to disembark safely.

Talking to Rangers supporters years later, many made the point that the breaking of the window was the act of only one person, and how can a club or a support be held responsible for the act of any one drunk daft individual, however outrageous and dangerous? But none of those who had been there denied that many more had been involved in the hostile mobbing of the bus.

It was outrageous that a team bus less than half a mile from its own stadium should be physically attacked by opposition supporters. Villarreal CF chose to play the incident down. Pellegrini, the Villarreal Manager, made it clear, both before and after the game, that his players were not mentally adversely affected by the incident. The Villarreal President Fernando Roig, with his team safely through to the Quarter Finals of the Champions League, opted to respond in a low key manner, leaving it up to UEFA to decide the appropriate response. Thanks largely to this low key Villarreal response, a consensus emerged that it would be treated as a minor rather than a major incident. Rangers FC were very lucky no player was seriously injured, or even affected enough to be put off their stride. Otherwise the rating of seriousness would have been much greater, with corresponding much greater adverse consequences for the Ibrox club.

The best estimates of final numbers of Rangers supporters in Vila-real on 22nd March put the numbers around 6,000, rather than 10-15,000 feared. Many spent a few days in Benidorm before the game, where at least 8 were arrested for a variety of disorder offences.

What is undoubted, was that there were far more Rangers supporters in the crowd than the 3,000 ticket allocation. The section in the Fundo Norte set aside for Rangers supporters was full, with 3,000 fans. But around as many again were scattered throughout the rest of the ground.

Vicente Arneu told an interesting story that helped explain some of the mechanics of what happened. According to Vicente, based on the experiences of the Celtic game some people, when they heard Rangers were coming in possibly similar numbers to Celtic, saw an opportunity to make money. Vicente was sure they were from outside Vila-real, from Castellon. He described them as "Wide Guys, opportunists, not football people." These people came to Vila-real before the game and paid young people, students from the local college, to stand in the ticket queues and buy tickets for the Rangers game, with their money, for a small commission. These people then, on the day, sold these tickets at greatly inflated prices, well above the face value, to Rangers supporters. Since the ticket sale limit was two tickets per person, it meant that Rangers supporters were spread out in pairs all around the ground. It seems the chancers made a killing, getting rid of all their stock. There were no stories at all of any Villarreal fans giving Rangers supporters their tickets to the game for positive reasons of friendship. But Vicente confirmed there had been no trouble inside the ground from this lack of segregation.

It needs to be stressed that Vicente's assessment of the behaviour at the game itself was supported by many people, and confirmed by the police. Despite the considerable dispersal of Rangers supporters throughout all four stands, there was no trouble at all caused by this breakdown in the formal arrangements for complete segregation. Nor was there any trouble in the town after the game. There was no post match intermingling, with the Rangers supporters escorted by riot police to the station and funnelled safely out of town. Given the level of disappointment created after their early lead and their ultimate elimination on the away goals rule, the Rangers supporters displayed a commendable restraint in their response to the ending of their own Champions League dreams.

The Celtic supporters at the Ibrox first leg game, at least those who were not evicted for being Scottish, reported that there was a definite degree of sectarian singing in the first leg game, particularly of the 'Billy Boys' with its "we're up to our knees in fenian blood" lines. Not one of the Villarreal visitors reported being the slightest bit upset by the singing. For them it was just part of the not always pleasant atmosphere at the ground.

Luis Broch and Vicente Arneu who both have a good ear for English, confirmed that the Rangers supporters in the Fundo Norte spent some of the game singing lustily, including the same sectarian songs that had been belted out at Ibrox. They reported this with no sense of outrage. Not a single other Villarreal supporter even mentioned it at all, except to say that they were not as good singers, collectively, as the Celtic supporters had been, and that their singing had not had the same emotional impact on them as the Celtic choirs had had in 2004. It does raise a question about whether behaviour can be said to be offensive if no-one takes offence.

The UEFA Response

That query was not a philosophical question that appeared of much interest to UEFA, who very quickly announced after the second leg match that Rangers were being charged with the assault on the team bus, and also with regard to sectarian singing at both legs.

The assault charge was dealt with easily, and Rangers were given a fine of 13,000 euros (around £9,000), which was very mild in the circumstances. The Ibrox Club did not appeal against this decision.

The issue of sectarian singing proved more difficult to resolve. The initial finding is of considerable relevance now in 2011, given the events of the past year. Rangers were not fined by the UEFA Control and Disciplinary Body. This outcome has regularly been described by Rangers spokespersons and their supporters as meaning they were cleared of the charge of sectarian singing. This is not the case. The finding was that while sectarian singing did undoubtedly take place, at both legs, it had taken place in a Scottish context of tolerated behaviour and therefore the club could not be punished for this.

It is worth quoting some of the text of the finding - "The Control and Disciplinary Body accepted that the nature of the song 'Billy Boys' related to a social problem in Scotland. The Body believed that the disciplinary decision in this case had to be taken in the context of Scotland's social and historical background. After studying the evidence at hand as well as the statement of Rangers FC, the Control and Disciplinary Body conceded that supporters have been singing the song 'Billy Boys' for years during national and international matches, without either the Scottish football or governmental authorities being able to intervene. The result is that this song is now somehow tolerated. Given this social and historical context, the Control and Disciplinary Body said it considered that UEFA cannot demand an end to behaviour that has been tolerated for years."

So Rangers supporters were definitely found guilty but, through weak logic, the Committee decided against punishing them. Wiser heads in UEFA were appalled at this poor logic of the Committee, and ensured that the organisation in effect appealed against the findings of their own Committee. Failure to do so would have potentially compromised many future examples of bad behaviour, if the defence of "local custom and practice" was to be allowed as acceptable. The UEFA leadership were right to challenge that bizarre conclusion. On appeal, the decision not to fine Rangers was overturned and the Ibrox club were fined a further amount of 19,500 euros (£13,000) in respect of sectarian singing and abusive and discriminatory chants at both games. UEFA stressed that Rangers "have been severely warned about their responsibility for future misconduct of their supporters in relation to sectarian and discriminatory behaviour". They described Rangers supporters as having been put on 5 years probation.

Although the Control and Disciplinary Body ruling was overturned, it proved to have an enormous significance. The Villarreal Rangers games will enter into historical reckoning because it was the first time the notion was tabled that somehow the behaviour of football supporters is the responsibility not just of the club that they support, but of the governing bodies of both the football world and the society from which they come. The ruling clearly put on the national agenda that both the SFA and the Scottish Government were seen in Europe to have a degree of complicity in the acceptance of sectarian behaviour in Scotland. Through not just a failure to have vigorously tackled it, but actual tolerant collusion. The swift response of UEFA to make clear that such complicity is not an acceptable excuse ensured the whole issue of sectarian behaviour within Scottish football had to become to be seen as a political issue. This point was not lost on the Scottish Executive or on the SFA, and an issue that had been largely dormant started to be given a much higher political profile.

A more tangible and positive legacy of the visit of Glasgow Rangers adorns a wall in Vila-real. Since March 2006, a Villarreal-Rangers half and half scarf has always proudly brightened the wall of the Celtic Submari Penya, taking its place alongside those on the other clubs who have visited Vila-real. Unfortunately it has not consistently been the same scarf, since one or two Celtic visitors, including a local Glaswegian who should know better, have thought it smart, funny, appropriate or their place to remove it. Ernesto Boixader, however, will have no truck with such bigoted nonsense and has always ensured a similar one has been restored to its place of honour.

ChapterTwenty Four   A voyage around the Celtic Submari

The first 23 chapters take the story of the Celtic Submari up to the point in May 2008 when they are active participants in the celebrations of Villarreal CF's achievement of finishing second in the La Liga and earning the right to have another attempt at achieving the ultimate dream and winning the Champions League.

At that point, I signed up for what turned out to be a three year voyage aboard the Yellow Submarine. During that voyage, I continued to have regular contact with the Celtic Submari, both in Vila-real with many pre and post match trips to the Penya and regular Friday night sessions there, and on their trips abroad, particularly the two trips made back to Glasgow. In addition this period saw the return of Rangers supporters to this part of Spain, to take on Valencia in the Champions League, giving me a chance to observe their behaviour abroad at first hand.

All this three year contact, which appears in the next few chapters in the form of Diary or Notebook entries written at the time, allowed me to observe the principles behind the Celtic Submari in action. And to heighten the lessons, both positive and negative, that the Celtic Submari can offer as an antidote to the negativity, hatred and sectarian hostility that continues to blight Scottish football. These lessons are spelt out in later chapters of this book, where a theory is offered to explain the continued difference between the behaviour of Celtic and Rangers supporters abroad, and solutions offered to the continued unacceptability of the behaviour of both sets of supporters at home.

Season 1 2008-2009

12th May 2008

Today I joined the Celtic Submari members in a day of celebration of the Vice Championship. The central feature of the day was the march through the streets of Vila-real of all the 39 Penyas, the Villarreal CF Supporters Clubs, of which the Celtic Submari is by far the biggest. The Celtic Submari Penya were prominent in the march with a huge banner glorifying both Villarreal CF and Glasgow Celtic. Prominent as the Penya banners were, it was clear from other banners that the march was also a celebration of the Vila-real patron saint, Pascual, a celebration that begins every year the week before his saint's day and continues daily until its climax on his big day, the 17th May. So the march was a peculiar mix of football and religion. In a Scottish context that inevitably would mean sectarianism, with all the ugly ramifications associated with it. But in Vila-real the conjunction was entirely positive and natural. No-one present seemed to see any contradiction between a football celebration and a religious one, the two merged together seamlessly.

After this entertainment, Ernesto insisted Gerry and I should join him and Maria Dolores, and Angel and Encarnita, for a late dinner. Ernesto wanted to take us to a restaurant beyond the Madrigal, but was stunned to be turned away at the door, every table occupied at almost 11pm. In the end we adjourned to the large Italian Restaurant near the railway station often frequented by Celtic Submari members. Good food, good wine, good company, a pleasant way to extend a good evening. The evening finally finished with a concert in the Plaza Del Labrador, the big square near El Madrigal with its statue of the Hero Workers. A Vice Championship well and truly celebrated by the whole population.

July 2008

It was clear from early June 2008 that Roig, Llaneza and Pellegrini had all agreed Josico's time in the Villarreal first team was up, and that he should go with the dignity his contribution had earned, and with their blessing. The Celtic Submari took the eclipse of their hero badly. Josico is a member of the Penya, one who popped in regularly and mixed well and easily. He is by far the favourite player of the Celtic Submari. The Submari refused to accept the possible loss of their hero. A huge banner, with his name spread over three lines so that the middle one read SI (for YES he must stay), was hung in the main street, indicating their public support for his retention. Josico hung on in grimly during preseason, but as it became clear to him that he would not be played at all, he reluctantly accepted the inevitable. Fortunately a wise old man, Luis Aragones, knew his worth and offered him a two year contract to come with him to Turkey, to his new club Fenerbahce. Aragones had wanted Senna, but when that was stymied by a new contract, he took the next best thing, his partner Josico. There were a few tears shed in the Celtic Submari Penya the night that transfer was confirmed.

31st August 2008 the Champions League Group Stages Draw

In football terms it was a quietly satisfactory draw for Villarreal CF, with them rated behind Manchester United but well ahead, in football terms, of the other two clubs, Celtic and Aalborg. But in social terms it is a brilliant draw, allowing the special relationship between Villarreal and Celtic to be further enhanced. There was dancing in the streets of Vila-real, or at least on the floor of the Celtic Submari Penya club, that Friday night with Estrella, Domingo and Pepe Mansilla leading it. Their beloved Celtic, with all their old friends and thousands of new ones, would be coming visiting again. And there would be another guaranteed trip to Glasgow.

As soon as the draw was made, Ernesto, Saul, Angel and the other key Submari members started planning the events, activities and entertainment they would lay on for the visiting Celtic supporters, as well as the bonus Celtic Submari trip to Glasgow.

The order of games was away to United, home to Celtic, then home and away to Aalborg, before receiving United and finishing off with the trip to Glasgow in December.

The first I knew of the draw, sitting on my terrace enjoying a beer with a Barcelona fan Francesc, was a text message on my mobile phone from Glasgow, saying "Jammy bastard." Decoding the Glaswegian, I knew that must mean a pairing with Celtic. In terms of the book I knew that was very good news, strengthening the Celtic social connection while not threatening qualification. Sorry but Celtic are a poor team. Aalborg are near enough to go to, and no threat. And a glamour trip to Manchester is much preferable at this stage to

Anfield or Stamford Bridge, with Arsenal being saved for knockout stage revenge.

I realised as a side reflection that the draw would give Celtic supporters an opportunity to show Manchester and England whether or not they were different from Rangers, with all the horrors that had attended the Rangers invasion for last May's UEFA Cup Final, disgrace, drunkenness and violence. If my developing theory is right, the forthcoming Celtic visit should all be love and peace, mutual friendship and a marked contrast to the Rangers visit.

15th September 2008

Today the official Villarreal CF party fly into Manchester. In 2005, flush with the excited newness of the situation, the Celtic Submari had organised its own well-subscribed trip to Manchester. This time, with the main Submari officials Ernesto, Saul, Jose Luis and Angel all tied up in work commitments, no separate Celtic Submari trip was organised, and the members who were able to attend, went with the main Agrupacion party. Indeed one or two of the more well-heeled members went with the official Villarreal CF party, posh hotel and all, for a mere 2,000 euros a head.

With Celtic playing at home against Aalborg the same evening, there is no repeat of the 2005 experience when hundreds of Celtic supporters had made the trip south to swell the ranks of Villarreal supporters. However some English based Celtic supporters do attend, to ensure a smattering of green and white amongst the yellow.

Back in Vila-real there were two communal ways of watching the match. The Agrupacion de Penyas organised a giant screen at Casal de Festes, the chosen site for the Celtic Party in two weeks time. There was a good turnout of several thousand excited supporters and the happy party atmosphere lasted until well after the final whistle. The Celtic Submari screened the game, on its own big screen in the Penya premises, to a full and patriotic crowd of several hundred. The noise when Franco backheeled the ball goalward was ear splitting, the contentment at the final whistle only marginally quieter.

Chapter Twenty Five Celtic Back in Villarreal the run-up
Friday 26th Planning for a Fiesta of Brotherhood

As soon as the draw for the Group Stages was made, pairing Villarreal with Celtic again, the whole machinery of the Celtic Submari had sprung into full planning mode. Everybody in the Celtic Submari had got very excited. Thousands of their friends would be coming back to visit them again. There would be an opportunity to recreate that magical day of April 2004. The main planning group comprised Ernesto, Saul, Jose Luis, Angel and Gerry. Tonight they reviewed all the arrangements and checked everything was under control. Ernesto had quickly negotiated with the Agrupacion of Penyas that the Celtic Submari would organise the main event for all the visiting supporters, but do it on behalf of the Agrupacion rather than get into competition with them. That meant some of the money the club gave to the Agrupacion could be used to subside the activities.

It has been agreed that the main event, the centre piece of the whole day, will be a massive party to be held in the huge barn like Casal de Festes, from noon on the day of the game. With an 8.45 pm kickoff, that would leave plenty of time for partying and mass mingling. The central feature of the Party will be a massive Paella, provided free, as would all the entertainment. Drink will be provided on a subsidised basis but it has been agreed that any monies made from the drink and from associated activities like sales of scarves and jerseys, and raffles and auctions, will go to Aspanion, the Spanish charity for families of children with cancer. A couple of bands, the Irish Rovers and Peas and Barley, were booked to provide entertainment, with a 'surprise' guest appearance arranged from the Mourne Mountain Ramblers.

Recognising that most supporters would either base themselves overnight in Valencia or arrive there early on the morning of the game, and in either case travel to Vila-real by train, the Celtic Submari are making arrangements to provide a constant stream of free buses from the Vila-real railway station to the Paella Party, and then further free transport from the Casal to the stadium.

The new Visitors Stand will be used for the first time for the game, meaning that Celtic have been given 3,000 tickets by Villarreal. After consultations with the Huddleboard and other well-informed Celtic sources, Gerry Martin and the local police together came to the expectation that anything up to 6,000 Celtic fans might make the trip. This would be a significant decrease since 2004 but still way above any other travelling support ever to come to Vila-real. Arrangements are made to erect a giant screen in the Casal for fans unable to get tickets.

Gerry Martin is taking responsibility for publicising the event in Celtic circles in the home country, and I volunteered my friends Mairi and Bill Alexander, over from Inverness for the game, to distribute free tickets for the event to Celtic supporters in Valencia the night before the game.

This Friday night in the Penya, there is a tangible feeling of joy and excitement and a certainty that Tuesday 30th September 2008 will be as memorable a day in Vila-real history as 14th April 2004 had been. Indeed, surely it will be even better, given the now explicit nature of the longstanding friendship between the two sets of supporters.

Saturday 28th

Saturday night we pick up Bill and Mairi from Valencia airport, the first arrivals for the Celtic game. Living in Inverness, they had found it cheaper to book a flight from Aberdeen to Dublin for pennies, and another from Dublin to Valencia for further pennies, rather than pay the inflated prices being asked for flights from Glasgow, up to £700. There were only 4 other obvious Celtic supporters on the Dublin plane.Very few Celtic fans were visible in the city centre that evening. I had learned that most of the many hundreds of those making an extended holiday around the game, had arranged to go to Benidorm or Torrevieja for a few days rather than Valencia. The two expat Celtic Supporters Clubs, in Benidorm and Guardamar, are handling looking after them as best they can.

Sunday 29th

Bill and I go to the Mestella to see Valencia beat Deportivo 4-2. That win kept Valencia top of La Liga with Villarreal, after their 1-0 away win the previous day, secure in second place, the same position Celtic were occupying in the Scottish League. We clocked a group of noisy but happy Celtic supporters sitting at the very top of the Grada Del Mar stand behind us.

Monday 30th

Bill, Mairi and I go to Valencia with several thousand tickets for the Paella Party, looking for Celtic supporters to give them to for free. Valencia is structured such that most visitors tend to congregate in the Old Town with its three main squares and many side streets full of great cafes and bars, so finding them was not likely to be a problem. And so it proved, with the numbers of Celtic fans in the Old Town being well into four figures. I spoke to many Celtic supporters that night about their relationship with Villarreal, with a range from some of who had been there in 2004, to those whose only previous involvement had been seeing the Celtic Submari visit Celtic Park.

Martin Wilson the hippy vegetarian was not surprised that the events of 2004 had turned out to be the beginning of a long friendship. He had not been involved in this developing but had watched it with interest and had shown his appreciation when Villarreal fans came to Parkhead. When Celtic drew Villarreal a second time, he persuaded several of his pals to take holidays and hire a car, so they could travel together, and this time spend more time in Vilareal. I had clocked him on the Sunday night at the Valencia game, right at the very top of the Grada del Mar stand. They stood out as several of the party were sporting Celtic colours. The accents helped too. He was delighted with the invitation and tickets Bill and Mairi gave him and his gang to the free Paella Party. Although he became slightly disappointed when he discovered that this biggest paella in the world would contain rabbit and chicken, and therefore not be acceptable to him. He liked the fact that the beer at the Celtic Submari party would be much cheaper than the ones he was drinking all that night in Valencia. He complained that he was fed up as a Celtic supporter with foreign bars ripping off Celtic fans on their European travels by doubling or trebling their usual prices.

Larry is a train driver, from Dunfermline, a Celtic supporter all his life. Through his railway background Larry gets reduced rail travel throughout Europe and, as his mate Tam doesn't like flying, they tend to follow Celtic across Europe by Rail. This season they decided that they could only afford to go to one of the two European Group stage games (Manchester not counting as a trip abroad). So the choice facing them had been 'Villarreal in sunny Spain in September' or 'cold Denmark in November'. A no-brainer, so here they were in sunny Spain. It was their first trip to Valencia. They had been to Spain before with Celtic, Seville of course, and Barcelona a couple of times. Exhausted and bankrupt after Sevilla in 2003, they had missed the first Villarreal game in 2004 although they had watched it on TV and marvelled at how good Villarreal were. Some of their pals had made the 2004 trip and came back raving about how good a time they had had, and how friendly the Villarreal people were. Larry and Tam had read about the Celtic Submari with interest and seen them at Parkhead. Larry is a great fan of Spanish football on Sky TV and he stated that nothing gave him greater pleasure than looking for the Celtic Submari banner always on display behind the right hand goal at every televised home game of Villarreal.

The coordination of their travel arrangements required a Saturday teatime exit from Glasgow, which meant that Tam and Larry could not take in the whole of the Aberdeen game due that afternoon. Despite their close friendship, Larry and Tam sit in different parts of Celtic Park, due to a long saga involving the inheritance of season tickets. This meant they had to communicate by mobile phone to coordinate their sharp exit from Parkhead at the Aberdeen game. With Celtic 2-1 down but pressing furiously for an equaliser, Larry had been reluctant to leave, but by Tam's third frantic phone call, he finally agreed to leave and meet up outside the ground. By the time Larry reached the pie stall it was 2-2, but he had missed the goal. They jumped into a passing taxi and, within minutes, heard on the cab radio it was 3-2 Celtic. They had missed the heroic fight back, not their best start to the weekend. The cab arrived at the station 10 minutes before the train left, so they tortured themselves with the thought that maybe they could have hung on, seen the goals and still made the train, but as a loyal railwayman Larry knew he could not have relied on the train leaving late. After a tortuous journey with an overnight in Crewe and a change of train in London and then Paris, they had finally arrived in Barcelona the previous evening. They had had a good night on the town, marred only slightly for Larry by the looks given to him by both local males and fellow drinking Celtic supporters after he bought a colourful pink handbag for his daughter Laura to go with the smart new coat she had just bought for his forthcoming wedding. He bought it off a stall that didn't do shopping bags, so he had to carry the pink handbag with him round the many bars they sampled that evening.

The evening ended well except that they couldn't find their hotel, despite having worked hard to memorise where it was. As Larry put it, "We were in that state we couldn't find our own fingers!" Finally in despair they hailed a Spanish cab and asked the bemused driver to take them to their Hotel. "You mean that one there" he said pointing out the cab window to the hotel across the road. "Aye, that one", they admitted sheepishly before scrambling back out.

Then the next morning, this morning, they had gone to the wrong station in Barcelona and wondered why there was no train for Valencia. Only a desperate scramble in a taxi enabled them to scurry to the proper station and get their booked train. So they were happy to be spending a quiet night in Valencia relaxing over a drink. Like most of the Celtic supporters I talked to that night, Larry and Tam are expecting Celtic to get beaten in Villarreal.

One Celtic supporter insisted on telling us the story of how he had just christened his son Charles Henrik Larsson Kelly. He had agreed with his wife to settle for Charles, but in the Registry Office with the help of a previsit drink he couldn't resist adding the middle names as a tribute to his all time favourite Celtic player. His wife almost killed him we when he got home but as he said, "But what could she do? And the boy will thank me later."

While most of the evening was a very pleasant experience talking to so many happy friendly travellers, interesting and delightful people, there were a few encounters that proved the truth of Veggie Martin's assertion that not all Celtic supporters are nice friendly pacifists. Two or three groups proved incapable of believing that there could be something for nothing being offered to them. Bill and Mairi were on a couple of occasions aggressively accused of being on a scam, and probably being paid commission by a bar owner to get unsuspecting Celtic supporters to pay over the odds for his beer, with the 'charity' angle a pure con. One group in particular were quite physically and verbally aggressive in their negative response, the women in the group pushing them away with foulmouthed abuse. It is sad to see such a negative mentality that cannot conceive of people doing them a favour for free because of their inherent goodness.

I know that on many of their foreign travels, Celtic supporters are regularly ripped off, particular by publicans. Gerry Martin who speaks perfect Spanish, tells the not untypical story of standing in a Barcelona Bar with a Spanish friend, talking Spanish, when a group of Celtic supporters came in to order copious amounts of drink. The bar owner quietly but clearly instructed the barman to charge them all double the normal prices. Gerry being Gerry had intervened, fruitlessly, but ended up leading the group to a neighbouring bar and ordering their drink for them while announcing the normal price in a loud Spanish voice. So a degree of suspicion and scepticism is not totally surprising. But in the context of organisers called the Celtic Submari, and the known history of the friendship between the two sets of supporters, such a strong blinkered desire to feel victimised is truly sad, and indicates souls not at peace with themselves or the world.

Fortunately such negative responses were very much a small minority. Almost all of the Celtic supporters encountered in Valencia the night before the game were absolutely delighted to hear that the Villarreal Celtic Submari Club are planning something welcoming for them, in the way of free food and entertainment. They were excited at the opportunity to be part of something so positive and friendly.

The very last encounter of the evening was a particularly sour one. As the three of us were gently evicted from the last open bar by staff wanting to go home (in Valencia that meant it was about 4am), we met up with the last 3 Celtic supporters we could see on the streets. We started to tell them about the Party, the free paella, the music, the cheap drink and the rest. Their response was the laid back assuredness of those in the know. "It'll be that Gerry Martin behind this, and that so called Cancer charity. We know all about it, him and this scam of his. The whole cancer collection thing is a giant con." In vain I argued with them that that was cynical nonsense, that Ernesto's son had indeed died of cancer, and that all the Celtic Submari were committed to raising money for Aspanion as well as other charities, and that only the previous year I had been present when a large cheque was handed over by the Celtic Submari to Yorkhill Hospital. No, they knew better, Gerry Martin was running a sophisticated con game and the Celtic Submari were all in on it. They would definitely not be going to the party and contributing to this scam, no thank you, not them.

I am sorry for the cynical trio, and the few other doubters I have come across in the past couple of years, but their cynicism is misplaced, their suspicions unfounded. The charitable aspect of the Celtic Submari is a force for good, delivered by good people, and supported fully by the many thousands of Celtic supporters who can recognise goodness when they encounter it.

While Bill, Mairi and myself were in Valencia, there was a party unrolling in the Celtic Submari Penya involving the several hundred Celtic supporters who had made their way to Vila-real the day before the game. Many of them were survivors of the 2005 visit to Vila-real, who knew what kind of welcome they could expect, and there was much renewing of old acquaintanceships. For the rest, there was the usual introduction to the wonders of the Penya, the friendliness of the natives, and the wondrous inability of Celtic supporters to be allowed to pay for their drinks.

As proof how much this rule was appreciated, Ioan the Romanian offers a story. Early on the next morning, Ioan noticed two Celtic supporters lying sleeping in a doorway, where they had flaked out at the end of what had been an obviously hard night. Some kind Spanish lady had come down and put a blanket over the two of them. For Ioan that summed up the two sides of the relationship well.

Chapter Twenty Six   30th September   Celtic back in Villarreal

For the Celtic and Villarreal supporters present, Tuesday 30th September did indeed turn out to be a very special day, a lesson to the rest of Europe, indeed the whole world, into the finer possibilities of friendship and brotherhood that football can offer. It was a perfect Valencian September day, a clear blue sky, the temperature warm but not oppressive. The Casal de Festes has a large forecourt, where the Paella was prepared in the most enormous dish ever seen. Most revellers stayed outside enjoying the sun, venturing into the cavernous Casal only to replenish their drinks, at least until the main business started indoors. All the hard work put into the preparations for the Paella Party turned out to be worth it. It ended up being an unforgettable experience for the thousands of supporters, of both teams, who attended it. It might not actually have been the biggest paella ever, but it can not have been far off, certainly it was big enough to feed everyone there who wanted fed.

The main recollection of the whole day, reinforced by just about everyone, was the spirit of friendliness and the mutual affection shown by both sets of supporters. It seemed to me walking the Vila-real streets that the whole town was determined to welcome Celtic supporters back into their midst. Everybody smiled, everybody said hello, many stopped to offer handshakes or hugs.

At the Casal itself the atmosphere was wonderful. At the beginning, there were more Villarreal supporters, with all the Celtic Submari members on volunteer duty and many from other Penyas too, happy to be hosts. But as the day wore on, and busload after busload of Celtic supporters arrived, the green began to dominate over the yellow. Although as 4 years earlier, there was so much shirt and scarf swapping going on that colour was not the best indicator of affiliation, but accent. There were dozens of taps at the bar, again manned by Celtic Submari volunteers. There was a ticket system in force, and a one euro ticket could be exchanged for a large beer that would have cost 4 euros in Valencia the day before. The Irish Rovers, Peas and Barley and the Mourne Mountain Ramblers kept up a steady stream of Celtic music, much of which was accompanied by enthusiastic singing from the floor.

Celtic TV were there, shooting footage for a forthcoming documentary "Friends Reunited" about the phenomenon of the Celtic Submari and their friendship with Celtic. Ernesto was interviewed at some length, as was Gerry Martin. Others stalwarts of the Celtic Submari like Javi Salas and Jesus Del Amo were also interviewed along with a string of Celtic supporters. Anyone wanting a sense of the excitement, and pure happy friendliness of the day should seek out a copy of the Friends Reunited DVD, which contains much footage of the friendly intermingling going on there.

A notable part of the Vila-real memory of the 14th April 2004 had been how the green hordes had drunk Vila-real dry, literally, consuming all the beer at the Paella Party, then moving on to drink dry bar after bar. So Saul, Jose Luis and Angel had determined they would not be caught short this time. On the basis that up to 6000 Celtic supporters were coming, they ordered 30,000 litres of beer, hoping that (at roughly 10 pints a head) would be enough. It was just. There was some beer left at the very end, but not much.

Monica Broch was on scarf and shirt selling duty with half and half versions of both scarves and tops doing roaring business as well as the Celtic Submari t-shirts and tops. There were various raffles throughout the day and the selling of tickets was led by an indefatigable Hope Wightman who, dressed all in white, hobbled about around the cavernous hall going from table to table gently persuading eager supporters, Scots, Irish, English and Spanish, to part with the cash, to buy more raffles tickets on her assurance it was all for a good cause. She was in her element.

The singing was amazing. Pepe Mansilla added to his legendary status by fronting many of the songs, in both languages. The highlight was probably a rendition of "You'll Never Walk Alone" sung lustily by absolutely everyone in the hall as they held scarves of both teams aloft. At that point, about 4.30 pm, people were only slightly drunk and the impact was oddly moving.

Speeches were kept to a minimum but both Ernesto and Gerry Martin had their shot at the microphone. Ernesto's speech, towards the end of the party, was the main serious part of the business. He talked of the principles of the Celtic Submari and the great mutual friendship that had developed since, and the many exchanges of visits over the past four years, something he was confident would continue for ever. He concluded, in both Spanish and English, with the motto he had developed which already was on the back of many Celtic Submari t-shirts, "Rivals for 90 minutes: Friends for Always", to great emotional applause.

Ernesto had worried that the original phrase 'enemies for 90 minutes' might be too strong a word and that 'rivals' might be more appropriate, but fortunately opted for the softer version before the t-shirts were printed. His moving speech focused minds on what was going on and how special it was, and proved to be the high point of the Party.

The Celtic supporters who had been in Vila-real before, either in 2004 or the visits since, were quietly proud that the relationship started so wonderfully, had developed so well. Those visiting for the first time were amazed but even more delighted. Liz Brownlee from Greenock summed up best the sense of what Celtic supporter after Celtic supporter told me - "I have been to many European games, and enjoyed most of them, but I have never known anything like this. It is wonderful to be so welcome, so appreciated, to be made to feel part of their family". Danny from Linlithgow added a dimension also felt by many - "What made this party so great was that it was not just Celtic supporters. There are so many Villarreal supporters here too, mixing with us like true friends. I never expected that, it's wonderful."

There was one discordant note where I was probably in a minority of one. At various points throughout the day, there were several enthusiastic choruses of "If you hate the fucking Rangers, hate the fucking Rangers, clap your hands." Every Celtic supporter present seemed to join in enthusiastically to the slight bemusement of the locals. No-one seemed to see an irony in the supporters who were taking such pride in an image of themselves as spreading brotherly love everywhere they went, fostering hatred and hostility in their own backyard. But I have been around Scottish football too long, and been to too many Old Firm games, not to know that indeed, for many, not a small minority, but many Celtic supporters, hatred for Rangers is a part of the reality. The primary lesson the people of Vila-real took from Celtic supporters was that football can be about friendship between opposing supporters not inevitable enmity. But that appears to be a lesson taught only on their travels, not one to be applied at home. I will return to this contradiction in the later chapters on Rangers and Celtic supporters and their different behaviours and their different identities.

Eventually around 7.30 pm Gerry declared the party closed and ushered the last remnant celebrants up the short road from the Casal to the main square around the stadium, where another orgy of friendly drinking and cross-dressing was taking place, in the Plaza Llabrador and all the bars around it.

Then it was time for the main attraction, the game itself, in front of what turned out to be a record attendance for El Madrigal, of 25,400. This increased capacity was made possible by the bringing into use, for the first time, of the new Away Supporters Stand built over the summer above the Fundo Norte. It is slightly ironic that the first time it was used it was for the one large set of visiting supporters, the Celtic friends, for whom its safety features or its total segregation were not required. Nevertheless it was 3,000 Celtic fans who filled it to full capacity for its debut. Despite its plastic glass front and its side nets it did not interfere with the togetherness atmosphere felt by all supporters of both teams.

As well as the 3,000 in the new Stand, there were about another 1500 Celtic supporters in the rest of the ground, most of them situated in the Fundo Norte but others spread throughout the other 3 stands, all integrating perfectly and without problem. They were welcomed, everyone was very friendly and there was no hostile atmosphere at all. All the Villarreal supporters were genuinely touched when the Celtic fans several times before the match started, launched into a chorus of "Villarreal, Villarreal", the only song the home supporters seemed to have. And many Villarreal fans reciprocated by joining in choruses of "You'll Never Walk Alone" and "Hail, Hail, The Celts are here" led by the Celtic Submari members who of course know all the words of both well. It was a strange feeling being at a match where there was so much obvious affection between the two sets of supporters. The friendly atmosphere continued throughout the game. At the end of the game I found it genuinely moving as the 4 stands of Villarreal supporters all stood and chanted "Celteek, Celteek" for several minutes in tribute to their visitors.

Just before the end of the game, an announcement was made requesting Celtic supporters to stay in their seats for 15 minutes after the game. Two seconds into the announcement I realised it was the dulcet tones of Gerry Martin. He had persuaded the normal announcer, Alfonso Salas, a Celtic Submari member who speaks very good English, that Celtic fans spoke Weegie rather than English and that it would be better if he, Gerry, made the announcement so that they could all understand it. Later in the evening Gerry also told the story of his work at the official prematch lunch, where he had again been on translating duties, translating for John Reid, and suppressing the desire to publicly introduce him as "a warmonger with blood on his hands". He also reckons he has disgraced himself for good by asking the Spanish Ambassador to take a photo of the top table group including Gerry, with Gerry's camera.

As in 2004, the Celtic supporters took their defeat well, with dignity and magnanimity, but this time to no surprise. In the bars around the Madrigal there was much friendly exchange of drinks and good wishes and happy embraces and scarves, until at last all, or almost all, of the Celtic supporters were safely ushered onto the special train to take them back to Valencia.

By my reckoning there were somewhere around 4,500 Celtic supporters who made the trip this time. Everyone managed to get a ticket so the big screen showing in the Casal was cancelled, although several of the Penyas did show the game for locals without a ticket. The reduced numbers from 2004 was a combination of several factors, one of them being the economic climate. Another factor was the lesser importance of the game, a Group Stage match instead of a quarter final. And a sense amongst Celtic supporters their team was a poor one. None of the 4,500 who made the effort to come to support their team seemed to regret it. For the Celtic supporters who had been there in 2004 this day was even better, with the explicit evidence that their previous trip had produced such a positive product. For the Celtic supporters visiting for the first time, it was a mind-blowing experience to find themselves so welcomed, so appreciated, so looked after, instead of the more normal exploitation.

In the end it was not quite as memorable and wonderful a night for Vila-real as the 14th April 2004 had been. Then there had been the extra ingredients of fear, tension, surprise and astonishment. This time the amazing friendliness and mutual affection was expected, anticipated and delivered upon. It will still go down in Vila-real history as a truly great day, the day they repaid Celtic supporters for all the positive experiences of 2004. And for all the Celtic Submari, there was a new element this time around, the confirmation of the correctness of their commitment to Celtic and Celtic values, and to eternal friendship with the Celtic family. The main organisers Saul, Jose Luis, Angel, Pepe and the rest felt well satisfied at the way their hospitality was offered and received. Everyone will have as many positive happy stories and memories as they did 4 years ago. There was no sense of anti-climax or disappointment.

Perhaps the most eloquent comment of all came from Javi Vilar, a Celtic Submari member not known for his imagination or articulateness. At the end of the evening he turned to Ernesto, gave him a great big bear hug, and said to him "You have created something wonderful here. Thank you so much."

And oh yes, there was the game of football too.

It was the first home game in the Champions League since the Riquelme penalty miss 889 days earlier. A chance for all the Villarreal supporters to feel the swell of pride as once again the Champions League hymn was played out across their stadium. In a football sense it turned out to be a quietly satisfactory day for Villarreal.

I found it wryly ironic that Strachan played the Rangers way. He set out his stall not to lose, with only Samaras up front, and McDonald and Vennegor on the bench. It was the 4:5:1 system Rangers had used last season in their UEFA Cup run. Almost all the Celtic supporters I knew had been very critical of Smith for this negativism, and claimed moral superiority for their own more attacking style. Yet here, in the first away European game of the new season, Strachan was imitating the negativity of Rangers. And it did not even work. Villarreal without playing brilliantly, outclassed Celtic and outworked them. Celtic were restricted to a couple of half chances which Samaras fluffed. Villarreal patiently created more and more chances, and although it was still scoreless at half-time, it was obvious where the match was going. The Yellow Submarine eventually got their reward in the second half, with a cracking goal from a Senna freekick. Thereafter as Celtic were forced to open out a bit, Villarreal began to crucify them with slick football, pace on the wings, balls inside tired fullbacks, and could have had several more. Unlike Smith, Strachan did not stick rigidly to his new system, moving to playing with 2, then eventually 3, forwards, without ever looking likely to score.

For a 45 minute spell, from the 35th minute onwards, Villarreal played football of high class, using possession, speed and width to outplay Celtic. Senna and Pires were the best two men on the park but all the Villarreal men played well. For Celtic only Boruc and a gritty McManus passed muster.

A lesson for the World

The positive events of 2004 had caught the world by surprise and while they were widely reported locally and in Spain, it was as a rushed reaction to a surprise event. This time round the local, national and international media were better prepared, and from the day before the game Vila-real was flooded with reporters, commentators and cameramen eager to capture any repeat. And capture it they did.

Javi Mata, writing then for the Valencia Community paper Superdeporte, captured the prematch mood well with his headlined article "Celtic Submari prepara la fiesta de hermanamiento" (preparing for the celebration of brotherhood). The day of the game, the same paper had a full page spread featuring an interview with Ernesto and pictures of happy Celtic fans enjoying the hospitality of the Penya. The article stressed the amazing friendship between the two sets of supporters and highlighted both the family nature of the Celtic Submari and its strong charitable focus.

The day after the game all the local papers, and all the major national papers, ran features about how amazing the joint prematch celebrations had been, how great the atmosphere at the game had been, and what a lesson this represented for football fans all across the world. It showed how an important competitive game could be played with such sporting togetherness being demonstrated by all the supporters on both sides. Javi Mata's phrase, "Fiesta de Hermanamiento", was picked up and repeated by many papers and one paper had a headline "Amigos para Siempre" (Ernesto's slogan Friends for Always)

Local police later confirmed that throughout the whole day there not a single incident of trouble or violence involving anyone of the Celtic support. The Head of the Police Operation, a man who knows Gerry Martin well, confirmed the strong sense of shame felt that while the behaviour of the 4,500 visitors had been impeccable, there had been several instants of theft and aggression from one young Spanish man with a severe drug problem.

1st October

I bumped into a few Celtic supporters still in town. Tosh McLaughlin lost his glasses, an expensive pair, in the excitement, mayhem and drunken splendour of the Villarreal Celtic game last night. When he realised this the next morning and told Ioan about it, the big Romanian took Tosh up to the Madrigal to look for them. At the front of the stadium they had by pure chance met Fernando Roig. Ioan explained the situation to Roig, and the President had insisted on opening up the ground, taking them to where Tosh had been sitting and the surrounds, and then even onto to the pitch in a vain search for the glasses. Tosh had been so impressed by the whole experience, he insisted on giving his Celtic top to a very grateful Ioan. He has worn it every Friday night since then.

2nd October   A sad epilogue   Hope takes a knock

Later on that night of the Celtic game in Vila-real, Hope and Willie were walking home to their accommodation, in their usual slow unsteady way, when Hope was assaulted by a man who grabbed her bag and threw her to the ground. Willie tried to hit him with his stick but it all happened very quickly, the man was gone and Hope was left lying on the ground with what turned out to be a broken hip. She was taken to the new De La Plana hospital in Vila-real where she was kept in and eventually operated upon. Apart from the obvious impact on Hope, the town of Vila-real was traumatised. It would be naïve to pretend that there is no crime in Vila-real, but robbery with violence just does not happen. Even normal theft is far below Glasgow levels, and Hope herself had commented on the numbers of people who left their doors open, even when they went out. Ernesto could not believe such a thing had happened, and to Hope of all people, a symbol of all that was good about the relationship between these two sets of fans. The initial response was the suggestion that the perpetrator was a South American. But that only slightly comforting notion was soon replaced by a harder reality. While not a local from Vila-real, the perpetrator was a Spaniard from nearby Almassora, only 5 kilometres up the road. He was from a 'good' family, but had become heavily involved in drugs and had been desperate for money for his next fix. He had come into Vila-real attracted by the presence of thousands of very drunken Scotsmen and went on a rampage. As I understand it, he was later charged with several crimes of theft, but not the actual assault on Hope, because of the lack of identificatory and other evidence. His safety could not be guaranteed if he were ever to show face in Vila-real again, given the massive nature of the affront he caused the reputation and self image of the town.

The Celtic Submari swung into full action and a rota was drawn up to ensure that Hope was never without a visitor. When I along with Gerry visited the

Hospital today, Willie, Pat, Francis and the others stated they were bowled over by the kindness and care shown by so many people both to Hope, and to them as her bedside companions. When Willie and Francis had to go home, Hope's son Paul flew out to ensure that family as well as friends were ever present with her at the hospital. Elena Roig visited Hope in the hospital on behalf of Villarreal CF, which pleased Hope enormously. Elena also arranged for Giuseppe Rossi, the Italian from New York who speaks excellent English, to come and pay his respects on behalf of all the players. As well as the never ending stream of Submari visitors, and more flowers and fruit than she could ever consume, Hope received 23 individual cards, which she has kept as treasured mementoes of the kindness of Vila-real people. She said "They treated us like royalty, me like a Queen. I will never forget that."

Hope developed a particularly strong relationship with Marissa, one of the nurses, who spoke passable English and showed her repeated kindnesses. Saul's cousin, a nurse in the hospital, also was very good to her. Hope also developed good relationships with the hospital cleaners, one of whom gave her a card in which she wrote in Spanish "No hay nada mas bonito que la amistad" (There is nothing nicer than friendship).

When Hope got back home to Bathgate she sent a note of thanks to the Penya and asked that it be circulated widely in Vila-real.

"Muchas Gracias, Thank you to all the residents of Vila-real

On a recent trip to Vila-real I was unfortunate to end up in hospital with a broken hip. However, it was proven that "you'll never walk alone" in this world. Although I could not speak a word of Spanish, throughout my stay I was never without visitors.

Thank you to the Nurses, Doctors and Support Staff of De La Plana Hospital in Vila-real for all the excellent medical care and treatment I received. To the Alcalde (Mayor) of Vila-real; to President Fernando Roig Alfonso's daughter Elena and Giuseppe Rossi of Villarreal CF; thank you for giving up valuable time to visit me in hospital.

To all members of Celtic Submari CSC, Gerry, Jesus, Juan and Saul, I would not have been able to communicate without your help. To Ernesto, Jose Luis, the extended Del Amo Bort and Ramos families, thank you is not enough for the love and friendship you gave me. To Wullie, Paul, Franny, John, Martin and Pat, my travelling party, thank you for being there in my time of need and to all well wishers thank you for your fantastic cards and gifts.

No hay nada mas bonito que la amistad (there's nothing nicer than friendship), God Bless you all,

Hope Wightman".

If Ernesto's wife Maria, or any of the other Celtic Submari women, had been similarly assaulted in Glasgow, I have absolutely no doubt that the response to her would have been just as spontaneous, generous and caring as that received by Hope in Vila-real. But it would have lacked the element so powerfully present in Vila-real, that of total shock, bemusement and shame. It would not have been more acceptable but it would somehow have been more predictable, more expected, more part of the less than perfect fabric of Glasgow life. But for it to happen in the quiet peaceful conservative law abiding town of Vila-real created a genuine traumatic sense of horror and disbelief in the ranks of the Celtic Submari. And for it to have happened to Hope, who had somehow become the grand old lady of the Celtic connection, heightened and intensified the sense of shock, shame and pain.

Chapter Twenty Seven Pursuing the Big Dream
4th October

It has been fascinating over the past few days talking to the members of the Celtic Submari about Villarreal. Not one of them thinks they will win the league. Not one of them believes they will win the Champions League, even the ones who thought they might in 2006. But they all believe they can do well in both tournaments this season. Almost to a man they do not think their team is playing as well as it did last season, despite the positive results. I am beginning to understand a little more about the Vila-real character. They are not dreamers, but realists. In conversation, even over a few beers, they are much more detached and realistic about their team than the groupings I am used to in Glasgow, of Celtic, and Rangers, Thistle and Clyde supporters, where equal measures of bombast, beer and boasting tend make a much more potent, positive and excited mixture.

21st October

Socially it was a better night. I went up to Vila-real with Val, who works for Clyde, on the restaurant side. We started in the Celtic Submari club, where Gerry had brought his Danish friends from the night before. Pedro the bar man, was selling raffle tickets, first prize a trip for two to a game in Madrid. Gerry and I agreed if we won we would take each other rather than partners. Val agreed if she won she would nominate us both. Val had been slightly worried before hand that it might slip out that she was a Rangers supporter. It did, but no-one bothered and Ernesto and the others were very nice to her.

After the game in which Villarreal beat Aalborg 6-3 without playing well, we hit the Bar Madrigal for beer and tapas. Pepe Mansilla was there in jubilant form. He advised me to forget the poor football and focus on the result.

Tuesday 25th November 2nd leg v Manchester United at the Madrigal

The atmosphere in the streets of Vila-real before the game had its lively moments, although there was absolutely no trace of any trouble. There is only so much "Glory Glory Man United, Glory Glory Man United" a non-United fan can take, although the faithful would appear to have no problem repeating it endlessly. Add the occasional enigmatic reference to "Knick Knack Paddy Wack, give the dog a bone" coupled with various rude comments cum suggestions about Manchester City, and the shared intent about "We're going to Wemberlee, Wemberlee" and this appeared to represent the sum of a very limited repertoire.

Very few of the 3000 United fans came straight to Villarreal or stayed there, almost all seemed temporary residents of Valencia and they did not really appear on the streets of Vila-real until just about 2 hours before the game. Despite the numbers involved, there was no party organised along the lines of the Celtic Jamboree and most of the Submari settled for friendly mingling. Most of the 3000 seemed in a good mood and there was no sense of potential violence or even aggression simmering below the surface. The bulk concentrated around the square and the fountain and the myriad of little pubs surrounding it. Much beer was consumed but probably a reflection of the lesser time involved, few seemed to reach the level on merriness attained by a fair number of the Celtic fans. It was noticeable that there was much less interaction with the locals but there a flourishing trade in 'half and half's' the scarves made to celebrate both teams.

Ever eager to test the reality of myths, I sought to establish whether any of them in fact hailed from Manchester. All had flown in from Manchester and lived there or thereabouts. Not really different to Celtic, whose followers are as much from west central Scotland as from Glasgow itself. The Myth is another lie told by Manchester City fans as consolation for their second place status.

A couple of the groups I spoke with, had combined the trip with an opportunity to spend a night or two in Barcelona, not yet having caught up with the reality that Valencia is a more beautiful and more active city for a few days break.

Friday 22nd November

Marcos Senna brought his wife and young son, Pedrito, onto the pitch at the end of training. The boy was hardly bigger than the ball but showed good skill in kicking it for one so young. Senna, a thoughtful, serious and caring man, has just launched his charitable Foundation the other day, and Gerry used the opportunity to explain to him that the Celtic Submari Penya regularly raised money for charity and it would make sense to link up with Senna and channel funds into his Foundation. Senna seemed genuinely pleased at the prospect.

6th December International Congress of Villarreal supporters

A big day for the Celtic Submari as the first ever International Congress of Villarreal Supporters starts in the Auditori with a Panel Session. There are Villarreal supporters present from all over the world, representing the growing number of Villarreal penyas based outside Spain. The Celtic Submari is still by far the biggest of all the Villarreal penyas, and members are determined to be as welcoming as possible to their counterparts. After the opening ceremony, many of the visiting delegates ended up in Celtic Submari Penya Club just across the road from the Auditori. It really is one big happy family. And family is the appropriate term, since there were many women, many children and a good few babies. Both the Villarreal Fan Club Finland and the Flamencs Grocs (from Belgium) have placed huge banners at the left hand goal, which can be easily seen as you watch a game from El Madrigal on TV.

Chapter Twenty Eight   The Celtic Submari return to Glasgow

As soon as the Group Stages draw had been made in August 2008 many of the Celtic Submari began planning for this great opportunity given to them to return to Glasgow. At the time of the draw it might well have transpired that the game, the last one in the Group Stage, could be vital, with hopefully both teams still having the chance to qualify. The romantics like Domingo and Estrella dreamed of a situation where they would be present at Celtic Park with a drawn game being enough to see both teams through. The realists like Jose Luis saw it as more likely Villarreal would get a result that would eliminate Celtic. The timing of the game, in midweek in the second week of December, meant that many of the previous travellers, particularly the teachers, would not be able to come this time. That unfortunately ruled out both Ernesto and Saul. They both very reluctantly settled for helping plan the trip, knowing they would not be joining it. This left Jose Luis Broch and Angel as the effective leaders of the invasion force, with Domingo and Estrella as chief cheerleaders. Around 100 of the Celtic Submari members were able to commit to coming, although the school week clash meant that it was adults only, unlike the 2005 and 2007 expeditions, but at least 40% of the travellers were women. Gerry Martin handled the Glasgow end arrangements, again, with help from Derek Rush. I took the opportunity of the game to arrange a week back in Glasgow.

Monday 8th December

The Celtic Submari party arrived at their hotel in Ingram Street. There was much excited meeting up with old friends, and socialising well into the night. At one point Domingo put on a false moustache, and impersonated a BT technician in an elaborate ruse to divert hotel staff as part of a cunning plot to enable the hotel bar to be kept open longer. It worked.

Tuesday 9th

All the Celtic Submari party went in two buses on a trip to Loch Lomond and Luss. The highlight, for most, was a guided tour of the Auchentoshan Distillery. Many of the Submari have begun to develop a palate that appreciates good malt whisky and they had specifically asked if a trip to a Distillery could be arranged. Auchentoshan did not disappoint them, neither in the tour nor the generous samples provided at its end. After a full and lengthy lunch on the banks of Loch Lomond, it was back to Glasgow and some free time before the main social event of the trip, a Buffet cum Dance in the Corinthian Bar, which Derek Rush had been able to book through the same contact who had set up the Arta event on a previous visit.

Most of the Celtic Submari were very impressed with the Corinthian and its many impressive features, even after being told it used to be a Court House.

Elena Roig and her brother Fernando Roig Negueroles, were there along with their cousin Trini, and some of the local journalists already familiar to me. Elena brought with her a jersey signed by all the first team players as a contribution to the charity fund raising activities of the evening, with once again, all monies raised being promised to Yorkhill Children's Hospital. It turned out to be a very happy and enjoyable evening. The emotional highlight of the evening was the presentation of a Ceramic Plate to Hope Wightman, in recognition both of her many services to the Celtic Submari, and as a further apology for the attack that had landed her up in the Vila-real Hospital a couple of months previously.

After we were all finally, and relatively politely, thrown out of the Corinthians, groups of the more hardy revellers continued round the fleshpots of the Candleriggs area in search of more excitement. Gerry Martin and I were surprised but pleased that Fernando Roig Negueroles, normally slightly reserved and formal, showed himself sufficiently relaxed to join in and tag along, ready and willing to go with the flow.

Wednesday 10th

I went round to the hotel in Ingram Street to see how the Celtic Submari members were coping with the pace. They had been in Edinburgh in the morning to the Scottish Parliament, where they were given a formal reception by Scottish Minister for Education, Fiona Hyslop. The Submari members were very impressed with the Holyrood parliament building.

Two stories emerged from the reception which have already permanently entered Villarreal Celtic Submari Penya folklore. The Carfin crew have a friend who works for Porcelanosa in Glasgow, and when this friend heard they would be going to the Scottish Parliament with the Celtic Submari, they offered to provide a cake to be presented to the Minister. It was agreed that the cake was to have the Villarreal crest and a St Andrews Cross on top along with the Hope Wightman motto "No hay nada mas bonito que la amistad". Jesus Del Amo had linked up with his Carfin 'family' and travelled through to Edinburgh with them and the cake they had picked up the day before, securely in its box. Jesus was standing beside the Minister when the cake was presented to her. The box was opened and the cake was proudly displayed on the table for host and guests to admire. The crest, the flag and the motto all turned out magnificently, and were rightly much admired. But as eyes travelled to the top of the cake there were literally gasps of horror heard in the room from many distraught members of the Submari. Across the top of the cake, in very prominent icing, was printed PORCELANOSA, the deadly rivals of Pamesa, the Roig Ceramics company. It was a bit like Celtic Supporters presenting a cake with the Rangers sponsors in pride of place on it. "Muy mal" was the immediate general consensus, quickly followed by "Nobody better tell Fernando Roig or we're all in trouble."

Poor Jesus, whose only crime was to be standing beside it when it was presented, was immediately and irretrievably given the full blame for this massive faux pas by all the other Celtic Submari members.

Spanish ham was made the probably equally innocent fall guy for the second story. Domingo told it best but it was also verified as true by enough other Submari members present for me to include it without fear of legal problems. According to Domingo, just as the Minister turned to walk away after the presentation by the Alcalde of a Villarreal Plaque to her, she let out a highly audible fart. Now just as Spanish women never get drunk in public, it is also an unchallengeable rule of nature that Spanish women never ever fart. Domingo was hugely amused (and still is two years on) and was generously prepared to put it down to the ham consumed at the reception. The rest took it as a welcome sign of the directness of Scottish politicians.

I joined the whole Submari party in the short walk round the corner to the City Chambers for the reception with the Lord Provost. We were joined for this event by Juan Rubert, the Alcalde of Vila-real, and his Minister for Sport. Gerry Martin was conscripted into his role as official translator for the party. The Celtic Submari members were impressed with the grandeur of the City Chambers, which they compared favourable to the world famous Ayuntamiento Town Hall in Valencia.

Bob Winter, Lord Provost of Glasgow, handled the formal reception with his usual political skills in full play. Being a staunch Celtic supporter, he probably regarded welcoming Villarreal people as one of his more pleasant civic duties. Brian Wilson was there representing Celtic, and Jose Manuel Llaneza, Villarreal CF. Rubert and Llaneza each were presented with a bottle of very exclusive Malt Whisky, to the chagrin of most Submari members who knew they would see none of the contents of either bottle. So they made do with the Provost's fine wine, made freely available. In return the Provost received a signed Villarreal jersey from Llaneza and a Ceramic Plate from the Alcalde.

Bob did his welcome act very well because Angel remembers in particular the trip to the Scottish Parliament and to the Glasgow Lord Provost's office. "I remember having the distinct impression that the words of welcome in both places were not just the usual politician's hot air, but that the warmness of welcome and feelings of affection were real. So did the rest of us. We felt appreciated and loved."

After the Lord Provost's reception, it was time to begin the prematch preparation with several pints. I ended up in O'Brien's in the Candleriggs Centre with many of the Celtic Submari who had opted to walk to Celtic Park rather than take the buses.

For the meaningless game Pellegrini played 9 reserves, with only Senna and Gonzalo from his first eleven. For the first 15 minutes Villarreal reserves were the superior team and several times carved open the Celtic defence only to squander the chance created. Then Celtic scored, possibly from an offside position. Quickly thereafter Franco was sent-off for no perceptible good reason and the Villarreal heads went down. Celtic got a second goal just before half time and the second half was a dreary bore. The 60,000 Celtic supporters enjoyed it. Many of them seemed totally unaware they were facing a reserve team and the few who did, didn't care. The Bhoys enjoyed themselves, gaining their first and only victory of the Champions League campaign.

I felt sorry for the Submari fans who had paid £500 for the trip but to be fair, few of them objected and they had the sense to concentrate on the social aspect of the experience rather than the football one. Which, after all, was why they had come. And they all loved the whole experience of being at Celtic Park. Afterwards it was another happy Submari night in Glasgow. Once again Arta proved a hit, with Celtic supporters and Villarreal supporters mingling, buying each other drink, and trying to communicate any way they could.

Like almost all of the Celtic Submari party, Estrella has good memories of the December 2008 trip to Glasgow. The trip was special for Estrella because as a Bar owner, Easter is always a bad time for her, so she had missed the 2005, 2006 and 2007 trips, but was determined to make the 2008 one in December. She loved it, from beginning to end, and is determined she will return to Glasgow one day. "We went to the Scottish Parliament, which was very impressive, and there was a great party in a big bar in Glasgow. Because the game was in effect a friendly, I was not bothered that Celtic beat Villarreal, but it was great to party with the Celtic fans". And party she had, never stopping dancing for the three days.

The trip went well, and the Celtic Submari members loved the whole experience. Gerry Martin felt slightly annoyed that Celtic organised nothing for the Villarreal supporters to compare with the day long celebrations organised in Vila-real for the visiting Celtic Supporters. He did raise it with the club but was told that if they did it for one, they would have to do it for everybody, so no. They sent Brian Wilson to the Lord Provosts reception, and entertained the Club Directors, but offered nothing social to the supporters.

Chapter Twenty Nine   The push for Europe
2nd January 2009

Raising money for people in need, particularly children, has always been a very important part of Celtic Submari activity from the very beginning. Every event they organise includes a determination to raise some money for their charitable activities.

All this effort comes to a culmination every year centred on the annual Children's Party held in the Christmas New Year holiday period. Invitations are made not only to children of members, but to local children known to Aspanion, the charity supporting families of children with cancer. When the Club Groguet for young Villarreal supporters was formed, invitations were extended to include some places for their members. The result is that each Party has hundreds of excited young children in attendance, all of whom are guaranteed a present from one of the Three Kings in attendance, who tend to be Villarreal players in fancy dress. Spanish children are much better behaved than Scottish children, not in the over polite English sense, but just in terms of their demeanour and respect for others. But while the behaviour is better than it would be at a similar Scottish function, the noise generated at these parties is phenomenal.

Tonight Celtic Submari had their annual Christmas celebration to distribute the funds raised during the past year for Aspanion. This year, Cani, Pires and Guille Franco attended as the Three Kings and a great time was had by all. Robert Pires handed over a cheque made out to Aspanion, and 2 other local charities also received donations. It was held in the Instituto Francesc Tarrega, the school linked with John Ogilvie High in Hamilton.

13th January 2009
Shedding blood for your club

Many supporters throughout the world claim to be willing to shed blood for their favourite football team, but Villarreal are one of the few clubs to put that boast to the test. Several times a season they set up blood donation facilities in the Ground, and reward all donors with two free match tickets. This week was the first of the year, and over 400 supporters gave a half-litre and were rewarded with tickets for Sunday's game against Mallorca. Three of the players Gonzalo, Capdevilla and Viera turned up to personally thank the donors. Celtic Submari members were well represented in these donors, in a gesture which fits well with the general ethos of the Penya.

Friday 6th February 2009

Tonight we went to the Celtic Submari Penya with Richard and Margaret over from Scotland on a visit. Like all our Scottish visitors, they were overwhelmed with the friendliness and hospitality shown by the locals. Saul and Vicente both speak good English so they talked to Margaret, while Richard, who speaks Spanish, was able to integrate better with the non-English speakers including Jose Luis Broch whose friend's son is currently with Clyde's Youth Team in Cumbernauld. There was excited talk in the Penya that Willie McStay, Head of Celtic Youth Development, was coming over next week to watch Villarreal play and to study their facilities. The Submari Committee have arranged a meal with him. The talk gave Richard, a lover of rotten puns, the opportunity to rescucitate the old 1980s Glasgow Celtic joke, when Greig's Rangers were struggling, much to Celtic delight. "Actually there are 3 of them McStays not 2, - there's Paul McStay, Willie McStay and Greig Muststay". It's the way you tell them.

Celtic Submari announce their plans for the trip to Athens. They will fly out with the team, and spend 2 nights in a 4 star hotel, all for 520 euros. Seems like very few of the Submari sign up, much less than made trip to Glasgow for the Rangers game at the same stage 3 years ago. Of course there was the Celtic dimension operating there, but even so, the novelty of the Champions League seems to have worn off quickly.

Tuesday 10th February

Went to Vila-real tonight, interviewed Willie McStay, then we both went to a working dinner with the Committee of the Celtic Submari Penya. Ernesto, his brother Jose Manuel, Pepe Mansilla, Pascual and Vicente were all there, plus Willie McStay, Gerry Martin, and myself. The Head Waiter was a member of Celtic Submari, so star treatment was guaranteed, along with free beer and wonderful food. Despite the language problems, the communication was good. Wille McStay handled himself very well, accepting the hospitality and homage with good grace, and contributing many good stories about Celtic and its people.

24th February

There are expected to be 3,000 Greek fans coming over for the Panathinaikos game, as many as Manchester United brought. Only Celtic and Rangers have ever brought more. The atmosphere and expectation are likely to be completely different than for the Celtic game, which was seen as an opportunity to demonstrate the universal brotherhood already existing between the two clubs. 90% of the Greek fans will arrive in Spain on Wednesday, the day of the game. They will be kept in Valencia until a couple of hours before kick-off and then ferried into Villarreal in special trains. They will be escorted up to the Stadium and all packed into the new Visitors Stand. After the game, the Greeks will be escorted by a large police presence straight back to the station and returned to Valencia. So not much of a Greek bonus for Villarreal publicans.

Again in contrast to the Celtic game, where the Submari Penya organised a massive and brilliant party for the 9 hours before the game for thousands of Celtic supporters, this time the Celtic Submari have organised something for only Villarreal supporters. There will be a party in the Penya club followed by a mass march up to the Madrigal. The Celtic Submari phenomenon happened largely because the two sets of supporters were allowed full access to each other in the bars and streets of Vila-real, and each was amazed and impressed by the attitude of the other. The authorities had been caught by surprise in 2004 and had not expected anything like the 10,000 or so supporters who travelled to their little town from Scotland. It was about 9000 more than they had experienced before in the Intertoto and UEFA history. One of the costs that has come with the subsequent Villarreal success in Europe has been a loss of that kind of spontaneous interaction, and it is almost certain that the events of 2004 will never be repeated. The chances of a Panathinaikos Submari emerging from the next few days would seem non-existent.

25ᵗʰ February 2009

I went to the Celtic Submari Penya Club well before the game started. The Penya Plan was to invite all Villarreal supporters, not just Penya members, to assemble in or outside the Penya, then march in unison to ground led by Batuca Groga, a drum band dressed in yellow with several of the loudest drums ever produced. They were practicing inside the Penya, leaving little opportunity for civilised conversation.

I did manage to talk with Willie and Hughie, two lads from Paisley. Willie was wearing a Celtic top with the 1967 European Cup logo on it, which attracted envious glances from many of the Submari faithful, but he would not be seduced into the usual habit of swapping it for a Villarreal one. Willie had been in Villarreal in September 2008 for the Champions League game and had been blown away by the welcome and friendliness. Hughie, who spoke some Spanish after having lived in Barcelona for a couple of years, had never been in Vila-real before but had heard all about it. With Celtic prematurely out of Europe they had decided to invade Europe themselves and the obvious game that jumped out for them was Celtic-friendly Villarreal playing at home against green strip with shamrock Panathinaikos. So they had flown to Alicante and made their way up to Vila-real.

Inside the Club, Domingo was in fine form, dancing frenetically to the drumbeat, glass in hand, without ever spilling a drop. Estrella was manic, as if on drugs, leaping wildly to the incessant beat of the drums, whirling her arms and shouting rather than singing the Villarreal song. After half an hour I could take the noise no more and I sought refuge from the drums and went in search of Greeks.

It proved harder than I had expected to find any, the tight security shepherding being obviously effective. The first two lots I found did not speak English or Spanish, so our communication was not very productive. In the next Bar I met up with a couple of young men who had come over with the main party but had managed to escape and were determined to sample some Villarreal Bars before the game. It was the first time in Spain for both Panaotis and Yoros. Panaotis was the more flamboyant of the two. He was wearing a huge green wig with hair several feet long and had a voluminous and luminous green and white raffia scarf cum coat wrapped around himself. Within seconds of finding a seat, the transformation was incredible, and he sat at the bar as sedate presentable young man, dressed in pale denim. Then when he left bar it was again as a combination of the Jolly Green Giant and the Incredible Hulk. His English was very good but he claimed he had only learned it at school and not practiced it since then. Yoros was more sedately attired, only a green top with Panathinaikos emblazoned across the chest gave the clue to his affiliation. I confirmed with Panaotis that he would not have been born when Panathinaikos got to the final of the European Cup, to be beaten by Cruyff's rampant Ajax side. He desperately wants to be part of the next stage of the history of his club. He was adamant that the score tonight would be 1-1, and that Panathinaikos would win 1-0 in Athens. His pal Yoros had less good English but was still able to tell me that they would definitely get the valuable away goal tonight in a 1-1 draw.

I met Domingo after the game. The dancing fever had left his legs but he was still upbeat and his eyes still had their usual sparkle. I attempted to commiserate with him, but he had a more positive perspective on what he had seen than I expected, with plenty of hope. "They'll have to come at us more in Greece and that will open up more room for our front players, it's far from over yet" was his assessment.

8th March 2009

This time round the Celtic Submari supporters were not engaged to the same extent as in the first adventure. While they all expected to beat Panathinaikos, they did not expect to win the Champions League. They all assured me they would be going to the Quarter Final away leg. In the end only 20 of the 700 Celtic Submari members made the trip to Athens and they were absorbed in the Agrupacion group travelling with the team. The Celtic Submari hotel, the Titania, while 4 star, was rather less luxurious than the Hotel Grande Bretagne favoured by the Club and the richer supporters.

Back in Villarreal, there were several all night parties going on. The Plaza Maior had been full for the game. The screen looked bizarre. It was an EcoPanel system which looked uncannily like a giant eyeball, a round white blob with a black centre. The screen at the front of the eyeball was curved rather than flat but the picture had great clarity and the sound was excellent. Row after row of white plastic seats were filled from the Eyeball at the far end of the square, right back to the other end. About 8,000 people must have been packed in to watch their team. Around the edges, many were standing but even from the back rows the view was very good. Only a few philistine young children were uninvolved, running up and down the two side green ramps rather than becoming absorbed in the game. The square is surrounded by blocks of flats on all three sides, and many residents chose to watch the game on the eyeball screen from their terrace rather than on their television indoors.

Although the square has several bars on three sides, there was little drinking going on. Once again the contrast with Glasgow was hard to avoid. Such an event in Glasgow would have had many people under the influence of alcohol but in Vila-real there was not one drunk person to be seen the whole evening. The crowd were well-behaved and very good natured. They clapped good moves which at the ground is one way to show the players some appreciation, but which is funny concept, and maybe wasted effort, to do to a giant eyeball.

One slightly bizarre element was exposed the two times Villarreal scored. Either the screen process imposed a few seconds time delay allowing radio listeners to be ahead of the game, or sections of the crowd were psychic, because on both occasions the wild cheering started marginally before the final shot was struck. With each goal there was an eruption of collective joy, with yellow balloons being released and thousands of scarves waved, with much chanting and singing and communal hugging. Towards the end of the game, a Mexican

155

Wave started at the front and made its way up to the back of the square, to be picked up again by the front row and continued onward again. It only stopped when a particularly penetrating Villarreal attack started. The delight at the end of the game was tangible. For the second time in four years the small town of Vila-real celebrated its team reaching the Quarter-finals of the biggest and most important Club tournament in the world.

The Celtic Submari Penya had its biggest attendance of the year as members crowed in to watch the game on their Big Screen rather than walk round the corner to the Plaza Maior. Ernesto was acting as resident host and must have personally greeted about 400 people. Every now and then, in the midst of the game, Franco the barman would put the Villarreal song full blast on the Club sound system, and Estrella and her mates would leap up, whistles blasting and dance up and down on the spot.

Chapter Thirty   Gunning for Revenge, the slow death of a dream
Saturday 21ˢᵗ March

I went to the Celtic Submari Penya club before the game against Athletic Bilbao to see what the general view was about the Arsenal draw. The place was buzzing, busier than usual and with a very happy atmosphere. Ernesto was in good form. With the Arsenal away leg taking place during the Easter holiday break, he and the other teachers and professionals are going to be able to go. The Committee had set up a table at the end of the main room, manned by Jose Luis and Saul, to sign up people interested in going to London and in the half hour I was there they got 42 signatures. One good thing about Gerry Martin being stuck in London is that he can organise the trip and the entertainment. Everyone I spoke to seemed at least quietly confident that Arsenal could be beaten and that revenge could be gotten for 2006.

I walked up to the Madrigal with Saul. As a teacher, he is free for the Arsenal game and looking forward very much to his first away trip of this campaign. He had been in London in April 2006.

Friday 27ᵗʰMarch

I drove to Villarreal for a quiet night in the Celtic Submari Penya Club. The main surprise of the night was that Pepe Mansilla, known for his exploits on away trips, will not be coming to London with the ever-growing Submari party (now over 80 and rising). He was rather shamefaced when Ernesto told me in front of him that this was because his wife Antonia would not let him, but he offered no alternative explanation. Not exactly the stuff of legend.

Tuesday 7ᵗʰ April

My friends Richard and Tim arrived on Monday for the match. Richard is an Arsenal fan who has travelled to most of their Champions League away matches. He still has not fully recovered from the emotional strains of his recent trip to Rome, the penalty stress and then the two hour wait in the stadium before they were allowed to leave. I assured him Villarreal would be much more civilised and that he would be able to join us in the Bar Madrigal within 15 minutes of the game ending.

We went to the Celtic Submari club well before kick-off time but had missed the two giant paellas that had been prepared as part of the pre-game celebrations. Richard, with his Arsenal top and scarf, was warmly welcomed by Ernesto, Vicente, Saul and the others who remembered him from his previous trip to the Penya. Richard had brought with him a large Arsenal pennant which he presented to Ernesto, who seemed chuffed and hung it prominently on the wall. Several of the Villarreal supporters wanted photographed beside Richard who seemed to be the only Arsenal supporter in the Penya. The general mood was relatively quiet, there was no great sense of confidence about the result to come.

After the game, a 1-1 draw which has left Arsenal favourites to go through, we went to the Bar Madrigal for some food and drink, then made our way back to the Celtic Submari Penya. Patrick Barclay, Chief Football Writer for the Times, was there, Gerry having met him at the game and invited him back to the Penya. He told a story of coming down on the train for Barcelona sitting next to a group of Spaniards, who turned out the family of Cesc Fabregas. He seemed genuinely impressed with Villarreal and the Celtic Submari.

It was obvious from the conversations that somehow the Villarreal supporters knew the moment had passed, from half time. The Dream was over, gone. They would not be winning the Champions League this year, or even reaching the semi-final. But many of the Celtic Submari were still determined to go to London, and enjoy the experience.

Tuesday 14th April 2009

Since I was in France on business I made my own way to London, flying from Carcassone rather than travelling with the main Celtic Submari party. We are all staying at the Melia White House, in Regents Park, a good class hotel that specialises in Spanish visitors.

The Tuesday evening was the one free night for the Celtic Submari in London, with the Arsenal game on Wednesday and the flight home on Thursday. So where and how did they opt to spend it? In the West End, taking in a show, or in Soho? No, in an outcome no-one would ever guess, the evening was spent in Hayes, a 40 minutes bus ride away from London. Ernesto had agreed with Chris, a regular visitor to Vila-real Fiestas, that the whole Celtic Submari party would be guests of the Hayes Bhoys CSC. It just emphasises that they are people persons for whom communication with like minded people, particularly Celtic supporters, is more important than any bright lights.

The Hayes CSC is based in Captain Morgan's Bar, a friendly pub near the main street. Hayes Bhoys CSC is a relatively new club started by four mourners in the emotional aftermath of the death of Bobby Murdoch 8 years ago. It meets every week in Captain Morgan's, which used to be owned by the Club's first treasurer. Four different owners since then have all honoured the commitment to let the CSC meet there and decorate at least the back room walls with Celtic memorabilia. The club currently has about 120 members with a normal weekend attendance of around 60-70, with the Celtic game on TV the highlight. The Club is the home base of the Bible Code Sundays, a Celtic Rock band with a growing international reputation. The group have played at Celtic Park before a full crowd and were well received.

Chris Harley, the main man behind the visit to Hayes, had made a big impression on his several visits to Vila-real for the Fiestas, and you could tell many of the Submari people were pleased to meet up with him again. Chris was born in Greenock, near the Cappielow ground of Morton, but grew up an avid Celtic fan. Living and working in Madrid, it is easier for him to keep in touch with the Celtic Submari. Indeed he is one of the very few Celtic supporters the Submari have met who speaks good Spanish. Like everyone else Chris fell under the spell of Ernesto on his first visit and has worked hard at remaining a friend ever since. When back in the United Kingdom he is based in the South and links up with Hayes CSC as his nearest branch. There was a good turnout to welcome the Spanish guests and as per normal practice language differences were not allowed to prevent good intermingling. The Hayes CSC has a very cosmopolitan membership with Scots and Irish predominating, but most parts of the globe represented, and even a few Englishmen. I talked to David, a Swede who became a Celtic fan when he worked with Chris in Alaska. It was an affiliation confirmed for life when his all-time favourite Swedish player, Henrik Larrson, signed for them. David travelled to Celtic Park several times to see his idol, but was finally barred as a jinx when the pattern emerged that Larsson never scored on his visits. From the other end of the globe was Adrienne, a Chilean living in Madrid, where she had been converted to Celtic by Chris who lives and works there. Like most intelligent Chilean women, Adrienne is a great admirer of Chile's most famous citizen, the Villarreal manager, and thinks Matigol Fernandez is pretty cute too. Like several others there tonight, she will be going to the Emirates tomorrow night, but her support of Villarreal will be more passionate, and more longstanding, having been to El Madrigal on her own several years ago to pay homage to Pellegrini.

The Bar has two big television screens. In deference to the nationality of the guests, one was tuned in to the Barcelona Champions League game with Bayern Munich, the other to the Chelsea Liverpool quarter final second leg match. This turned out to be one of the great Champions League games of recent years, with the lead changing hands several time. Most of the Submari faithful including Ximo, Javi and Javier elected to watch this match rather than the Barcelona game. And most felt either English team would beat Villarreal or Arsenal if they met in the Final.

The full Bible Code Sundays line up was not present, but those who were agreed to perform for the Submari, in a performance which was much appreciated. Andy Nolan played the accordion, and Ronan McManus, the lead singer for the group, provided the vocals. To suit their audience, they played many of the Celtic classics.

Wednesday 15th April

I had a pint at lunchtime with Jose Navarro Martinez. Jose was a midfield player in the Villarreal team that won promotion to the Third Division in 1951, so he is no spring chicken, being born in 1930. He played for Villarreal for 10 years and has been a supporter ever since. I also had a long conversation with Felix, who has friends who live in Naquera.

The expedition to the Emirates set off early and after several pub stops, makes a final base camp in the Quay pub about a mile from the ground. Gerry Martin has booked tables and food there for the whole party. All the Arsenal supporters encountered, both here and everywhere else that evening, are friendly. At one of the pubs, we rendezvous, by arrangement, with Gerry's son Matteo and an Italian pal of his, Valerio, from Liverno. Matteo, an Arsenal supporter, is a bright, smart, attractive kid. A Gerry Martin but well-educated, charming and with the rough edges planed down.

After the game there was a major problem with the bus supposed to take the Submari party back to the White House Hotel. It just disappeared and no amount of telephone pleading could solve the matter. Celtic Submari trips tend to have a history of problems on the bus front. Most Submari members appear to firmly believe this is because Gerry Martin associates with cowboys. Gerry robustly defends himself with the obtuse argument that he could lay on a fleet of Rolls Royces if the Submari had the money, but they don't, so they should gratefully settle for the miracles he does with the limited budget. About half an hour after everyone else has left the Emirates, the main Celtic Submari party is still standing by the side of the road not far from the Stadium when the official Villarreal CF Team Bus passes by slowly. Roig, Llaneza and the other occupants recognise their supporters and acknowledge them, but do not stop to offer assistance. Gradually the braver spirits start to drift off to make their own way back. Eventually back at the hotel, I sit with Ernesto and Maria Dolores, Saul and Ximo, and drown the sorrows of the ended dream.

No-one is surprised at the outcome of the game. Ever since the second half of the first leg, everyone seemed to know the dream was over and there would be no second semi final for them. There is disappointment however at the cravenness of the surrender and the lack of 'Villarreal' football. Ximo summed up the general view well, "I wouldn't have minded so much if we had played really well but been beaten by a better team. But to go out without a whimper, without having a go, without playing attacking football, that was just pathetic."

Friday 8th May

None of the Celtic Submari members seem to be planning to go to the Barcelona game in the Camp Nou this weekend, a marked contrast to the first ever trip to the Camp Nou only 10 seasons ago. And none of the ones I talked too seemed to have any great hope that a similar result to ten years ago might be achieved, despite the astounding improvements over the past 10 years.

16th May   Real Madrid game

Before the game there was a mass march of penyas from Plaza Maior to El Madrigal. Around 40 penyas were represented, all with their own banners and flags. The atmosphere was vibrant, full of excitement and anticipation for one of the great days of the season, when the official "greatest club in the world" come to little Vila-real. There are very few Real Madrid supporters in view, far less visitors than for the Barcelona and even Espanol games.

For the main May Fiesta, the Celtic Submari have temporarily moved to new premises, in Calle Luis Vives, a big barn much better for drinking parties. This week for the Fiestas, every night the Celtic Submari are raffling off, at 1 euro a ticket, some of the shirts worn by Villarreal players including those of Pires, Capdevila, Gonzalo, Diego Lopez, Nihat and Matigol. The proceeds from this, along with from all the extra beers sold, will as always go to local charities, as part of the never ending Celtic Submari commitment to help others.

The highlight of the late Saturday night was the special Bull run. For this one, the horns of the bulls are set aflame, and burn for hours. The bulls roam unfettered through the Vila-real streets for hours, angry and outraged. Every bar and most houses have temporary grills erected to offer pedestrian protection.

Sunday 24th May 2009

A sad day for Celtic Submari members as Rangers win the Scottish League on the last day. The Celtic game was shown on the big screen and few of those watching denied that Celtic were poor.

Friday 5th June The Penya End of Season Dance

Last night was a wonderful night in Vila-real, as the Celtic Submari Penya celebrated with their now traditional end of season dance. For once I had the sense to know that driving home would not be an option, so Gerry and I booked into La Masia, beloved of regular Celtic Supporter visitors, to share a twin room.

The dinner dance took place in the Jardi Alaska, a brilliant venue quite near El Madrigal. There were well over 200 Submari members present, including most of the usual suspects. The first half of the evening we were basically sat at our pre-selected tables, as course after course of food appeared, with endless supply of red and white wines. Then the tables were pulled out from the centre, the wine was dispensed with to be replaced by a bar selling spirits at cheap prices, and the singing and dancing began. The stars of the evening were Pepe Mansilla and Estrella, who exhibited enormous amounts of energy dancing, leading community singing and cheerleading.

The one semi-serious part of the evening was a presentation to all time Submari favourite Josico, back from his season in Turkey with Fenerbahce. In his six seasons with Villarreal, he had been the midfield grafter that fans love and opponents fear. He had been the player who most appreciated the values of the Celtic Submari and identified with it, visiting frequently, and getting on with all the members, who in turn idolised him. The circumstances of his transfer and departure to Fenerbahce had been such that no proper farewell had been possible, but tonight remedied that. Ernesto made a great speech emphasising Josico's humanity as well as his ability, then he was presented with one of the Submari special statutes, commissioned from a local sculptor, of a globe or football supported by three hands representing Solidarity, Friendship and Respect.

Once again I found it impossible to ignore the contrast with similar Scottish events where a high level of drunkenness would have been guaranteed. Here people got happy, but no-one, not even Gerry and I, got drunk, despite hours of continuous intake. So maybe it is cultural not genetic. The party didn't end till after 4am, quite early by Spanish standards, then it was a happy walk back to La Mesia.

Chapter Thirty One Voyage Two and the R word returns
13th July 2009   Nilmar presentation

The first main event of the new season was the presentation in the Madrigal of new signing Brazilian international forward, Nilmar, already known to the Submari as Nilmaradona. Around 5000 people turned up. After the Presentation, which involved nothing more than Nilmar mingling happily on the pitch with the couple of hundred kids in Villarreal strips, I met Saul and Sisi, sitting outside the Bar Madrigal. Both are pleased with the Nilmar signing and are looking forward to a positive season. Saul, now the Secretary, reported that membership of the Celtic Submari is still growing, and is now well over 700. He confirmed there is a full programme of events planned for throughout the coming season, with the first main highlight being the mid September Fiestas, where the Penya will have something planned every day.

Thursday 20th August

The official season begins with a trip to Holland, for the first leg of the Europa League Final Playoff Round qualifier. Very few of the Celtic Submari made the trip, most of Vila-real still being away on their month long summer holiday. The game resulted in a comfortable 3-1 away win in Breda against the local NAC.

Thursday 27th August

There were an amazing number of Dutchmen, and women, in Villarreal tonight for the second leg, despite their team Breda being 3-1 down from the first leg. At least 2,000 of them. As one of them put it , in the perfect English which they all seemed to speak, "We don't get out often. So we were not going to miss the chance of a trip to Spain, even if we have no chance. We are here to be happy and enjoy ourselves." And they were true to his word, filling the Plaza Llabrador and surrounding bars in a happy mood. Intelligent, opinionated friendly people quite happy to talk freely. The Celtic Submari were out in force on their best integrating behaviour.

August 29th First Villarreal B game in El Madrigal

Today proved a memorable day for the Celtic Submari. Most of the core members are children of the 1960s who as they grew up, if they supported Villarreal at all did so as their 'Wee' team, in the lower leagues, while giving a primary loyalty to a 'Big' team in La Liga. Some like Angel and Javi supported Real Madrid. Many, like the 4 Boixader brothers and Ximo, supported Valencia. Most like Saul Ramos, Vicente, Jose Luis Broch, Monica, Estrella and Sisi were Barcelona fans. A fair number, like Pepe Mansilla, Enrique Navarro, Luis Broch and Juan Luis Botelha were Atletico Madrid followers. As Villarreal took a place in the First Division, all of them went through a dramatic metamorphosis with the Yellow Submarine replacing their First Loves as the premier club of their heart, their new 'Big' Club. By 2008 the transformation had long been complete, and apart from a couple of surprising Atletico renegades, all the adult members of the Celtic Submari were absolutely clear that Villarreal were now the undisputed team of their heart. For their children, life had been much less complicated, all of them growing up with Villarreal as their First Love, their Big team.

In June 2009, 14,000 Villarreal citizens, including just about every Celtic Submari member, had been present in El Madrigal when the Villarreal B team played the first leg of the double header that saw them gain promotion to the Second Division. Most of them had turned out on the streets of Vila-real for a giant celebration a week later, when that promotion was confirmed and the B team toured the narrow streets of their town on an open topped bus.

Today saw more than 8,000 turn up at El Madrigal for the first game of Villarreal B in the Second Division, against Levante. What this meant for the Celtic Submari, and many thousands of other Villarreal supporters, was that once again, or in their children's case for the first time, they now had another 'wee' team, Villarreal B. All future B team games will be played in the Cuidad Deportiva complex, in the Mini Stadium that has been upgraded to seat around 5,000 in modern comfort. The Villarreal CF Season Ticket allows free entry to all Villarreal B games. Some Villarreal supporters, like Juan Luis and Domingo, have always watched the B team and even the C team and junior teams. But from now on a significant number will go to a game every weekend, alternating between the main team and their new Wee team, Villarreal B.

There is one important organisational implication of this for the Celtic Submari. It has opened up another 23 clubs with whose supporters the Celtic Submari can begin to make their special arrangements and offer their unique hospitality. Given the low numbers of visiting supporters common in this league, it becomes much more feasible that the Celtic Submari can actually issue a blanket invitation to all of them, to come to the Celtic Submari Penya for food and drink before or after games. And sure enough, over the season this is what began to happen, and supports like Huelva, Cartagena, Cordoba, Gimnastic, Huesca, Las Palmas and many others experienced with shock and delight the kind of friendship and camaraderie offered by the Celtic Submari as part of their new model of how to relate to other football supporters.

13th September

The game against Mallorca showed the fickleness of fate. One minute we were sitting shirt sleeved, the next minute we were swimming for our lives as the most phenomenal deluge arrived. It continued unrelentingly for the next 75 minutes and turned the pitch into a swimming pool. The nature of El Madrigal Stadium is such that both ends, the Fundo Norte and Fundo Sur, are totally exposed. The rain was so ferocious that it was impossible to stay and watch the game. Even those few who came prepared with umbrellas and waterproof capes were soon totally soaked, so from the two separate ends, all the drenched congregated in the many bars around the stadium to watch the second half on TV. They didn't open the stadium gates until halftime, so thousands milled about inside the ground, unable to escape.

I chose the Bar Deportivo where, as well as the Villarreal regulars including Gerry, Ernesto and Estrella, there were some regular visitors from Glasgow and Liverpool, Tam O'Hare the Abuelo, and Tosh, and Billy Spencer, the Everton supporter. From the dry Bar we watched amazed as the referee allowed the second half to be played as a kind of water-polofootball. We watched dismayed as the three points seemingly guaranteed by Rossi's goal were reduced to one as a shot from Borja Valero skidded past the Villarreal keeper.

14th October

It was a bit of a surreal night in the Celtic Submari Penya tonight, the night Valverde came for tea. The team under his leadership had been doing badly. Domingo would have sacked him after the 4th game, before he came to Penya. Almost all of the Submari members there tonight think he is already doomed, and that sacking him is a necessary step, but being the decent people they are they treated him with respect, friendliness and kindness. It was an impressive demonstration of that central Celtic Submari value, respect for others. It would have been alien to that value to give the man a hard time, whatever their personal views. Valverde couldn't believe how well they treated him, despite how badly the side were playing. The new players for this season, Oliva, Marcano, Escudero, Jonathon Pereira and Fuster were also there, all bar Nilmar, and it was less of a strain to be nice to them. Valverde does seem a nice man, confused and bemused but not a bad man. However his personal qualities did not convert a single Submari member to the "Valverde must stay" camp. They know their football too well for that.

Wednesday 21st October

Whether it was the economic recession or the football depression, far fewer Villarreal supporters than originally anticipated made the flight today to Rome for tomorrow's Europa League tie with Lazio. The Celtic Submari had weeks ago abandoned plans to organise their own trip and only a few linked up with the official Agrupacion party.

Sunday 1st November Home to Tenerife.

Gerry Martin had planned to come with me but got confused about clocks, put his forward rather than back and missed the lift. 47 years old and still cannot tell the time. The 5-0 win lifts the club out the relegation places after 5 miserable weeks in them, but the Submari members are still unhappy. The 5 goal win reassures no-one. Incredibly Tenerife seemed the better team for most of the game.

5th November Home to Lazio Europa League

After 2 losses in the previous two Europa League games, Villarreal could not afford another slip up tonight, at home against Lazio. A defeat would leave them effectively eliminated.

In the Penya before the game, most of my regular analysts, Ernesto, Angel, Jose Luis, Pascual and Domingos, were present and quietly confident. Not on the basis of the last two league games, which had left them unimpressed and still critical of Valverde, but on the basis of the excellent football produced the previous week in the away game. And so it proved. Villarreal played well again and won comfortably.

Afterwards in the bar, the Celtic Submari supporters I drank with were quietly pleased. I talked to Fermin Font who told me his father, Supporter Number One, was doing well, but had not been able to go to the game

13th November 2009

Tonight I had an enjoyable Friday night in the Celtic Submari Penya. With Ernesto, Saul, Vicente and others there was some serious football talk. The consensus amongst them was that Valverde has confused the defenders and midfielders who don't understand what he wants them to do, while getting the message that he wants something different than the Pellegrini way. The good periods of play this season have been when they have given up on his theories and reverted to the concepts taught them by Pellegrini.

Friday 20th November 2009

For first time ever in my visits, Ernesto was not in Penya, reportedly suffering from a bad stomach. There was a suggestion the constant strain of being responsible for everything was maybe getting to him.

Tuesday 1st December 2009

Villarreal fly out to Sofia for the penultimate Europa League game, against Levski. Only a handful of supporters have joined the official party. For the first time, not a single Celtic Submari member I know travels with the team. This is definitely not Celtic like behaviour.

January 2010

Yet another successful Children's Party with more large cheques handed over to Aspanion and other charities, and more unforgettable memories created for the hundreds of children in attendance.

Friday 5th February

The general mood in the Penya is quiet satisfaction that Valverde has gone, and more positive pleasure that he has been replaced by "a man of the house" in Garrido, who took the Villarreal B team to 4th place in the Second Division, giving Vila-real, population 50,000 two clubs in Spain's Top 24. In the way of the village that is Vila-real, most of them feel they know Garrido well, have known him for the 10 years he has worked with the club and most have bumped into him around the Cuidad Deportiva in his various roles over these years.

Thursday 18th February Europa League KO Stages Home to Wolfsburg

There were supposedly 300 Wolfsburg supporters in town for the Europa League first leg game but well regimented and behaved. The first half of game was miserable, due to a combination of both the heavy rain and the poor performance by Villarreal. Wolfsburg missed several good chances, then Senna scored a freekick just before half-time to give Villarreal a slightly undeserved half-time lead.

The second half proved even more miserable; Grafite scored twice, Marcano was sent off, and then Marco Ruben equalised. The general consensus in the Bar Madrigal after the game was that it was not looking good for next week.

16th March 2010

There was quiet satisfaction in the ranks of the Celtic Submari tonight at the news that Vicente Belles has "resigned" as President of the Agrupacion de Penyas del Villarreal and been replaced by Vanessa Martin (no relation to Gerry), the President of the Penya Santi Cazorla. The Belles resignation was described as being for personal and professional reasons, but the Celtic Submari consensus is that he jumped before he was pushed. The key Submari members have always felt his primary objective was to help himself rather than the mass of supporters, and that he was pettily jealous of the size and significance of the Celtic Submari and blocked many of their positive suggestions. They are looking forward to a much more constructive working relationship with the new President.

Sunday 28th March

Bill Alexander and I went to Vila-real with Gerry, for the Sevilla game. Before the game we met up with Sisi who invited us into her house for a beer. Her flat is very well furnished and laid out in an attractive minimalist style. She wasn't going to the game, so in best Submari fashion, she gave her season ticket to Bill to use.

After the game we all met up again in Bar Madrigal for a few beers and much happy analysis, of a 3-0 victory against one of the other Big Six clubs. This has put Villarreal back in the hunt for a European place which had seemed lost after Valverde's failures.

Saturday 10th April

The members of the Celtic Submari like Neil Lennon. As a player he reminded them of their all time idol Josico, with a similar hard, uncompromising total commitment to the cause. When he was in Villarreal on Celtic business, Lennon came to the Submari Penya, was very friendly, and happily posed for photos with Ernesto and others. So they were pleased when he replaced Mowbray. But they watched with sadness today on their Big Screen as he failed to motivate his team against Ross County and Celtic slide shamefaced out the Cup.

After the Gijon game it was off to a Bar to watch El Clasico. Most of the watching Villarreal fans were ambivalent. They want Barca to win the league but they want Pellegrini to prosper. Barca won comfortably, 2-0, and it looks like Pellegrini is doomed, despite these being the only three points dropped at home all season.

Friday 30th April

It is a good night in the Penya, with people happy at the recent progress of the team under Garrido. Despite this, the usual stalwart analysts, including Ernesto, Jose Luis, Angel and Vicente, are not confident about the imminent game against Barcelona.

1st May

In the Penya before the Barcelona game, I met Barca supporter Alex Ximo. Alex has a German father and speaks good English, but is a fervent Barca fan, who travels to many away games. The whole group of Barcelona supporters, pulled in off the street as per normal Penya procedure, are blown away by the friendliness of the Penya and its members. As Alex put it "I have never, ever, in all my travels, met such a bunch of friendly people who go out of their way to make you feel so welcome. This is what football supporting should be all about. Sadly, it is unthinkable that Barcelona supporters would treat visiting fans this way."

Barcelona win the game, 4-1, but the Celtic Submari members take consolation from the fact that their team are still in 6th place, with only three rounds to go. So after all the turmoil of earlier in the season, and the flirting with the bottom of the league, European qualification is still in their own hands.

Saturday 8th May Entertaining two groups of visiting supporters

Saturday was a busy day for the Celtic Submari Penya, but one which demonstrated what this Penya is all about. First they had a group Paella at lunch time to which all visiting supporters from the Canaries that could be found were invited. Then it was onto the Cuidad Deportiva to see Villarreal B play Las Palmas. Josico their old hero should have been playing for Las Palmas, but never got on the park. It was a mad game, with the Villarreal keeper Juan Carlos sent off .Villarreal B, with only one previous home defeat all season, ended up losing 5-2 but none of the Submari seemed to mind. Then there was a frantic move en masse to El Madrigal, with Josico tagging along, for the Valencia game. There was good mingling with the Valencia supporters after the game. The Celtic Submari definitely do not hate their closest neighbours and rivals. How could they, with Ernesto, all the rest of the Boixaders, and many others having been brought up supporting them? So while there is rivalry, it is of the friendly variety. Not all of the Valenica supporters feel the same way back, some of them bitterly resent the presumption of their upstart country bumpkin neighbours who dare to claim an equality rather than accept the long standing subservience. But enough overcame this instinctive reaction to respond positively to the overtures made by the Submari to create a good atmosphere of friendliness, even despite Villarreal having played them off the park.

Wednesday 12th May

Tonight, Forlan showed his best side and helped his old club, by helping his new club win the first Europa League Final with a 2-1 win over Fulham. The brilliant Uruguayan scored both goals. One happy Atletico supporter tonight was a certain Pepe Mansilla, the Celtic Submari legend, he of the dual allegiance. He went to Hamburg to see the Europa League Final. Muy Feliz. He was invited by friends in Madrid, friends he had made by inviting them to the Celtic Submari Penya in Vila-real when Atletico visited several years ago. He has told me that he joins them in Madrid for every Atletico Villarreal game "And in Madrid my money is no good. They buy me food and drink all day long and all night!" Just as well he has a big heart capable of loving two teams at the one time!

Thursday 13th May

Another demonstration of what the Celtic Submari is all about. Tonight over 200 of the 700 members of the Villarreal Celtic Submari Penya squeezed into their club room to pay a last tribute to their two departing heroes, Javi Venta and Robert Pires, who last Saturday played at the Madrigal for the last time. Both players received a very warm and emotional reception from the Celtic Submari faithful. The Submari President Ernesto Boixader helped Submari youngsters hand over two specially designed "Hands round a globe" statuettes to the players, who patiently participated in individual and group photos until everyone was sated.

Javi Venta knows all about the Celtic Submari, which he has visited many times. He feels an affinity with Celtic. He spoke with a very positive regard of playing at Parkhead, and the wonderful atmosphere generated by the amazing Celtic supporters and their songs.

26th May 2010

Pellegrini was sacked as manager of Real Madrid despite leading them to their most successful ever league campaign, at least as measured in points gained, 96, a record number for the Madrid club and a total never before matched in the history of Spanish football. Over the past few months, many of the Celtic Submari members have been getting increasingly annoyed with the way the Real Madrid club ill-treated and abused their ex manager. For most it confirmed for them, as it did for many Celtic supporters, just why they actively despise rather than just dislike Real Madrid. The arrogance, the snobbery, the elitism, the assumed right to eternal superiority, all jarred, as did the cruelty perpetrated on a man they so admired. When I asked for a Celtic Submari perspective on Pellegrini's time at Real Madrid Vicente Andreu wrote me the following comments

"León de ojos verdes"

Two years ago Manuel Vicent, a very well-known Spanish journalist and writer, published a novel entitled "León de ojos verdes" –meaning in English "Lion with green eyes". This novel, which I strongly recommend reading, narrates several short stories that happen during summer-time in a beach resort on Castellón's Mediterranean shore, around the Hotel Voramar. The several plots and dramas take place under the attentive look of a plaster lion that guards the main staircase of the hotel entrance. Another famous Manuel, Manuel Pellegrini, is also a frequent guest to the Voramar. At least during the five years he managed Villarreal CF's first squad. Now, he has just finished his spell as Real Madrid's coach. The job that half the people in Spain dream of and the other half would accept without hesitating in spite of the feeling that it would involve cooperating with the enemy. The statistics of his performance with Real Madrid during the season are unquestionable -: ninety six points, and one hundred and two goals. Last season, Barcelona, the winner of everything, got eighty seven points. Six years ago, Valencia, obtained the championship with seventy seven points. But that has not been enough, he has not been capable of obtaining a championship and was beaten in the Cup and in Champions League by minor rivals, and that is a sufficient reason for having been dismissed as manager of what many people considers the best club in the world. The real thing is that price is often mistaken for value. It is commonly assumed that a squad needs time to adapt to the philosophy of its coach and Pellegrini has not had enough time to proof that he is one of the very best in his job. We, Villareal supporters, know it quite well. Next season Real Madrid will have again a great squad with renowned players and a new manager, and, sure enough, they will be fighting again for the championship. But that won't happen under the smart, elegant and polite look of the Chilean lion with green eyes. Good luck, Mr. Pellegrini. I hope to see you again at the Voramar.

Chapter Thirty Two   Voyage Three European Joy and Disappointment at the Celtic Submari

Many of the disappointed Submari members had consoled themselves after Celtic's surprise defeat to Braga in the Champions League qualifiers with the fantasy that with Celtic and Villarreal both playing in the Europa League, there could be another repeat of the wonderful days of 2004 and 2008. However Celtic and Villarreal had contrasting fortunes in the final Playoff Round for the 2010-11 Europa League.

I had thought that Celtic would be too strong for Utrecht, Celtic's opponents in the final qualifying round, a sentiment shared by 90% of Utrecht even after the first leg. Celtic threw it away in the second leg, being craven and incompetent beyond belief, to the surprise and delight of an astonished Utrecht and their delirious supporters. And Barry Maguire delivered on his promise of driving Celtic to the 'eve of destruction' with a cracking goal. Reality returned to Utrecht that weekend, as they were hammered 4-0 by Twente in their league game, a reminder that they are not secret world beaters, just a decent enough team very lucky to get Celtic at their absolute worst. But even that dire Celtic performance against Utrecht would have been enough to see off Villarreal's opponents Dnepr Mogilev. Villarreal beat them 5-0 in the first leg at the Madrigal literally without breaking sweat on a warm Spanish evening. The immensity of that gap proved to be accurate over the two legs as Villarreal complete a 7-1 aggregate win. Mogilev were so poor that even the most disillusioned Celtic supporter would have felt confident in putting their house on Celtic to beat this team. And would have got his money back. So there will no repeat this season of the previous two clashes.

The Celtic Submarine gear up for Glasgow

Sometime early in season 2010-11, partly after the disappointment mentioned above, the decision was taken, by Ernesto, Saul, Jose Luis and Angel, that their longstanding plans to visit Belfast, with a ferry trip over to Glasgow for a Celtic game, should once more be put on hold and replaced with a direct trip to Scotland. The fixture list around the Easter break was consulted, but due to the Scottish system of a divide into two mini-leagues for the last 5 games, then for the final chosen dates of 22nd-25th April, there will be no guarantee that Celtic will be at home that weekend. However the Easter weekend suits people best, so it is fingers crossed for a home game and on with the planning.

Planning for such a trip takes months and months of effort. The early indications were that probably around 100 of the Celtic Submari would sign up for the trip. Since it was to be during the Easter holidays, teachers and children would be included. So the plans were made for full family participation, just like the original trips of 2005 and 2007, rather than the more restricted ones of 2006 and 2008.

Every year the Celtic Submari have a standing invitation to all their Celtic friends, Scottish and otherwise, to visit Vila-real for the annual Fiesta in mid-September. In 2005, flush with the excitement of the first Submari trip to Glasgow a few months previously, well over 200 Celtic supporters took advantage of that offer. In subsequent years the numbers have not arrived at this level but what the visitors have lacked in quantity, they have tended to make up for in enthusiastic determination to enjoy themselves. This time, September 2010, the population has been swelled by some 40 Scots making the pilgrimage.

Today's Spanish papers provide gruesome pictorial evidence that one element of Spanish Fiestas can be fatal. Last night some poor soul out enjoying himself, was gored to death at a bullrun in another Fiesta. Over the weekend several full grown bulls will roam the main streets of Vila-real.

Friday 10th September

Up at Villarreal, the Penya were running several events a day over the three key days of the Fiestal. There were many Scottish visitors in town, including Linda, Tosh and 19 young girls from John Ogilvie High, Tam 'the Abuelo', Floppy and the 67 Bhoys from Carfin. And they all saw Ernesto as the spiritual centre of their visit and wanted a piece of him. I wondered again, as I often had over the past two years, how he coped with the incessant demands on his time and his emotional energy. He responded as always to every request, every demand, every approach, with calm courtesy and positive engagement. But there comes a time when even the deepest well runs dry, and I have feared for some time that Ernesto is approaching that point. Not seeing him daily, as most of the Submari seem to do, I had more opportunity to notice almost imperceptibles changes in him over time. He looks older and tired. He seems to have been ill very regularly over the past two years, often with stomach problems. He confessed that some of the peripheral activities he has been trying to create around the Penya, have consumed far more of his time and energies than he had thought or wanted. Some of his closest friends in the Penya have had their worries about him too. Collectively they feared their charismatic friend was taking on ever greater commitments and paying the price, and they identified a pressing need to pull him back and share his load. Some like Saul have tried to take more of the weight of work, others like Vicente and Jose Luis have tried to counsel him to do less. Ernesto attributed his tiredness over the past year to the massive amount of work he has been doing on the Young People's Disco. He has been disappointed and disillusioned at his failure to bring this to fruition.

Saturday September 11th

As a bonus for staying overnight, Gerry Martin was allowed on the back of a small open top van dishing out free beer to the workers on behalf of the Submari, his idea of heaven on earth. At night there was a posh do in the Penya, or at least as posh as it gets without getting formal. As always, all the Fiesta visitors were made to feel very welcome and very special.

Sunday 12th September 2010

I spent time in the hotel bar with the Carfin people. They love their trips over, which they have been making regularly since September 2005. They feel part of the Del Amo family now, because of the links created following Jesus's visit to Carfin in November 2004. They are staying in the Palace Hotel, the only good one in Vila-real, but spend most of their time with the Del Amo family. On their 2008 visit Jesus's father had promised them a special ceramic Villarreal CF plate. They thought he would have forgotten all about it but yesterday he handed it over.

It was Hope's first trip to Vila-real since her injury in 2008. Like most victims of serious trauma, she was a little anxious about returning to the scene but she was determined that she would pay a visit to the hospital and thank the nurses and others who had been so good and so kind to her during her stay there. The visit turned out to be very successful. She got a great reception and the key people were there to receive her thanks and her flowers. Saul organised through the Penya and the club that she got to meet with Giuseppe Rossi again. Capdevila was there too, which gave her a good thrill, meeting a World Cup winner.

Hope was also given one of the special sculptures, of the three hands round a ball globe. Ernesto had altered the usual script slighty in telling her "the three arms represent faith, Hope and charity, and the greatest of these is Hope." She was greatly touched with this gesture and her only worry was how to get the sculpture, which, being solid metal, weighs about a quarter ton, home.

Pat told me an incident the previous night which summed it all up for her. The five of them had been round at the Del Amo family home for dinner and Jesus's mother had said "You must come to my granddaughter's first communion in May, the whole family will be there, and you are part of our family." For Pat, the whole Celtic Submari phenomenon is about acceptance and family, and how through football, families can become extended and enhanced.

Outside the ground before the Espanol game, I met Linda Orr as arranged. She had with her some of her19 young girls from Hamilton she had brought with her as part of the school exchange scheme. The ones I met were happy, obviously very fond of and respectful to Linda, and very much looking forward to going to the game with Espanol, which Villarreal won 4-0.

Often the good done by good people due to their goodness goes unrewarded, even unnoticed. So it was great to hear from Linda that the John Ogilvie High School in Hamilton has been named Spanish School of the Year 2010 by the UK Spanish Embassy. This award is made annually to the UK school that has done most to promote the teaching of Spanish in the United Kingdom. While this prestigious award is an honour for South Lanarkshire Council, South Lanarkshire Education Department, the Headmaster, the school and all its teachers, it is primarily a reward for all the good work done over the past 6 years by Linda Orr and Thomas 'Tosh' McLaughlin through the regular school exchange scheme developed between John Ogilvy High and the Francesc Tarrega school in Vila-real.

It grew out of a football relationship but while football has remained a central core in it, the scheme has passed well beyond football alone, to embrace full cultural exchange. It has allowed hundreds of youngsters from both cultures to learn about and enjoy life in another culture, and to appreciate that learning a language is not a dry boring chore, but an exciting mechanism for enhancing communication with friends. The parents of both communities have responded generously by letting pupils from the other community into their homes.

Friendships between young people, and with families, have been forged that will last a life time and ensure that the two communities remain inter-twined for generations to come.

Both football clubs, Celtic FC and Villarreal CF, have responded magnificently and generously to the opportunities the school exchange have created. Pupils on every trip are not only given free entry to the home Stadium for the games (and trips are only arranged after scrutiny of the fixture list has ensured there is a home game in that period) but the clubs lay on conducted tours, meetings with players and other related trips. In Villarreal, Elena Roig the daughter of the President, personally conducts the tours of the Stadium and Cuidad Deportiva with the Scottish young people. The Villarreal Alcalde (Provost/Mayor) and the Town Hall have always been so helpful and accommodating that Linda has become a very close friend of the Alcalde's assistant, Ester.

Although Linda is by nature shy, quiet, self-effacing, she has realised the full significance and importance of the Spanish School of the Year Award and has permitted herself to be seen and heard in public, receiving it, promoting it and increasingly in being engaged in related publicity efforts. She knows the award is very important to many people and has been able to see that these people want her to get her just credit for the achievement that reflects so well on so many people.

People at both ends of the Celtic Submari Scotland connection, like Derek Rush and Damian Kane, Ernesto and Saul, are very proud of the School Exchange initiative that has grown out of a football friendship and ensured that full links between Vila-real and Scotland have developed that will last for lifetimes, enhancing and promoting full understanding and real exchange.

The Glasgow connection

After the fiestas I returned to Glasgow briefly to tie up some of the Celtic and Rangers ends of the story. One highlight of my trip to Glasgow was Wednesday night at Celtic Park where Celtic demolished Inverness Caley Thistle 6-0. Two miracles happened, the Celtic crowd was less than Villarreal's the next night, and Samaras was the man of the match, working hard, tackling back and spreading play unselfishly. Maybe it is not too bizarre to see him as the new Forlan. Atletico Madrid what have you missed?

One reason the crowd was so low was that the League Cup game was not covered by the season ticket, a notion contrary to the Roig philosophy. Knowing the turnout would be poor, Celtic had closed off the whole top deck around three sides of the ground. With this top deck completely empty, the ground looked like the Madrigal Stadium would if Roig had gone down the road of having the capacity enhanced to 40 or 50,000. The eerie one third full stadium reminded me of many Celtic games of my youth where the club struggled to get crowds in five figures. I had thought these days had gone for good, but here was a stadium usually filled with more than the entire population of Vila-real for every game, actually attracting a crowd smaller than the one Villarreal drew to the Madrigal the next night for the game against Deportivo.

The interviews with supporters on both sides of the Old Firm divide went well, the only real difference being that more of the Rangers ones were cautious about being identified by name in the book.

Friday 22nd October

The Submari members are pleased with life at the moment. Their team is playing excellent football. There was some collective disappointment at the failure of their team to take the opportunity last weekend to go top of the league for the first time ever. Most agreed that the team had tightened up, and blew the opportunity against Hercules due to nerves. But overall they are pleased that their team is competing with Real Madrid and Barcelona by playing attractive "Villarreal style" football. They are all very positive about Garrido and some are even beginning to compare him favourably with Pellegrini.

Sunday 24th October

Watched the Rangers Celtic clash on Sky TV, where Celtic were abysmal, then off to the Madrigal for the Atletico game. I met up with Sisi for a quiet drink before the game. She was just back from a weekend in Madrid where she had had two contrasting cultural highlights, a visit to the Prado to take in the Renoir exhibition, and a trip to the theatre to see Mama Mia.

Tonight proved a hard test of loyalties for the 4 Celtic Submari 'colchoneras', and two of them failed. On the Friday Pepe Mansilla had shown me an email he had received from a group of his Atletico pals in Madrid, seeking to ensure his hospitality would be up to its usual high standards when they came for Sunday's game. Pepe had invited me and Gerry Martin to join him at the small party cum dinner he was organising. Then on Sunday I met Enrique who slightly sheepishly opened his coat to show me the Atletico scarf underneath. These two undoubtedly have failed the "Abandon the First Love test" and are still primarily Atletico men. Another good night despite another inhuman 9pm kick-off, on a Sunday night! Villarreal played really well, outclassing Atletico Madrid comfortably, and justified all the positive comments made about them in the Penya a couple of nights before.

26th November 2010

The highlight of the night in the Penya was a table manned all night by Maria Dolores and a string of helpers. It sold Navidad lottery tickets on behalf of the Penya. It did good business all night.

I heard a good story about one of the pictures in the Penya. Every one of the many items of football memorabilia on display has a provenance. I have already mentioned the Larsson portrait, and the signed Celtic jersey, both of which adorn the bottom wall. This story involves the huge panoramic photograph of the crowd taken at the Old Firm game at Celtic Park won 6-2 by Celtic, on 27th April 2000. It is not likely many of the 59,476 crowd present that day have forgotten the game and where they were sitting. The unique feature of the photo is that every single seat in the stadium is included, so anyone present at that game should be able to point directly to themselves. The very large photo, mounted in a good frame, belonged to a keen Celtic fan, Charlie Sharkey from Eaglesham. 'Big Charlie' made one visit to the Celtic Submari Penya and was so impressed with the hospitality he was given, he vowed to return one day bearing that framed photo as a gift for the Penya. Unfortunately Charlie fell ill with prostate cancer and was never able to make good on his promise to himself to deliver the photo to the Penya. Among the arrangements he made to follow his death in March 2010, was a request to his neighbour Hugh Lynch to take the photo to Vila-real on his behalf. Hugh moved last year to Benicarlo about 40 kilometres up the road from Vila-real. Last summer he brought the photo down but the Penya was deserted. Hugh got the cleaners from next door to let him in and left the photo with a wee note explaining how, why and from whom it was appearing as a gift. He returned several months later to find the photo in pride of place near the entrance. Hugh too was so beguiled by the friendship and hospitality of the Penya members that he joined, and bought a season ticket for Villarreal, and makes the round trip most Friday nights and for every home game.

30th December 2010

Another very successful Christmas Party organised by the Celtic Submari. This time the guest players were World Cup winner Carlos Marchena and new Submari hero, midfield genius Borja Valero. The night served as their formal introduction to the Celtic Submari, as the season's new signings, as well as allowing them to distribute presents to all the hundreds of children in attendance. Linda Orr, in town for the holidays, participated in the ceremony whereby the players handed another large cheque, for three thousands euros, to Aspanion.

9th January 2011

The Villarreal official party took the new High Speed Train to Madrid, publicly supporting the region's new transport infrastructure. It was quite a different experience, and about two hours faster, than the train Angel, and several thousand other Villarreal supporters had taken for the very first match in La Liga away to Real Madrid in 1998. Again the pattern of the recent away trip to Barcelona was repeated with the team being joined by less than a couple of hundred supporters. Of all the things Villarreal have learned from Celtic supporters, and of all the behaviours imitated, travelling in mass to away games, either domestically or in Europe, is not one of them. I suspect that only a Villarreal appearance in a Cup Final will ever recreate a situation where many thousands of Villarreal supporters travel again to a game outwith Vila-real. For those most dedicated and brave souls who did make the trip to Madrid, there were considerable consolations. Villarreal were brilliant in a dazzling first half display, outplaying Real Madrid and unlucky not to go in 1 goal up, having twice forced a lead. In the second half Mourinho showed why he is a winner, as he several times changed things to enable his side to end up as rather lucky 4-2 winners. Still Villarreal confirmed that are the second best football playing team in La Liga.

Chapter Thirty Three The Ran(gers) in Spain pisses mainly on the plain, but also on the righteous and the ungodly alike   Part Two

Since that disciplinary action of 2006 following the Villarreal games, Rangers have been subject to further sanctions from UEFA on several occasions. Following the March 2007 game against Osasuna in Pamplona, Rangers were fined £8280 for the "improper conduct" of the supporters who became involved in a brawl with Spanish police. In November 2009 after the "battle of Bucharest" Rangers were again fined, this time £18,000 for the "improper conduct" of their fans including throwing seats and brawling with local police. On both occasions, senior club spokesmen appeared to blame poor stewarding and heavy handed local police, rather than rigorously condemn the unacceptable behaviour of their own supporters. In between these two incidents there had been the events in Manchester in May 2008 at the UEFA Cup Final, when scenes of Rangers fans rioting had been broadcast around the world. Rangers escaped official action because the events took place well away from the actual stadium, but no-one was left in any doubt that the historical pattern of bad behaviour had been massively extended.

Since their trip to Vila-real in 2006, Rangers supporters had been in Spain on two occasions and both times their supporters were involved in trouble. They were fined by UEFA for the encounters in Pamplona in March 2007, and later that year there was further trouble when Rangers visited Barcelona on Champions League Group Stage business. Most of the Rangers fans who travelled did not manage to get tickets for the game, and throughout the day and evening of the game there was a series of incidents involving clashes with local residents. The actual game passed without major incident and UEFA took no action.

In season 2010-11 Rangers were drawn in the same Champions League Group as Valencia. I determined to go into Valencia the night before the game to talk to as many Rangers supporters as possible and to formally interview some.

Monday 1st November 2010

I go into Valencia to meet Rangers supporters. It transpired that most of the large Rangers travelling support has elected either to go to Benidorm for a day or two's 'rest and recreation' before the game, or to fly in for the night of the game only. So there were only a couple of hundred Rangers fans in the Old Town centre, all congregated in the main Plaza de la Reina Square. Indeed almost all there congregated in the one Bar, Finnegans.

None of the fans I talked to seemed to see any incongruity in Rangers supporters settling on a Irish Bar, clearly advertised as a Dublin Bar. They totally took over the bar, which is large with several separate sections; draping Rangers flags and banners inside and out. They also colonised all the pavement tables outside the Bar.

The general mood was light, positive and happy. Finnegan's is not a Bar Spaniards drink in anyway, and there were no natives around at all for potential integration. Even the Bar staff all tend to be Irish or English so language was not an issue. There was almost continuous communal singing in the bar which made casual conversation difficult.

A reflection of the relative lightness of the mood was that the most popular song was "Who'se got jobbie on their hands, jobbie on their hands; Bobby Sands, Bobby Sands", sung repeatedly and enjoyed as toilet humour, rather than the more vicious versions about famine, hunger and death which had persisted at the time of his death and subsequently. I found it bizarre, but strangely reassuring, that almost 30 years on, all that anger had been reduced to a dirty ditty sung almost affectionately.

"The Billy Boys" was probably the second most sung song enjoying regular coverage, of the full "We're up to our knees in Fenian blood, surrender or you'll die" version. It was clear that everyone felt this song is their song and they had every right to sing it, which they did, all night. There was no element or section present within the Rangers support taking the line that this song would be better not sung. No-one I asked considered it in any way provocative or offensive, and they all indicated that they would be singing it at the game tomorrow, as usual, as always. As the night wore on the ability of people to take part in constructive conversation deteriorated, but the benign mood did not. If it had been a points score situation, comparing the behaviour with that of Celtic fans almost exactly two years previously in the same square, then Rangers would probably have won narrowly, due to the absence of the aggression of the Celtic female group, but then I wasn't trying to give the Rangers supporters something for nothing.

The ones who had been in Villarreal in 2006 confirmed the accounts both of other Rangers supporters interviewed previously, and all the Villarreal natives. There was no hostility displayed to Villarreal as a club. Most expressed an interest in the central thesis of the book, of how come a team from such a small town could be so successful while much bigger clubs, including their own, struggled. The 'link with Celtic' element was a source of cynical scorn rather than overt aggression.

For years Rangers supporters have been telling me that much of the violence and mayhem around their trips abroad is not caused by Rangers supporters, but by right wing hooligans from England who use the Rangers support for Queen and Country as a cover for their dire deeds. "It was Chelsea supporters not Rangers supporters", or "It was Millwall supporters not Rangers supporters" are the two main variations of this theme. Much of the trouble in Manchester in 2008 was attributed to these groups. My normal response to these claims, bolstered by facts like the addresses of those charged with the Manchester offences, was that peculiarly Scottish use of the double positive to create a negative, as in "Aye, Right!"

However over the course of the evening I was forced to reconsider my attitude to this phenomenon. It was a bit like a disbeliever interviewing the Abominable Snowman, or in this case, more like the Abominable Englishman.

Alan Adair was only one of several I talked to but the one I interviewed in most depth. Alan was born in England and has lived in England all his life. He is not a Rangers supporter but a Luton Town supporter. If Luton were to play against

Rangers in Europe, Alan is 100% certain he would be supporting Luton. But for several years now, he has been following Rangers to away games in Europe, and to an occasional game at Ibrox. He does this because of the way they align themselves so positively with Queen and Country and wave the Union Jack. For Alan identifying with Rangers is definitely a political gesture.

Alan admitted to being present at just about every game over the past 5 years where Rangers fans have been in trouble. He was in Vila-real in 2006. He was not part of the attack on the Villarreal team bus but did not disassociate himself from it. He accused the Vila-real Riot Police of being heavy handed. He was in Pamplona for the Osasuna game and told me how he had been viciously assaulted by the Spanish police for "doing absolutely nothing".

In Barcelona, after a day's drinking that began at 4a.m., he was the victim of police brutality, being thrown down a flight of stairs by four Policemen, and ending up in hospital with a badly broken leg, again with no provocation on his part.

He had been in Manchester, "along with 200,000 other Rangers supporters". He described the aggression of Rangers supporters that night as understandable given the massive provocation of what he described as the 'deliberate' switching off of the Big Screens just before kickoff. He reckoned supporters of any other club would have exhibited even worse behaviour under these circumstances, and that the expression of frustration in which he had participated had been natural and unavoidable in the circumstances.

Alan claimed that on all his Rangers' travels, he had never assaulted anyone but several times had been forced to defend himself against attacks from police and rival fans. He acknowledged that he sang "The Billy Boys" at every Rangers game he went to. He saw it as song exalting Rangers' tradition of Protestant support for a Protestant monarch. Unlike almost all of the other Rangers supporters I spoke to, Alan had no problem about being identified by name. He told me he is also in the process of writing a book about his experiences with both Luton and Rangers, a book that will blew the lid of the kind of hostile discrimination Rangers supporters suffer unfairly. Alan was friendly, frank and not without a degree of rough charm and charisma.

Alan was with a group of fellow Englishmen, all Luton supporters. He told me that over the years he has come across a fair number of Chelsea and Millwall supporters who do the same as he does, and also mentioned Leeds and West Ham supporters as often joining them. Over the evening I met several other examples of this phenomenon of Englishmen supporters of other teams, here to follow Rangers. I think they were so visible that evening because coming from London they had flown straight into Valencia the day before the game and congregated in the one small area while most of the Scottish contingent came later via Benidorm.

So on the basis of these meetings, these conversations and interviews, I now accept that such followers rather than supporters do exist, and that it is likely they contribute a disproportionate, but small, share of the violence, mayhem and bigotry.

Tuesday 2nd November Behaviour on the day

By the time of the game the next day, Tuesday, the numbers of Rangers supporters in Valencia had swelled to about around 5,000, some flying in direct that day but mostly those who had been in Benidorm for a few days having a good party, finally making into the city.

Valencia supporters had not been convinced by the erratic performance of their team, and it was the poorest Champions League attendance for many years at the Mestalla, of just over 26,000. So Rangers supporters and their followers ended up being about 20% of the crowd. There was little integration or mixing with the natives before the game, but equally no major reports of bad behaviour in the city centre or the streets around the ground. There were many reports in the local papers the next day of the high level of drinking engaged in by the Rangers supporters, drinking several pubs dry and amazing locals by their capacity for drinking beer.

The Valencia police, perhaps mindful of the poor segregation in Vila-real in 2006, took a firm line and all Rangers supporters, whatever their ticket said, were allowed admittance into only one area of the stadium. Or at least that was the plan, which by and large was implemented successfully. The police funnelled them into ground well before kick off, and kept them there after, singing happily despite defeat.

The next day the main Valencia paper had a main page top headline which highlighted one major behavioural problem during the game. It read "Scottish hooligans urinate on the stands below". The article quoted local police sources as confirming that throughout the game Rangers supporters pursued a deliberate policy of urinating from their elevated height onto the stands below their reserved area. As well as this urination, police also reported that Rangers fans had brought bottles of beer into the ground and that there had been several fights within their own ranks. The police had in the main left them, once segregated, to their own devices but eventually had gone in and ejected 4 of the worst offenders, but only made one arrest. The police confirmed there were no problems at the end of the game and that the later evacuation of the Rangers supporters passed without incident.

There were also some examples of a similarly disrespectful practice with Rangers supporters displaying their manhood in front of largely unperturbed Spaniards. One Spanish paper the next day printed a photo of a Rangers supporter with his kilt proudly raised. The paper left his face untouched but pixelated his private parts.

Taken together these two activities are classic examples of behaviour based on a hostile lack of respect. Most Rangers supporters seemed to find both activities greatly amusing and there was no self policing attempts to get the perpetrators to desist.

Throughout the game there were regular choruses of "Hello, hello, we are the Billy Boys", but the next day no mention made anywhere of sectarian singing. The official UEFA Observer either did not hear it, or chose to give it no significance. Nor did they comment on the systematic urination. Nobody on the

Valencia side took any offence at the singing or made a point of commenting on it.

Later on in the season, in April 2011, the same Rangers supporters that sang without incident in Valencia, were reported for sectarian singing in Eindhoven of all places. That it is Eindhoven helps clarify one point. Rangers fans do not sing "The Billy Boys" just to antagonise the rival supporters, they sing it primarily to emphasise their own identity. So while they sing it in Catholic countries, exultantly, they also sing it equally strenuously when in Protestant territory. Following the Eindhoven games, Rangers were fined £40,000 and their fans banned for one away game with a further ban on one home and one away game suspended pending future behaviour. It was clear that the tolerance of UEFA was reaching breaking point and future offending would be seen as having extremely serious consequences for the Ibrox club.

There is a difference in the singing habits of the two sets of supporters abroad. Celtic supporters impress foreign supporters with the emotion, passion and positiveness of their singing. The singing by Rangers fans is seen as more negative, more hostile, more aggressive, even by people who do not understand the words or their sectarian significance.

The four trips to the Valencia area by the Old Firm invaders, Celtic in 2004 and 2008 and Rangers in 2006 and 2010, serve as a microcosm of the wider truth that there is a pronounced and considerable difference between Celtic and Rangers supporters in their behaviour abroad. As demonstrated in their two trips to Villarreal, Celtic supporters are well behaved. Celtic supporters seek to engage with the locals and be friendly with them. Celtic make friends and leave a positive impression everywhere they go. As demonstrated in their two trips, to Villarreal and Valencia, Rangers supporters display hostility or at best indifference, and engage in aggressive, unfriendly and disrespectful behaviour. The pattern since the late 1960s has been a consistent one, of Celtic supporters acting well and bringing credit upon themselves and their club, and of Rangers supporters acting badly and bringing censure upon themselves and their club. It is acknowledged that not all Celtic supporters have always behaved impeccably on their travels. Over the years there have been some incidents perpetrated by a minority of supporters that have not lived up to the normal high standards. The infamous encounter against Rapid Vienna for one. Equally importantly, it is acknowledged that the vast majority of travelling Rangers supporters have acted throughout their travels as the decent individuals they undoubtedly are. Yet there is no denying the validity of the pattern identified of significantly different behaviours between the two sets of fans, consistently over a long period of time.

It seemed to me that the urination on the Valencia supporters was a brilliant symbolic metaphor for the attitude and behaviour of the Rangers support, not just in Valencia but on all their travels.

From these two different Spanish experiences the difference can be summarised succinctly

Celtic supporters mix with the natives and drink with them.

Rangers supporters ignore them, then piss on them.

Chapter Thirty Four   Developing a Theory to explain these profound differences

The history of Celtic supporters abroad is a succession of good news stories, tales of well behaved mingling with locals.

The Rangers history is a much blacker one with numerous dark highlights, from Newcastle in 1969, Barcelona in 1972, Birmingham in 1976, right up to Manchester in 2008.

Celtic supporters have received considerable praise from both UEFA and FIFA for their excellent conduct including awards from both organisations for good behaviour and for setting positive examples.

Rangers supporters have behaved in away that has led to numerous reprimands and sanctions from UEFA. Since the two fines for their behaviour in their games against Villarreal in 2006, Rangers fans have been formally censured many times. The catalogue of bad behaviour abroad has continued with Pamplona and Barcelona in 2007, Manchester in 2008, Romania in 2009, Valencia in 2010 and most recently Eindhoven in 2011.

There can be little room for argument with the proposition that there is a considerable difference between Celtic and Rangers in their behaviour abroad, and that this difference has been longstanding but still is as strong today as ever.

Rangers fans travel and make trouble, Celtic fans travel and make friends. This has been true since fans could afford to travel. From the early days when England was a far distant land, the Rangers record is littered with riots, at Newcastle in 1969 and Birmingham in 1976, while Celtic were the team all English players wanted as their testimonial opponents because their fans were both numerous and generous.

Since European travel became more accessible the same pattern has been maintained. Celtic in their European Final triumph, captivated the city of Lisbon with peaceful friendliness. A few years later, when Rangers at last tasted European success, there was a riot involving Rangers fans and Barcelona police

This pattern was continued into the 21st century when both clubs reached the UEFA Cup Final in the same decade. For the world the difference was encapsulated in the divergent events of the two recent UEFA Cup finals. In 2003 100,000 Celtic fans invade Sevilla and captivate the whole city, without a single arrest. The pictures of a friendly invasion are beamed around the world. Celtic fans win awards from both UEFA and FIFA for their good behaviour and the positive example they set.

In 2008 100,000 Rangers fans invade Manchester and alienate and horrify the whole world, with many arrests. They won world wide condemnation for their riotous behaviour amid sickening scenes of mobs attacking policemen, with considerable numbers arrested. The pictures of mass violence and mayhem are beamed around the world. Rangers fans are roundly condemned by both football and governmental authorities for the shame and disgrace they brought to Scotland.

But it is important to be very clear that these two contrasting outcomes were just the reflection of two different behaviour patterns that have been active for the past 40 years. Leave aside Seville and Manchester, the pattern has been consistently displayed from the 1960s to the current day.

So how can such a pronounced difference in pattern of behaviour be best explained? I have always known that one danger is that a simple message will be drawn from this book "Celtic supporters good, Rangers supporters bad". Certainly that has been the moral many of the Celtic supporters I have interviewed have attempted to draw, that somehow Celtic supporters are genetically or morally superior to Rangers supporters.

So let us quickly dispose of both of those arguments.

The genetic superiority one is the easiest to dismiss. Although many of the more bigoted supporters on both sides would like to think there are massive genetic differences between the two sets of fans, any analysis of the matter soon completely dispels that myth. The narrow view is of two totally distinct and different tribes, Protestant Scots and Catholic Irish. In fact the gene pools of Scotland and Ireland over the past 2, 000 years have been subject to the same kinds of experiences, the same influxes and outgoings of new sources and the same mixing of existing characteristics, that random DNA testing has shown there to be no perceptible large scale differences. Protestant Scots, Catholic Irish, Protestant Irish, Scots Catholics are all genetically extremely similar, if not indistinguishable. In addition the massive interbreeding that has been such a feature of the 20th Century, in Scotland more so than Ireland, has blurred boundaries even further. Whether the purist bigots like it or not, the genetic differences between themselves and their hated neighbours are so small as to be not remotely sufficient to offer any part of the explanation of their different behaviours.

So if genetics is ruled out the answer has to be found in social and cultural terms. Moral Superiority is often proffered as an explanation, particularly on the Celtic side. On the religious side it would take a brave and extremely foolish man to claim any moral superiority for one religion over the other between Protestantism and Catholicism. The only sensible conclusion is that both these strands of Christianity are based on sound moral foundations and neither has a monopoly on moral goodness far less superiority.

There are distinct political differences, in general terms, between the two sets of supporters, with Celtic fans traditionally lining up on the left and Rangers fans on the right. Rangers have been identified with values around respect for authority, for tradition, for Royalty, for Country, for King and Empire, for Conservatism. Celtic fans have been identified with socialism, collective action, respect for human rights, for solidarity, for Labour.

These value stereotypes were truer in the past than they have become as the 21st Century has replaced the 19th and 20th century certainties with new alignments. In the 1920s and 1930s when sectarian hostility was at its greatest, most Rangers supporters and indeed most of the Protestant working class along with their managers and bosses, voted Unionist/Conservative or even for the more extreme Protestant Front organisations that were extremely popular in both the west and the east of the country. Celtic supporters, and indeed the whole Catholic community, both working and middle class, tended to vote solidly in support of the Labour Party.

That pattern continued right up to the 1950s and is one of the main explanations why in 1955 the Conservative and Unionist Party received more than 50% of the Scottish vote, the last time any party was to do so.

But as the impact of the welfare state took hold and the remnants of the worst extremes of anti-catholic discrimination began to disappear from Scottish society amidst a process of continuous economic and social progress, this crude political stereotype divide began to crumble, particularly on the Rangers side. A survey in 1990 indicated more Rangers supporters voted for the Labour Party than for any other political party. The support for the Conservative Party, who had quietly ditched the emphasis on the Unionist name, dropped to a small minority, less than a third.

The slow growth of a substantial Catholic professional middle class meant not so much a reduction in their support for the Labour Party but a more critical relationship.

It was perceived political wisdom in Scotland until recently that the SNP were more likely to take votes from the Protestant community than the Catholic community because of the latter's fear, always deliberately reinforced by the Catholic Church, of what might happen to them in a Protestant dominated Scotland. This occasional protest voting is of course different from Unionists coming out in support of the notion of Scottish Independence. Yet even the political boundaries on unionism and independence are beginning to blur.

It is too soon for detailed analysis of the voting patterns in the Scottish Election of 2011 by football allegiance, but most analysts seem to agree that the SNP received massive support from both religious communities and from the supporters of both Old Firm football teams. The old myth was that Rangers supporters owed their loyalty to the United Kingdom and Celtic supporters to a united Ireland, neither of them seeing themselves as primarily Scottish. This never completely true misconception is being replaced by a reality where the great majority of both sets of supporters have a primary political and emotional loyalty to Scotland, even to the point of contemplating its independence without paralysing fear.

But despite this slow process of political convergence at an individual level, the traditional concepts of the major value divides have continued to play a major part in patterns of collective behaviour. The explanation for the difference in behaviours abroad can be found not in genetic or moral superiority, but in social and cultural factors and attitudes.

Celtic supporters see themselves as being "of the left" with collective values of respect and tolerance for others. They feel a sense of unity and brotherhood with other peoples in other countries and other nations, a sense of equality rather than superiority. In a classic example of self-reinforcement Celtic supporters are very proud of their reputation abroad as well behaved well respected, welcome visitors and take care to act in ways to enhance rather than threaten this reputation.

Rangers supporters collectively feel a superiority over others, represented by their classic anthem "we are the peepil". They feel themselves part of the ruling establishment and superior to those not part of the Crown and Empire elite. They carry this sense of superiority wherever they go.

All non Rangers supporters have their own memory of first encountering this phenomenon. Two friends of mine have vivid memories of first being exposed to aspects of this superiority. One remembers being taken to Ibrox for the first time as a young boy, and seeing a wee drunk old man cavorting madly on the pitch screaming at the top of his voice "we are the people", a claim not possible by him in any other setting, but one loudly supported by all around him. My friend described it as "the end of innocence".

The other memory reinforces the economic dimension to this superiority. My friend tells of being taken to her first, and last, Rangers Celtic game by a Rangers friend. While she was appalled by the hate in all its manifestations, the most powerful single memory that remained with her was hundreds of Rangers fans waving £20 notes at the Celtic supporters while shouting, "Take a good look because you're never going to own one." It sums up the historical assumption that Celtic supporters are at the bottom of the economic chain, even below the poorer Rangers ones.

The inescapable reality for all those who have that common claim "We are the people"proclaimed to them, is that those to whom this 'truth' is broadcast to are not the people. Rangers supporters believe in their innate superiority. That is the view of themselves they take on their travels. Yet Rangers supporters collectively feel "no-one likes us and we don't care", a view most famously expressed by Donald Findlay before his resignation in disgrace, but shared by Rangers supporters everywhere. Put together, these attitudes do little to prevent behaviour that will confirm their superiority and others' dislike of them.

These different attitudes produce a qualitatively different way of behaving when abroad. One story illustrates this graphically. In a Spanish bar, over 50 Celtic supporters are singing loudly at 2am. A guy from a flat above the Bar comes down and says, in English, "We all have work to go to in the morning, please." so 55 Celtic supporters sing in whispers for the rest of their long night. A creative and positive "We'll work round about you" response. In a similar incident in another city, Rangers supporters were observed to respond in a "Fuck you, Jimmy" manner and upped the volume.

Self Policing

One factor that has emerged as relevant is the different degree of self policing amongst the two sets of supporters. It is much higher within the Celtic support than within the Rangers support. Explanations of this reality range from the higher standards of discipline and respect for authority set within Catholic schools, to the more likely one that Celtic supporters abroad have a very positive reputation they are proud of and wish to retain, and therefore they are motivated to act to squash potential threats to it. Rangers supporters with their "no-one likes us but we don't care" approach, are more resigned to the perpetuation of a bad reputation. Whatever relative weights these explanations have, there is little doubt that the degree of self-policing is much higher within the Celtic support. Many Rangers supporters, very similar in every regard to the Celtic supporters who do intervene to control their more hotheaded and undisciplined members, have told me that they do not do so because of the high risk that they will be turned upon, and get a doing. These are important cultural differences that becomes self reinforcing over time.

I have developed a theory to explain the different behaviours of Rangers and Celtic supporters abroad. Like all major theories and essential truths, it can be expressed succinctly and simply. Put simply the theory is derived from the different cultural histories of the two tribes of supporters, and is as follows

"Rangers supporters travel as a **Colonial Army**, invading foreign territory which they seek to subjugate. Their focus is internal, about imposing their will. It is no coincidence that their emotional anthem is 'We arra people'.

Celtic supporters travel as an **Immigrant wave**, treating the land they enter with due respect, seeking to blend in and make accommodation with the natives. Their anthem is "We are your friends, we come in peace."

Chapter Thirty Five The Celtic Submari dream of Dublin

From the beginning of the 2010-11 Europa League campaign many of the Celtic Submari felt it was preordained that this would be their year, that finally they would get to a European Final and get their hands on that elusive first trophy. One element was the background to their participation, when despite not qualifying, they were finally gifted an entry after energetic lobbying by the Roig father and son duo in Spain and at UEFA. The clincher was discovering the Final was set for the 18th May, the day after the Vila-real holy day, the day of the town patron saint, Pascual. When Villarreal fans had last believed they were going to win a European trophy, in 2006, the Champions League Final was set for St Pascual's Day itself, and only a last minute penalty miss had denied them their promised date with destiny. The fact the Final set for Dublin where their Celtic connection would ensure a warm welcome, local support and the presence of many of their Celtic friends was just an additional bonus.

This sense of destiny was reinforced by a very kind Final Qualifying Round draw when they were given the 3rd lowest rated team of the 74 clubs in the hat. Then the Group Stage draw kept them apart from all the major threats and gave them opponents as innocuous as Dinamo Zagreb, Paok Salonika and Bruges all ranked well below the Yellow Submarine. Only a few dedicated individuals made the trips to Zagreb and Salonika and early on the Celtic Submari decided to concentrate its travel efforts on a December trip to Bruges, where football could be combined with Christmas shopping and the opportunity to catch up with existing friends in the Grocs Flamencs, the Villarreal Belgian supporters club.

Wednesday 15th December2010

Even though qualification for the Knockout Stages was already guaranteed mathematically before the Bruges game, a fair number of the Celtic Submari signed up for the organised trip. Most excited of all the travellers was Ioan Nelu Bordean. Ioan had missed out on all the trips to Glasgow and all previous European excursions, but he planned for months to make up for all that disappointment by a memorable few days in Bruges. Ioan had to spend some of his time explaining to friendly Bruges supporters exactly why he was wearing a Celtic jersey, but once they got it, they liked the story. In the absence of competitive football, those that travelled settled for making even more Belgian friends, drinking Belgian beer, eating Belgian chocolate, doing Christmas shopping and generally enjoying themselves. The Celtic Submari travellers had a ball in Bruges, doing recruiting miracles for the Grocs Flamencs and winning friends everywhere by their enthusiastic implementation of the best principles of the Celtic Submari. And they saw Villarreal outplay Club Bruges with positive attacking football to get an away win and clinch first place in the Group.

When the full list of last 32 qualifiers was known, the Submari faithful saw nobody there that frightened them. Villarreal, with the high quality football they had been playing in La Liga all year, could fancy themselves against any of the other 31. The bookies agreed with this assessment and Villarreal were installed as one of the favourites. The favourite request of Christmas gift from the Three Kings for most Villarreal supporters was a May trip to Dublin.

The first Knockout draw sent the Yellow Submarine to Naples for an away first leg, with the likely reward for victory being a next round first leg trip away to Leverkusen. The club second in Serie A, followed by the club second in the Bundesliga, two opponents seemingly certain in be with Villarreal in the next Champions League, bring them on. Current economic realities in Spain are such that it was not seen feasible for the Celtic Submari to organise a trip for either tie. Particularly with around 100 members saving up for the long planned April trip to Glasgow. So there would be no repeat of the fondly remembered 2006 trip to Milan, not even a reprise of the much smaller sortie to Wolfsburg. A few hardy souls signed up to go with the official party, but instead most Celtic Submari supporters reconciled themselves to enjoying great European evenings at the Madrigal again.

And the Neopolitans did not let them down. The first leg had seen Villarreal play well and intelligently, to get a 0-0 draw that left the second leg tie finally balanced. Around 4,000 Napoli fans hit Villarreal for the return game, the biggest invasion since the visit of Celtic in September 2008. From anecdotal impressions, less than half of these invaders came directly from Italy, most seemed to be Napoli supporters working in Spain. But wherever they came from, they made a hell of a noise. The town was jumping from hours before kick off and the Plaza Llabrador became a sea of blue. The Italians were excited and not particularly keen on integration, but neither were they hostile, and the pre-match atmosphere was electric. The Italians completely filled the Away Support and had enough left over to claim a portion of the bottom end of the Main Stand as their own. The rest of the ground was a solid sea of yellow. Big time European football had returned to the Madrigal. Even the Italians scoring an early goal, requiring Villarreal to score twice to win, did not dampen the ardour and faith of the Celtic Submari members in the crowd. Not a single one recollected any feelings of doubt. Their absolute faith in Garrido's men proved fully justified, Villarreal got their two goals and the Submari faithful partied joyously well into the night, with dreams of Dublin to follow.

Even the delirium created by this result against Napoli did not engender an organised Celtic Submari trip to Germany for the next Knockout Round. Instead the Penya was filled to overflowing the night of the first leg as the Big Screen showed the brilliant performance realised by a tactically astute Villarreal as they achieved a remarkable 3-2 away victory against the second best team in Germany. Watching the body language of the dejected Germans at the end of the game, the whole Penya knew the tie was effectively over, and the Yellow Submarine was heading for the Quarter Finals. But that did not stop them all for signing up for the triumphalist second leg. On the night, the Madrigal was full to the brim of Villarreal supporters, with the only empty seats being in the Away Support stand where around a 1,000 German supporters still managed to make quite a noise. Although less numerous than the Neapolitans, they proved more open to friendly integration pre-match. The atmosphere and excitement in the town and in the stadium matched the heady days of the 2006 Champions League run-in. At the same stage in 2006 Villarreal had entertained Glasgow Rangers. The German supporters were better behaved than the Rangers ones had been, they didn't attack the team bus, they didn't abuse the natives and they didn't sing sectarian songs. But their team were even less successful than Rangers had been, losing meekly on the night to the great delight of 22,000 Villarrreal supporters who were beginning to fantasise about drinking Guinness on the banks of the Liffey.

The Quarter Final and SemiFinal draws were made at the same time. Most Villarreal supporters offered up prayers to St Pascual that they would be in the same half of the draw as Braga, Twente and Spartak Moscow. Their saint gave them 2 out of the 3 but provided the wrong Portuguese team. Even a first leg at home to Dutch champions and league leaders, Twente Enschede, in the Quarter Finals, did not prevent almost all of the Submari members thinking their team would be in the Semi Finals. But most of their hearts sank a little when the rest of the draw meant their likely opponents in the last 4 would be Portuguese league leaders Porto, almost certainly the best other team in the last 8. Still, with the second leg at the Madrigal and opponents who would let them play football, there was still a quiet confidence that this was indeed Villarreal's year and St Pascual's Day would be celebrated in Dublin, preparing for the Final.

Thursday April 4th

This turned out to be one of the most joyous night's in Villarreal's European history. A full house at the Madrigal saw Villarreal take a 5-0 lead over the Dutch champions, Twente, with a blistering display of attacking football. Most of the Submari supporters agreed later that while it was not their finest ever performance, in terms of pure attacking football it was as good as they had ever produced. The night was spoiled from being perfect by a horrendous and unnecessary injury to their captain Gonzalo Rodriguez, who suffered a broken leg after a criminal assault from behind by the big Austrian Janko. Gonzalo had started the season sidelined and available for transfer after his involvement in the events leading to the San Matias Day Massacre. But after responding with quiet dignity, he had been restored to the squad. He had quickly regained both his first team place and his role as captain, and had been a key factor in their fine performances both in La Liga and Europe. Many of the Celtic Submari, who had always rated him as a player and a person, wanted to see the season ending with Gonzalo Rodriquez lifting Villarreal's first trophy, the Europa League cup, high up in the Dublin sky. But then San Matias retook what he had seemingly restored, and now there would be no such happy end. Further injury was added to the wound when Janko scored a last minute goal to offer at least a glimmer of hope to the shattered Dutch.

But in truth even the most catious of the Celtic Submari knew, like all the Dutch players and management did, that Villarreal were in the Semi-finals, their third in the last 8 years. That night, after such an overwhelming first leg win, the thoughts of most of the Celtic Submari members began to turn towards Dublin. While no-one underestimated the semi-final task of overcoming strong in-form

Porto, a sense grew that maybe at last this was their time, for that elusive first trophy, and preliminary plans started to be made to ensure that the Celtic Submari would be well represented in Dublin. It was recognised that their Celtic connection would make them the favoured team of the locals, and also that many of their Celtic friends would also make the trip over to be with them.

Chapter Thirty Six   The Celtic Submari revisit Scotland
Thursday 21st April 2011.

After a break since December 2008, the Celtic Submari are preparing again to invade Scotland. Planning for this expedition has been taking place all season, and in recent weeks the excitement has grown to fever pitch as it dawns on everyone that not only is it actually going to happen, but it is going to happen soon.

A major change was that the detailed organisation of the Glasgow end would be undertaken by Tosh, Linda and Pat in Scotland rather than being done from Spain by Gerry Martin. Gerry was secretly relieved and looked forward to enjoying the trip as an ordinary member rather than the hard pressed organiser. This sense of pleasurable anticipation was considerably heightened when he reached agreement with his ex-wife to bring his son Matteo with him, for his first ever trip to Martin land.

After initial planning for anywhere between 80 and 100 travellers, the final numbers settled at 88. Many previous travellers were unable to attend, so the bulk of the party were first time visitors, looking to sample for themselves everything they had heard so much about from earlier visits.

The party were due to arrive late Thursday night, and leave around Monday lunchtime. A full programme was drawn up that left little time for individual exploration other than Monday morning. Because there were so many first time visitors, several of the highlights from previous trips were put in again, at the request of the new boys, like a visit to the Scottish Parliament, to Loch Lomond, to Stirling Castle, to a Distillery, to Celtic Park for the tour. A major social event was organised for each of the three evenings. Friday night, Tosh and Linda were organising an event in Hamilton. Saturday, Pat McGorry was organising an event in the Hibernian Club in Carfin, and Sunday night was set for the traditional big Dinner Dance in Celtic Park.

It is never certain until the very last minute exactly how many will make any of the Celtic Submari expeditions. This time 88 travellers are counted onto the plane, around the number expected, with the usual last minute additions and deletions. Tosh arranged the reception committee and the tired party were driven in luxury coaches straight to the Holiday Inn in central Glasgow, arriving well after midnight. With a crowded itinerary in front of them, most opted out of any late night revelry. Even the number one legend himself, Pepe Mansilla, was in bed before daybreak.

Friday 22nd April

It sometimes takes a foreign eye to help you appreciate fully the glories that are around you but too often taken for granted. On all previous visits by full groups, i.e. 2005, 2007 and 2008, trips had been organised to the Scottish Parliament. Everyone in the first visit in 2005 had been very impressed not just with the architecture but the ambience, the presence and the sense of a nation at political business. These positive impressions had been fed back and a repeat visit was demanded as necessary in future trips, some stalwarts insisting on going on all occasions. Again the feedback had been positive and impressed, so there was no dispute but that another visit would be required this time. There has been no expectation at the Vila-real end that Scottish visitors should be taken to see either the Valencian or Castellon equivalents. Not that the Submari members are ashamed of them, but just a recognition that they are nothing special either physically or in what they represent. But they do feel the Scottish Parliament is impressive at both these levels. So it was off to Edinburgh on the Friday morning. Perhaps this time, with Parliament not in session due to the impending elections, it was easier to be impressed since there were no politicians to lower the tone, only buildings to appreciate and atmosphere to absorb.

Lunchtime provided a football link. It proved difficult to find a pub cum restaurant prepared to take so many, including children, but finally a pub was found willing to accommodate the whole party. They were even allowed to bring in fish suppers with them, for those keen to try this strange way of eating fish. There was some initial confusion caused by the fact that almost everyone in the party was wearing a yellow Villarreal CF cravat type necktie, but the bar was assured they were not Boy Scouts. Once the football connection was revealed, and discussions on the beautiful game entered into, it emerged that this pub was the favourite watering hole of George Best in his time with Hibs and there were plans to dedicate a corner of the pub to his memory. Tosh was unable to determine if the focus of the shrine would be his football or his drinking, which by his Hibs days had become even more legendary.

Returning to the Holiday Inn most of those under 18 or over 58 were very tired, and I was touched to see tough Pepe Mansilla forsake an offered drink to gently carry his exhausted daughter up to her bedroom.

Within a very short time of their return, Tosh and Linda were shepherding them all onto two more luxury coaches for the trip out to Hamilton, where an evening of food, drink, dancing and friendly interchange had been organised. Those invited were friends, colleagues, family, football supporters and ex pupils and parents who had been involved in the regular school exchanges between John Ogiilvy High School and Francesc Tarrega in Vila-real. In all, several hundred turned up. Within a couple of songs the dance floor was full.

The gifts brought by the Submari were in great demand. As a recognition of all his immense efforts as the principal organiser, Tosh was presented with Santi Cazorla's boots, brand new and 42/8, just his size. However the boots must be made to measure as Cazorla must have the narrowest feet in the world, so Tosh was unable to wear them. They have been on permanent display at the front of Tosh's classroom, where they are greatly admired. Several other players contributed items, all of which became treasures for those lucky enough to end up with them after the raffles. Typical of a happy winner was one of the dinner ladies from John Ogilvie School, Isabel McGuinness, a Celtic fanatic, who won the first prize in the raffle. She was over the moon, absolutely delighted with the signed Villarreal top that was her prize. It made her night. Her beaming face summed up better than words what these Celtic Submari visits are all about. In the best Celtic Submari tradition, one of the main themes of the evening was raising money for charity, with Yorkhill Children's Hospital again the chosen charity, for whom a four figure sum was raised over the weekend.

Saturday 23rd April

Another busy day with the highlight being the trip to Celtic Park for the tour of the stadium. As always Celtic Football Club cooperated fully and did their Spanish soulmates proud. Ian Jamieson, the club Press man, arranged that as many of the party as wanted, could come to the Stadium on the Sunday at lunchtime when special arrangements had been made to beam back the Old Firm game from Ibrox. The 83 of the party without tickets for the game jumped at this generous offer, happy to be able to say they had been to the stadium twice in successive days. Another highlight was a trip to Loch Lomond and a short excursion on a boat, followed by souvenir shopping. They were delighted that their previous guide, Damien Kane, joined them again, this time wearing a jumper and jacket. Both buses were on the way back from Loch Lomond when it was suddenly realised that Pepe Mansilla had been left behind, in the Gents Toilet. If you had to nominate one Submari member whom it would be hard to leave behind without noticing, it would be Pepe. "I got talking to someone" said the man with no English, "and just got caught up in communicating" he explained when finally recovered. Another cultural highlight was the tour of a distillery. They enjoyed seeing the process, and testing the samples. Slowly they are acquiring a taste for whisky.

In the early evening the bus left for Carfin, where Pat McGorry had arranged a buffet dance in the Hibernian Club. The evening in the Hibernian club was another brilliant example of why the Celtic Submari phenomenon is something unique and very special. Pat McGorry, as usual, put in a power of work organising it, but it was a labour of love, and a task which was made easy by the full support of everyone who heard of it, thanks to all the positive memories still vivid from the last visit there in 2007. As Pat explained "When starting to organise the Fiesta on Easter Saturday, I contacted the Hibs Club to see if we could use the hall. The first thing they said when I told them who the event was for, was 'We will cancel our current event so that we can host the Celtic Submari', and then a long reminiscence took place on the previous event and how they were delighted to see them back again. The hosting deal they offered was that we got the hall and band for nothing, and they offered to sell tickets for us through the Torridon Celtic Supporters Club, who use the Hibs Club as their base. I found that the tickets sold themselves, as soon as we mentioned that Celtic Submari were coming over, everyone wanted tickets, from local Carfinians (as they took the guys from Villa real into their hearts from the last visit) to Celtic supporters. On the night you are always worried that things won't go well, but I don't know why I worried. From when the Piper played his first note to the moment when at the end, the Submari members all sang, 'You will never walk alone', everything was perfect, all I could see on people's faces was enjoyment and true friendship. To quote Neil Lennon, 'We don't walk alone in this world' not when we have a family the size of Celtic." In these words Pat succinctly captured the essence of another magical night, as Spaniards and Scots intermingled manically in perfect harmony.

Hope and Willie were there, along with Francis and Martin and the other family members of the 67 gang. Hope was rather subdued, worrying about her very ill sister. I had heard from Pat that Hope had had a heart attack a few months earlier, but she seemed to have recovered at least some of her old vigour. She is still an iconic figure for the Celtic Submari.

Among the many highlights of the evening prior to its emotional finale was Pepe Mansilla leading the entire dance floor in another rendition of his world famous Espumita dance. There was indeed something very moving about the last act of the evening as all the Submari members, all 88 of them, showed their solidarity with their hosts, by singing "You'll Never Walk Alone" in faultless English. It put real emotional tears in the mass outbreak of tearful farewells as the buses drove off back to Glasgow.

Sunday 24th April

With the help of Gerry Martin's friendly contact at Celtic, Stephen Frail, six tickets had been obtained for the lunchtime Old Firm game. It was agreed Tosh would accompany 5 of the Celtic Submari including Ernesto and Pepe Mansilla. None of the Spaniards had been to a Rangers Celtic game before, and all were a little apprehensive beforehand, after all they had heard, and after all the recent bad publicity in the build up to the game. They found the actual game a shocking experience, literally. Not because of the football, which turned out to be a mediocre game played in good spirit between two teams on their best behaviour but lacking the flair, ability and class of the Spanish version on offer every other week at the Madrigal. No, what they found shocking was the intensity of feeling on offer, the tension and the sense of suppressed hate. Pepe, an advocate of the philosophy that friendship is the answer to every problem, was particularly affected by its marked absence. They struggled with the information given to them that this was "good behaviour", that normally things were much worse, much more rancid and hateful. And that they were seated in the civilised VIP section of the Main Stand, immune from the worst excesses of baying crowd.

After the final whistle they were taken inside the Main Stand for some hospitality. There Izaguirre, the one Celtic player who, as a South American, talks Spanish as his native language, made a point of coming over and chatting with them. He was very attentive and could not do enough for them. While he was chatting one of the Spanish ladies noticed that his zip was down. He was discreetly informed and after initial embarrassment just got on with it. As it turned out the zip was not accidentally down, but actually broken. On a suit costing a fortune. Observing this, Tosh decided he would stick to Matalan, less smart but socially safer. So Izaguirre is not only a class player, but a class person, and shot up the Celtic Submari hierarchy of favourite players, replacing the recently departed Marc Crosas as number one. While pleased with the contact with Izaguirre, the gang of 5 enjoyed even more the hospitality they were shown in the Saltmarket Celtic Supporters Club, where they were treated as visiting royalty and made extremely welcome.

192

The rest of the Celtic Submari party watched the match in comfort and style at Celtic Park. They enjoyed the hospitality and the surroundings as much as the game, but they were pleased enough with the result which they assumed meant Celtic would go on to win the league. One person less than totally delighted with the final outcome was Saul Ramos, who had put on a bet before the game on Georgi Samaras as the first goalscorer. When the penalty was awarded, Saul began converting his winnings into Euros in his head, only to see his hard earned cash squandered by Greek casualness.

The Old Firm game was not the last football of the day. The main party arrived at Celtic Park for the Dinner Dance and were shown into the private top floor restaurant just as Villarreal were kicking off their La Liga match against Sevilla. This time Celtic had kindly, or cruelly, organised for a whole swathe of TV sets showing the game to be set up all round the dining area, so that every diner had at least one set to keep an eye on. The starter courses were ruined for many by Sevilla taking an early two goal lead. Most of the Submari party assumed that was that, and with the Europa League first leg semi-final against Porto only 4 days away, the team would take a rest for the remainder of an already lost game, and they could concentrate on the food and the company. However Garrido the Villarreal manager has a stubborn competitive streak and by the time pudding was served Villarreal were back in the match courtesy of much determination and a goal from Carlos Marchena. Even a lucky Sevilla goal a few minutes later did not slow the Villarreal momentum and the restaurant erupted in excited joy when Rossi scored to make it 3-2 with 15 minutes to go. However, although the in form Italian then went on to hit the inside of the post only to see the ball roll back into play, Sevilla managed to hang on desperately with the help of cheating ballboys throwing extra balls on the pitch to waste time and disrupt Villarreal momentum.

The Celtic Submari people were not too depressed. Frankly unlike their President, Roig, they would rather win the Europa League than attain Champions League qualification, but still remain quietly confident both are available.

However it did not take long for spirits to revive, and soon a good evening was in full flow. Every seat in the restaurant was sold out, with a good mix of Spaniards, friendly Celtic supporters and Submari sympathisers. Gerry Martin, with son Matteo, took one whole table for the Martin family, with his brother Terry, his Auntie Betty and various nephews and cousins making up the numbers. Matteo, who has grown markedly since I met him at the Emirates in April 2009, has turned into a fine looking, polite, intelligent young man who would have no difficulty in getting served in any Glasgow pub despite being only 14. That was probably one element in the mix of health and social reasons that saw father Gerry on the wagon for the duration of the trip. Matteo had been taken on the family origins tour of Shettleston which had been a quietly sobering experience for him. But being his father's son, when I asked him what his main impression of Glasgow was, he talked of the people rather than the places, and how delighted he was to have at last met the other side of his family tree. "I feel as if I have a whole new family overnight. I am really glad I have now met them."

Amongst the Celtic supporters who comprised about 60% of the gathering, were old faithfuls like Derek Rush and Damien Kane who had been actively involved in earlier trips, as well as many who were meeting the Submari members for the first time. Unfortunately Hope and the 67 gang were unable to be present as her sister was given the last rites earlier in the day.

The music was provided by the same band, the wonderfully named BJSUS, who had helped make Friday night such a rollicking success. They are fine musicians and set the pace and tone for the evening in a way that encouraged many onto the dance floor.

For Tosh and Linda, Sunday night had been meant to be a wee bit more sophisticated. It did not really turn out that way, but those present made it as emotional and fun-filled as the Friday and Saturday events had been, and everyone seemed to be enjoying themselves. Once again language differences were not allowed to stand in the way of full integration and enthusiastic communication.

Ernesto made another fine speech stressing how delighted the Submari were to be here, in their spiritual home, and how much the appreciated the hospitality and welcome being shown to them. Between Tosh and Gerry Martin, the various contributions were translated effectively into both languages.

The Restaurant with its stunning views into the stadium at night with the pitch and all stands visible was a great venue which enhanced the enjoyment of the evening. I don't think there was a single person present who did not at least once wander over to a window to study the impressive aspect of the lit stadium on view.

The night finished with more emotional group signing, which, though not quite as impressive as the Carfin 'You'll Never Walk Alone', still meant the event ended in high sentiment. And the buses started first time.

Back at the hotel there was a small group seeking continuing conviviality only to be told that the Bar was closed for the night. Matteo watched impressed as Pepe Mansilla, without a word of English, managed in his inimitable way to communicate well enough with the barman to have this decision reversed and the Bar declared open.

Monday 25th

In recognition of the hectic pace of the previous 3 days, nothing formal was organised, and most of the party had a quiet morning before the two buses arrived for a final time to take them all to the airport for the early afternoon flight back to Reus. The general consensus was that the trip had been hugely successful, a wonderful experience for all.

Chapter Thirty Seven Some reflections on the 2011 Celtic Submari trip to Glasgow

Overall the trip demonstrated that the 5 basic principles of the Villarreal Celtic Submari are still being applied in action. The first, and perhaps most basic, is that the aim of the Celtic Submari is to cherish and reinforce existing friendships while continually seeking to create new ones. This 2011 expedition succeeded fully in both aims. Many existing relationships, some of them by now of 6 or 7 years duration, were renewed and strengthened during this trip. And new ones were created, many of which are likely to last and endure. Many of them are also likely to result in further travel, as both previous visitors and new friends made strong promises to head for Vila-real either in September 2011, or May 2012 at the latest.

The trip also succeeded in its aim of helping travellers from Vila-real learn and appreciate more about the cultural and other attractions of Scotland; from its parliaments and castles; its distilleries and pubs; its lochs and its shops; its football grounds; its grottos and ghettos; and best of all its people. The first-time travellers returned home impressed even beyond their expectations with the attractions and delights of this once remote and shadowy country. 'Regressaramos', we shall return, was the unanimous cry.

The trip also fulfilled its aim of further integrating the Celtic Submari into the Celtic family. The friendship making described above was not restricted to Celtic supporters, but was an inclusive exercise open to anyone willing to respond. But identifying with Celtic, the club and its supporters, was a key aim of the trip, one engaged in very successfully. The sense of being active members of a big, happy and generous family was reinforced throughout the trip, including the three visits to Parkhead, but also the warm engagement with Celtic people everywhere they went. The reaction of the Submari members to being exposed to Old Firm atmosphere and tension will receive later exploration. But whatever reservations there were about that dimension, the trip reinforced for all its participants that the Villarreal Celtic Submari are a part of the Celtic family and proud to be so, even if they do have a better football team of their own. However this sense of belonging did not interfere with a crucial part of the Celtic Submari ethos, that football is about friendship not bitterness and hatred, and that positive feeling extends to Rangers supporters, Partick Thistle and Clyde supporters, and every other football supporter they met. They want no part of toxic rivalry.

The trip also carried out an inseparable part of the Submari ethos, that of the commitment to use all their social activity to help others. All three major events attended, on the Friday, Saturday and Sunday nights, were used to implement this belief, and over the three nights a great deal of money was raised. The monies generated on the Friday and Sunday nights were earmarked for Yorkhill, and the monies raised at Carfin for a local children's charity.

One significant social change I noted over the previous visits was in the social composition of the Scottish contingents. In the first visit, 2005, this had been dominated by young and middle aged males, reflecting both the composition of the Celtic support, and the expectation of the nature of their visitors. By 2011 these expectations had been redrawn after the realities of years on interchange and this was reflected in a consequent change in the composition of the Scots in attendance. Both the sex ratio and the age ratio changed, reflecting much more accurately the profile of the visitors. Children, young women, women and elderly people between them formed a majority leaving the traditional Scottish male football supporter in a minority, reflecting both the typical Villarreal CF crowd and the composition of the travelling party of 88 Submariners.

One consequence of this changed composition was reflected in a reduction in the number of drunken Scots on show over the 3 nights. And as always, while all the Spaniards did drink none of them ever seemed the worse for wear. So maybe somehow without even consciously trying, the Spanish visitors have exercised a civilising influence. Or maybe the more simple explanation was that Gerry Martin was on the wagon, depriving Pepe Mansilla of his constant drinking companion!

On the organisational front the trip was a great success. The secret suspicions of some of Tosh's more strident students, that really he is a fascist bastard, were possibly vindicated, in that at least all the buses ran on time, and everything else. He, Linda and Pat put in an enormous amount of work to make the trip a complete organisational success. but all were very clear afterwards that "it was worth every single minute." Ernesto and the Celtic Submari will accept with alacrity, their offer to continue to organise future trips.

ChapterThirty Eight   Villarreal Dream of Dublin   Part Two

After the first Twente game, Villarreal knew that it would be a rampant Porto that would stand between them and their first ever European Final. The foregone conclusion was used as a justification for not bothering to go to Enschede for the second leg, but most also opted out of a trip to Porto while swearing oaths of allegiance to travel to Dublin. The most honourable exception was Ernesto Boixader.

Ernesto has always been aware that there has been one area where Villarreal Celtic Submari members have failed properly to emulate Celtic supporters, as the Penya was set up to do. That has been around the commitment to travel regularly to away European games. We have seen that the Celtic Submari has had a good record in going to Champions League away games, but over the past two seasons very few Celtic Submari members have travelled to routine away games in the Europa League. For the Group Stages, the only organised Submari trip was for the Bruges game. Even for the knockout stages, not many made the trips to Naples, Leverkusen and Enschede, and Ernesto was not amongst them. As a teacher Ernesto has always found it difficult to commit to travelling to midweek away games, and was fortunate both famous Arsenal trips fell on school holiday weeks. So when the Porto game was set for his Easter holiday break, he determined that he would go. He also promised himself he would go to Dublin since as the Final fell around Vila-real Fiesta Saint's day, he would also be on holiday. But he could not persuade many others to come to Porto with him. For some, it fell too close to the trip to Glasgow. For most others, times are hard financially, people are working harder to try to stay in the same place, and while everyone committed themselves to go to Dublin, there was not enough volunteers for Porto to justify even a small bus. So of by car he went.

28th April Europa League semi-final first leg. Away to Porto

Ernesto Boixader was present for the game but he was not the only famous ex-player of Villarreal to be amongst the 300 Villarreal supporters that have made the trip to Porto. Also present is Toni Alapont the goalkeeper in the 1970 team that won that first ever promotion to the Second Division in the play-off game at the Bernabeu watched by Llaneza and his father. In some ways it is a disappointing turnout for a major European semi-final. Several thousand supporters of the Yellow Submarine had made the trip to Highbury in 2006 for the Champions League semi-final. Yet in 2004 very many fewer made the 40 mile trip down the road to Valencia for the UEFA Cup semi-final. However, if they are to believed, a fair percentage of the town, at least 10,000, are preparing themselves to commit to a trip to Dublin in what would be the greatest ever migration of Villarreal supporters. It might not compare absolutely with the Celtic invasion of Sevilla, but proportionate to population, it would not be dissimilar.

Ernesto and his fellow Celtic Submari member Tafol linked up in Porto with Jose Luis Lizarraga and Javi Mata and a couple of the other local journalists. They spent many happy hours before the game in their company, talking football and dreaming pleasant dreams of Villarreal success. Ernesto spent the game in the Press box alongside Jose Luis, and Tafol did the same with Javi Mata. Ernesto described it as a great place to watch the game, but felt the lack of his usual freedom to shout and cheer, particularly when Villarreal scored. Not that he or the two journalists sat silent at that point. After the game, the two journalists got them admission into the Main Hospitality Lounge and Ernesto was able to see first hand how sad and demoralised the players and officials were. In his usual way, he offered them help and support while assuring them of how much happiness they had already given him this season, and that there still would be good things to come yet.

Over the past three years I have talked to Ernesto about many Villarreal games. As an intelligent ex-player, he is a particularly astute analyst of the performances of his beloved club, and has always been able to provide insightful interpretation of what he has seen, unclouded by personal preference. I have come to respect his opinions and analysis greatly. Yet when I talked to him about what he saw that night in Porto something strange happened. He was good on the first half. He commented well on how Porto stood off the Villarreal players and pushed their back four staggeringly high leaving great swathes of open space behind them. He praised the way the Villarreal midfield, particularly Borja Valero and Cazorla, had spotted this and exploited it with incisive forward passes, liberating both Nilmar and Rossi for several great chances, which on other nights they would have converted into goals, as they both had been doing all season. He rejoiced in the move involving Borja Valero and Nilmar which culminated in Cani getting a vital away goal just before half time. He had leaped about with pure delight, then spent the 15 half-time minutes being truly happy. He really did think at that point that Villarreal and the Celtic Submari would be in Dublin, as would every member of the Boixader clan. But when it came to talking about the events of the second half, the rational words of analysis just did not come. He had no explanation for the disastrous last 30 minutes that saw Villarreal go from an advantageous 1-1 draw to a dire 5-1 defeat. All that he was able to do was just shrug his shoulders and turn his palms upwards, submissively. "What can you say?" was all he could say. For the first time ever in my acquaintance, Ernesto was speechless on a football topic. Even weeks later, he was unable to talk about it coherently. He did recognise that in the space of 60 minutes he had enjoyed 15 minutes of amongst the happiest times in his lfe, tasting Dublin, and 30 minutes of the most unhappy minutes of his life, as his team saw their advantage disintegrate into dust, and his dreams of a European final, so strong and vivid only an hour before, disappeared.

None of the rest of the Celtic Submari regulars I talked to later, were any more articulate or insightful than Ernesto. One impressive thing is that none of them sought to allocate blame, to make the disaster anyone's fault. Okay, boy wonder Andres Villas-Boas created a major improvement in his team for the second half, but the clear consensus was that Garrido had done nothing wrong. He had sent his team out for more of the same and within minutes Villarreal could have been 2-0 and on the way to Dublin. Okay, the team missed Gonzalo Rodriguez at the back and in Mario, Musacchio and Catala had three defenders whose first team experience was of less than a season's duration, all three having been playing regularly in the Second Division the previous season. But none of them, whose collective naivety and inexperience helped Porto score 4 times, were blamed. I found the dignity which they accepted the crumbling of their dream without the need to find a scapegoat to blame very impressive. And a model for others in Scotland, including many Celtic supporters, too eager to find excuses and scapegoats for every set back rather than accept that sometimes these things happen, you cannot win them all and defeat needs to be accepted graciously.

The 7 days between the two Porto games also taught me a great deal about the personalities of many of the Celtic Submari as they prepared themselves mentally for the second leg, where their team faced the task of winning 4-0 to keep the dream alive

Celtic Submari members, and indeed Villarreal supporters as a whole, passed the first test, buying up every available ticket for the second leg despite the magnitude of the task facing their team. In many other places such a disastrous away leg score would have resulted in a drastically reduced home leg attendance, if not a formal or informal boycott.

Garrido, his players and the management all made appropriate noises in the lead-up to the second leg, that the tie was still alive. They did not promise a miracle, or make false claims of certainty, but they did manage to communicate a degree of hope that the required result was a possibility, one they were committed to pursuing with all vigour. And a remarkable number of the Celtic Submari responded by believing that, yes indeed, it was possible. None but the very young went as far as believing it was likely, but a significant number believed that it was at least a possible outcome, and one their team would seriously attempt to achieve. Most football supporters in similar situations protect themselves from pain by taking refuge in cynicism and denial. But Villarreal supporters trod a more optimistic route. After all, when the past 14 years have been a permanent living miracle, encompassing many acts of a miraculous nature, then one more miracle would not be the stupendous thing it would be elsewhere, but just another part of the Villarreal mosaic of miracles.

I was a boy in Ayrshire watching Kilmarnock every other week, when they pulled back a 4 goal deficit on Eintracht Frankfurt. I was a youth present in Liverpool in 1966 at a World Cup game, where North Korea took a three goal lead over Portugal only for Eusebio to inspire a 5-3 victory. I was at Hampden in 1971 to see Partick Thistle beat Celtic 4-1 in a League Cup Final. So I do know miracles can happen in individual football games. But I have never before seen a whole town believe such an outcome to be possible. Not certain or likely, but possible. And to turn out 22,000 strong to wave 22,000 yellow flags. The atmosphere at this third European semi final in 8 years was far superior to the first one, against local rivals Valencia. It did not quite match the second one against Arsenal in 2006, but that had been born of more realistic expectation of triumph. This time, the whole crowd got behind their team and willed them on, creating an incredible atmosphere. Garrido delivered, setting out a team with

199

three forwards. At 1-0 up early on, it was 'one more this half, then the same again in the second half and we are there'. Then a cruel deflection let Porto back in and derailed the dream. But the team rallied from their disappointment and managed to beat Porto, stopping them from winning every away game. The crowd at the end were still waving their 22,000 yellow flags. They knew their team had not let them down, had done them proud. More fundamentally, they knew it was not a miracle failed, but a miracle delivered, that their team from a town of 50,000 had hosted their third European semi-final in 8 years, and were on course to finish 4th in the best league in the world.

Many of the Celtic Submari told me later of their pride at the end of that night, how they had stayed well after the final whistle, some as long as an hour afterwards, celebrating the miracle of Villarreal and the joy of their positive bond with their club. Saul Ramos put it best in perfect English "It was wonderful. We lost but we won. We failed to achieve a miracle but we did something miraculous. I was so proud to be a Villarreal supporter."

And so the dream of Dublin died.

Wednesday 18th May

The day after St Pascual's Day saw the Penya packed rather than deserted, as Celtic Submari members gathered collectively to think on what might have been, as they watched on the big screen as Porto inherited their destiny. They all knew that if it had been Villarreal playing Braga in that final, as it so nearly had been, then Villarreal would have definitely outplayed Braga and won the Europa League. In the real world Porto won much more comfortably than the 1-0 score line suggested.

In 2006 a fair number of Villarreal supporters including Ernesto, Saul and Pepe Mansilla had travelled to Paris for the Champions League Final anyway, having confidently made all the travel and accommodation arrangements before the second leg game against Arsenal. This time only a few Villarreal supporters had been so confident or so rash as to prebook, and most of even those hardy souls chose not to go, preferring to be part of the Villarreal Fiesta St Pascual Day celebrations in the town.Two Boixaders, Javi and Julio, did make it all the way to Dublin, as did maybe another three or four of the Submari. But the rest settled for imagining how it might have been and planning for the next European semi final to come, conscious that their President has promised them that Villarreal will be in a European Final one day. Munich 2012 here we come.

Chapter Thirty Nine   A final sail to the Celtic Submari Penya
20th May 2011

I went to the Celtic Submari Penya for the last Friday night session of season 2010-11. I wanted to check out a few last impressions about aspects of the season just about to finish, particularly the two Europa League Semi-Final games against Porto.

As a bonus, or as it turned out a penance, it was also a chance to watch Villarreal B attempt to secure their permanence in the Segunda Division, in their third last game of the season, away to an in-form Granada side, pressing to confirm a place in the Promotion Play-offs. The game was to be shown live on the big screen in the Penya. Most of the hard core of Penya members have watched the B team throughout their two seasons in the Second Division. And have been very proud of their achievements. They watched entranced as Garrido took a talented group of young players to 4th place at the halfway stage last season. They stayed proud as the team hung together after Garrido's promotion to the top team Manager's post, to finish in a highly creditable 7th place. They were proud rather than surprised when over the summer of 2010 Garrido promoted no less than 10 of that B squad into the first team ranks. They knew life would be harder this season for the denuded squad, despite the acquisition of new talent like Iago Falque, Nicki Bille and a couple of young Argentineans. They were amazed but delighted when new manager Javi Gracia, whom they remembered as a thoughtful player for the Villarreal side in the early 2000s, took them up to 5th place at the end of January, above a Barcelona B team filled with great talent, who had just denied them the title of the only La Liga side with a team in the Second Division too. They knew it would not last but they were all surprised by the speed of decline when the team went on a losing run of 8 consecutive games, slid down the table and suddenly found themselves struggling to avoid a slide right out the division. Javi Gracia was sacked a week ago and new manager Molina from the entertaining Villarreal C team some of them watched regularly too, took over, charged with keeping them in the Division. He stopped the slide with an away draw, and with 3 games to go the team are 6 points above the relegation positions. So a win tonight would almost certainly see them safe. However it was not to be, Granada were in much better form and ran out comfortable 3-0 winners, depressing the atmosphere in the Penya somewhat despite the recent celebration of guaranteed qualification for the Champions League. I watched the game on the big screen in the Celtic Submari Penya, along with many anxious Villarreal supporters who could hardly comprehend the speed and scope of the decline which now threatened their beloved B team with relegation.

Despite keeping one eye on this depressing backcloth, Ernesto was in fine form. He filled me in with more details of his recent trip to Porto. Everyone I talked to had a vivid memory of the second Porto game and a night that has entered Villarreal legend, but only Ernesto and Tofal had actually made it to Porto for the first leg. Ernesto seemed better mentally and physically, less tired and in better health than when I had worried about him last year. Maria Dolores and wee Maria were both there, talking excitedly about some memories of the recent trip to Glasgow.

Saul Ramos, still the Secretary of the Celtic Submari Penya, was also in good form, talking both about Glasgow and about the two Porto games. Vicente Andreu has been extremely busy the last few months, and had been unable to afford the time to come to Glasgow. As usual he was full of informed analysis of recent developments with Villarreal Club de Futbol. I was interested to hear from Sisi that she was just back from Paris, where she had been adding to some of the experiences described in her book. Fermin Font turned up towards the end of the evening, with his wife Claudia. Fermin assured me that his father, Supporter Number One, who will shortly be celebrating his 90th Birthday, is in remarkably good form and health. He is no longer allowed by his wife to attend El Madrigal but follows all the games closely on television and has been delighted with the form and progress of his team this season. He will still be renewing his Number One season ticket next season, aged 90.

Vicente told me that the other reliable work horse of the Penya, Jose Luis Broch, who had missed the Glasgow trip for health reasons, was recovered but unable to be present tonight for domestic reasons. His daughter is having her first communion next week, and many of the Penya regulars will be at that celebration.

Ernesto's brother Jose Manuel was in good jovial form, pleased with life and the progress of his team. His other two brothers had not yet recovered from their Dublin trip, so were not present tonight. I was able to catch up with Angel and Encarnita, who had missed out on the Glasgow trip because of a local problem or two, but they seemed to have matters back under control, and Angel seemed in good form.

I had met up with Ioan the Romanian for a drink in Luisos before the Penya, to catch up with him. Like many more recent migrant workers, he is finding life hard in the current climate, and was honest that he would have struggled to be able to go to Dublin even if Villarreal had got there.

Ximo was his usual solid reliable self. He compared notes with Cati about the hard times in the Ceramics Industry. Both of them work for Zirconio, which is having a hard time, laying off staff and cutting back in production but at least both are still in employment. Only Pamesa of all the Vila-real Ceramics firms, seems be riding the recession well. Further proof of Fernando Roig's impressive ability to take positive measures to protect and enhance his interests, be they industrial or football, while others flounder.

Pepe Mansilla was in fine form, and delighted with the pictures I showed him of some of his recent Glasgow antics. He has always scoffed at my determination to speak Spanish, insisting as he does, that language is not necessary for good communication. However he has become more impressed recently that after my slow start, I am actually able now to communicate with him and the others in something almost resembling Spanish. It amuses him even more that having made a tortuous effort to speak to him in Spanish and him getting it, I am so obviously unable to make any sense out of his reply to me. But as he says, it doesn't matter. We have learned to communicate well with each other, despite the languages rather than because of them.

I received further confirmation of my thesis that in some ways Domingo is the most Scottish of the Penya members. He was not here tonight but I learned that the reason for that is that he had so much to drink during the recent Fiesta events, that he sworn off all drink for the next 4 weeks in a desperate attempt to give his liver a chance to recover. In contrast, Gerry Martin has used tonight's visit to jump off the wagon and re-embrace the part of Spanish culture nurtured by San Miguel. I was assured by Pablo, brother of Estrella, that she had had a busy Easter period, but was well and happy. Pascual and Monica were not present and have not been seen in the Penya for some time now. Pascual keeps in touch with his pals like Pepe, but Monica seems to have abandoned social life altogether to concentrate on getting her two sons safely through the Spanish schools exam system. After the Penya closed, Maxine, Gerry Martin and I went with Fermin and Claudia, and Cati and Rafa, for further discussion of the main themes of the evening over some Italian food and good Spanish wine.

Friday nights in the Villarreal Celtic Submari Penya mixing with all these wonderful people will always remain amongst the happiest of my memories of the past three years.

Chapter Forty Some reflections on the Celtic Submari Penya 7 years on 25th May 2011

Today is the 7th anniversary of the founding of the Villarreal Celtic Submari Penya, when its formal constitution was signed by Ernesto Boixader, Jose Luis Broch, Saul Ramos, Enrique Navarro and Vicente Llop. Looking back on these 7 years, it is clear the Celtic Submari has been an amazing success. It has quickly established itself as by far the biggest of all the Villarreal CF Penyas. Given the system of membership where whole families counts as only one member, the nominal membership figure of 671 greatly underestimates the actual numbers of people who consider themselves members. Ernesto's determination from the start that it would be a family concern, has meant that not only do most individual memberships include several family members, they all actually attend as active members. For example Vicente Andreu appears as 1 membership but that 1 includes himself, his wife Marie Carmen, his son Vicente and his daughter Paula. Taking account of this factor, the number of people in membership will actually be nearer 1,000, or almost 2% of the population of the town. And equivalent to 5% of all season ticket holders. That is in comparative terms like one Glasgow Celtic Supporters Club having 10,000 members. Members once recruited have tended to stay faithful members. And demand for membership has continued so that a waiting list has had to be set up to ensure controlled growth.

Ernesto took on board the original advice he received from the likes of Saul Ramos, Vicente Andreu and Pepe Mansilla that it would be very important to exercise control over applications for membership, so that it would be restricted to people who shared the values that lay behind the organisation. From the start, there has been a process of selection and testing for adherence to the values of the Celtic Submari.

The rules of the Celtic Submarí Penya declare that good behaviour, solidarity with others, mutual respect, opposition to racism, peaceful behaviour, a friendly attitude and conviviality are values that must be shared by all members and are to be enforced by the collective membership. Having good times around football, and sharing experiences with people from different parts of Spain and Europe, are pillars of the club, as is the commitment to help others wherever possible. People with triumphalist or aggressive attitudes or histories are not welcomed into membership. People looking for a drinking or social club are pointed in another direction.

In conversation with Francesca, a friend of mutual friends, who had decided after several positive visits that she wanted to join the Celtic Submari Penya, she told me she was amazed to find that it was not just a matter of signing a form. First of all there was a waiting list, something no other Penya has. Then, more surprising to her, it was made clear to her that before she could be accepted for membership, she would have to meet the established criteria as outlined above. The vetting process has worked very well. I have never seen a single example of aggressive behaviour or drunkness inside the Penya and have been struck by the decency, kindness, friendliness and care of all the members I have come across.

There has always been a conceptual confusion around about what exactly the Celtic Submari is. What it is not, is a Vila-real Celtic Supporters Club. What it is, is a Villarreal CF Penya, but one dedicated to supporting the values of Glasgow Celtic. In the beginning there was an attempt to be both. The new Penya was quickly registered with the Agrupacion as a Villarreal CF Penya. Steps were also made to register the Celtic Submari as an official CSC.

Some Celtic supporters are disappointed when they realise the Villarreal Celtic Submari is not a CSC, but they are wrong to be so. The two games in 2008 brought home clearer realisation for everyone. You cannot have a Celtic Supporters Club that does not support Celtic, does not want them to win, that actively encourages their opponent to beat them. Out of this clarification was born Ernesto's great slogan "Rivals for 90 minutes, Friends for Always". So now there is clarity. The Celtic Submari is a Villarreal Supporters Club. But its reason d'etre is to honour Celtic, to emulate Celtic and to teach Villarreal supporters to become like Celtic supporters, embracing the traditional Celtic values of respect for others and care for others. Imitation truly is the sincerest form of flattery. The point of the Celtic Submari is for Villarreal supporters to learn to act as well, as magnanimously, as positively as Celtic fans.

Even more important than its success in attracting and keeping members, has been the success in meeting the goals set out by Ernesto at the very beginning. The Penya was set up to prove that football could be about friendship not hatred, and that supporters of different clubs could learn to relate together in a positive, peaceful and friendly way. Throughout the history of the Penya they have sought to put this philosophy into direct action, and establish a new model of football relationships. Ernesto is rightly very proud of the fact that the Penya has delivered on its goal of being friendly with all other supporters. Almost every time Villarreal have played at home, Penya members will scour the streets for opposition fans and insist they come to the Penya for hospitality, food and drink.

Over the past few years they have, through this habit, made friendly relations with the supporters of most of the top teams in Spain, and it becomes an annual ritual. Two years ago they had had an impromptu party for Barcelona supporters and last year, the week before the Barca game, Ernesto received a email asking if the Penya were going to be doing the same this year. To which the answer was a resounding yes. At that party, several Barcelona supporters told me incredulously that in all their years following their club throughout Spain they had never encountered anything like the Penya. That happy story has been repeated with club after club. Supporters of every La Liga club in Spain over the last 7 years have been surprised by the hospitality and friendliness offered by the Celtic Submari. Once they have got over the shock of being warmly welcomed rather than the more normal routine of abuse and hostility, they have responded very positively, and there have been happy pre and post match parties. As illustrated by the story about the Barcelona fans, a pattern has rapidly been established whereby groups who enjoy this hospitality once, start requesting it on every visit, and the Submari members strive to oblige.With Villarreal B being in the Second Division for the past two years, the litany of welcomed supports has extended to include much smaller clubs like Cartagena and Huesca and Gimnastic, who have also responded very well and quickly established strong relationships.

On the European front, every Champions League or UEFA/Europa League tie has been used as a welcome excuse to organise hospitality for visiting supporters. While the massive party offered for over 4,000 Celtic fans in September 2008 was by far the biggest one organised, smaller versions have been offered to a range of bemused but delighted foreign visitors.

The single thing Ernesto is most proud of is the way the Celtic Submari have fully embraced the original Celtic values and raised so much money for good causes over the past 6 years. "When I went to Glasgow and learned how central this was to Celtic and its traditions, from the very beginning of the club, I brought it back to Vila-real and ensured the Submari did the same."

Ernesto will never forget the first Christmas Party the Penya ran, to raise money for Aspanion. "As well as all the children of our members, we also invited children known to Aspanion, and I will never forget the happiness in the room that day." The Celtic Submari Christmas Children's Party has become an annual highpoint and over the years many of the Villarreal players have cooperated willingly, dressing up as the Three Kings and distributing presents.

If Ernesto has one regret about the last 7 years, it has been about not having been able to convey to everyone just how important the fund raising aspect is to the whole identity of the Celtic Submari. As the club has grown from the original core group who knew well, understood and supported all its founding values, some of the people who have come in have not always understood why the fundraising element is so important. The Penya take a small annual subscription from all members. Every event they run is subsidised for members, and any income raised at all is directed 100% to charitable causes. Yet he still gets some members who will say things like "Three euros for a plate of paella, that is a disgrace!" which sometimes makes him despair.

However overall, over the past 7 years, the incredible generosity of the great majority of Celtic Submari members has made him feel him very proud. Over these 7 years the Penya has raised large sums, not just for Aspanion but for a whole range of local charities. To give just a flavour, in the last few years, main donations have included:

- 9/11/2007 ASPANION (Association of Parents of Children affected by Cancer) 3,300€
- 31/12/2007 JOVENTUT ANTONIANA (Local charity association of young people) 1,400€
- 4/11/2008 ASPANION (Association of Parents of Children affected byCancer) 4,000€
- 4/11/2008 ASOCIACIÓN DE ESCLEROSIS MÚLTIPLE DE CASTELLON(Multiple sclerosis society of Castellón) 4,000€
- 18/12/2008 MANOS UNIDAS (Catholic NGO) 2,500€
- 18/12/2008 Children from Cuba 660€

- 5/01/2009 ASPANION (Association of Parents of Children affected by Cancer) 1,500€
- 05/01/2009 SAN VICENTE PAUL (Local charity association) 1,500€
- 05/01/2009 JOVENTUT ANTONIANA (Local charity association of young people) 1,500€
- 12/04/2009 ELS LLUISOS (Local charity association of young people) 675€
- 03/06/2009 CARITAS INTERPARROQUIAL (Catholic NGO) 1,000 €
- 03/11/2009 LA PANDEROLA (School for children with special educative needs) 2,000 €
- 03/11/2009 ASPROPACE (Cerebral paralysis society of Castellón) 2,000 €
- 08/03/2010 ASPANION (Association of Parents of Children affected by Cancer) 3,015 €
- 16/06/2010 ASAMANU (NGO for Develoment focused in Africa) 1,500 €

In addition Yorkhill Hospital, in Glasgow, has benefited from every Celtic Submari visit to Glasgow, as have several other Scottish children's charities.

Ernesto is also proud of the fact that the Penya has generated a momentum of its own which has turned it into a major social centre, sponsoring many offshoot activities. The first of these was English classes, to assist in the communication with Celtic supporters. These have always been very well subscribed and have included activities like learning traditional Celtic (as opposed to celtic) songs. Over recent years other offshoots have included a Wine Appreciation Club; an Athletics club; Football teams for children of members; a Hiking Club; Dance classes; and a class in the Traditional Valencian Flute. Ernesto has spent much time in the past year trying to set up a Kids Disco, which would be a first for what is still a socially conservative town.

A very important positive outcome of the Penya for Ernesto has been the cultural exchange visits between schools in Vila-real and Hamilton. Ernesto thinks they have been a wonderful example of the values of the Penya being translated into positive action. Hundreds of young people from both communities have had the opportunity to get to know the other community better, to make friendships that will last for life, ensuring the bonds between Vila-real and West Central Scotland will grow and strengthen.

I asked Ernesto straight "Do you ever get tired of the responsibility of running the Penya?". His answer "Yes, lots of times. It is the good we do with the likes of Aspanion that keeps me there when I might otherwise have walked away." He acknowledged getting fed up with the constant grind, and more irritated with those who do not share his passion for the charitable side. Incidents like the 3 euros complaints leave him increasingly annoyed and deflated, and he has considered walking away. When asked what he thought would happen to the Penya if he did walk away, he said "I don't know", but did not demur when Gerry said it would collapse without Ernesto as the central force.

Following that exchange I asked a few of the key Submari people what they thought about the furute of the Penya. When asked about the future of the Celtic Submari, Pepe Mansilla replied with one word "Ernesto". Asked to amplify he said "Ernesto is Papa (The Pope).". When asked to amplify further, he said, "As long as Ernesto is there, the Penya will flourish, after that who knows?" What the Penya is about for Pepe is loyalty and friendship; it is a Union of Friends. Pepe is one of those in no doubt about the central importance of the charitable element. "One word 'Give, Give, Give.' That is what we learned in the Penya from Celtic supporters, the importance of giving without asking anything back."

Saul, a naturally thoughtful and intellectual type, has spent time trying to work out why the Celtic Submari has been so successful and why there is such a bond between the sets of supporters. He highlights three elements of a shared background as key factors in this. "Vila-real is a religious town, where religious observance, of the many saints' days rather than regular church attendance, is an important feature. I have been surprised over the years not by the religiosity of Celtic supporters but their quiet respect, including many taking the time to visit the Basilica and main church in Vila-real". The second shared interest is more straightforward, a common love of the drink. Whilst accepting that "Celtic supporters drink more, more than any group I have ever met", Saul points out that Vila-real people are historically known as the "Borrachots" (the drunkards) and the town has a history, ever since an influx of Basques in the late 19th Century, of illegal poteens and legal drinking.

The third one which he acknowledges freely the Celtic Submari have learned from Celtic supporters, is the ability to use football to generate income for deserving causes. Saul is now well aware of that strand having been present around Celtic since its very inception and has always been impressed with the natural generosity and giving nature of the Celtic supporters he has met over the past few years.

When asked about the future, in his heart Saul does not believe the Villarreal miracle will last for ever. "Everything has an end. And a town of only 50,000 cannot possibly sustain a top team for ever. But I am determined to enjoy it while it is here." Saul does see the Celtic Submari surviving. "Its values are still important to many people, it is in a healthy state and I can see no reason why it will not last."

For Vicente Andreu the answer to the question "Will the Celtic Submari survive?" also had a one word answer, "Ernesto". Amplifying, he said "Ernesto keeps interest and motivation strong. He is so charismatic and motivates people who might otherwise drift away. There is only one Ernesto in the world. He attracts people from all environments, both as a teacher, and a footballer. The Submari relies to a high degree on Ernesto. We are committed to Ernesto rather than the Celtic Submari as such." Vicente explained that most Villarreal Penyas are formed and run by younger supporters than the 1960s generation that form the backbone of the Celtic Submari. "Frankly very few of us would be in a supporters club in other circumstances, it is only because of Ernesto we joined, and stay involved." Vicente is a strong supporter of the notion of a Nobel Peace Prize nomination for Ernesto.

Coming from a slightly different perspective, Angel was insightful when talking about the jealousy the Celtic Submari sometimes arouses in other Penyas in Vila-real, and in particular with the Agrupacion of Penyas who feel threatened by the active nature of the Celtic Submari. While the Celtic Submari just get on and do things, the Agrupacion, a bureaucratic beast by nature, will have meetings about what meetings to have. Angel likened it to planning Paella Parties, "By the time the Agrupacion have had three meetings, with 2 votes, about what kind of rice to have and what to charge for it, the Celtic Submari will have cooked the Paella and be giving it away free." He despaired of the Agrupacion mentality response to any new idea or suggestion "It can't be done", compared with the Celtic Submari record of just going on and doing it. In 2009 Angel stood against Vicente Belles as President of the Agrupacion. He lost by one vote when the most basic organisation and preparation would have left him a clear winner. Vicente Belles 'resigned' in 2010 and the new President, Vanessa Martin seems a much more progressive type who has already shown she will work more positively with the Celtic Submari.

It is appropriate that Ernesto should have the last word on his creation. When I offered him that opportunity, he thought carefully, then said "Looking back, the Penya is the best thing I have ever done in my life. The important thing is the people I have met and the relationships I have made, both here and in Scotland."

I ended the whole process by revisiting previous discussions in which Ernesto had stated that he sees the Penya as a form of memorial and homage to young Ernesto. Once again he reiterated the importance of this element. "Yes, I believe that for me that sense of homage has been a great part of it. It has not been the same as spending time with him, but it has gone some way to fill the gap. Whenever I am involved in the Penya, my son is always in the background for me."

Chapter Forty One   A paradox for the Celtic Submari, a lesson for Celtic supporters

The Villarreal Celtic Submari have demonstrated that a new model of relating to fellow supporters, based on affection and respect rather than hatred and rivalry, can be a positive force for good. Seeing this phenomenon in action helps other people be better themselves, and behave better towards others.

There is a misconception shared by many Celtic supporters that the Celtic Submari was set up to glory in supporting Glasgow Celtic. It was not. It was set up to help Villarreal supporters apply the positive principles demonstrated to them by Celtic supporters in 2004, to their relationships with all other football fans, whether in Spain or Europe. These principles included friendship, respect, camaraderie, (defined as friendly comradeship), sociability, a desire to mingle peacefully and a care for others. They included a recognition that these positive qualities should be displayed in both victory and defeat, that football was only a game and the important thing was always to relate to other football supporters as equal human beings. They were taught football need not be about hatred, bitterness and negativity, but could be about positive feelings expressed with humanity.

That was how Ernesto and the whole of Vila-real saw Celtic supporters behave in April 2004, in a display that inspired them to set up the Celtic Submari and apply these principles in their own actions. That is how they saw Celtic supporters, as the prime exponents of a model of behaving that they wished to embrace and share with others.

And because it was Celtic supporters who taught them this model was possible, they knew they would always have a special relationship with Celtic and its supporters, but it was never meant to be an exclusive one. Celtic would be their second team but the motto "Rivals for 90 minutes, Friends for Always" would embrace many others.

Attendance at the Old Firm game on Easter Sunday 2011 had a profound effect on Ernesto Boixader and Pepe Mansilla. They had both been at several previous Celtic games, not involving Rangers, where the behaviour of Celtic fans was everything they had expected it to be, friendly and generous, a credit to the principles that lay behind the formation of the Celtic Submari.

However both were profoundly shocked by the experience of being at an Old Firm game, as well as disappointed, saddened, appalled and disillusioned. The shock came from encountering, first hand, the mutual hatred and bitterness that always soils these occasions. They found it hard to believe what they were told that this was both sets of fans on their absolute best behaviour following the recent adverse publicity, and that normally the atmosphere at these games was much more rancid, the behaviour much more rancorous. Nor were they reassured by being told that sitting in the "posh" VIP section of the Main Stand, they were insulated from the full intense power of the hatred being generated in the less civilised sections of the ground.

Shocked is definitely not too strong a word to describe the feelings of Ernesto and Pepe that Holy Sunday day. At the core of their shock was the realisation that the Celtic supporters they so admired, and whose positive qualities they had set themselves up to imitate, were capable on their home territory of all the worst aspects of negative behaviour that the Submari strove to eliminate. They saw them exhibit hatred, bitterness and sectarian bile. They were disappointed that the Celtic supporters that day had displayed as much anger, bitterness, hate and sectarian ill-feeling as the Rangers supporters. Ernesto and Pepe were both shocked and disappointed that their behaviour did not live up to the standards that the Celtic Submari believes in, about friendliness, respect and affection rather than hatred and anger. They were surprised, saddened, disillusioned and disappointed that Celtic supporters who behave so well when abroad could behave so badly at home.

Over the years since 2004 they had been exposed to some sense of the negativity Celtic supporters felt about Glasgow Rangers. They and the rest of the Submari members had been bemused, rather than offended or amused, by this seeming obsession, by the occasional anti-Rangers chants and songs, the "Fuck the Gers" scarves and other manifestations of hostility to the other Glasgow club. But these had all been seen as minor eccentricities that did not detract for the essential positive message sent out by the friendly behaviour of the Celtic fans both in Spain and around Parkhead.

But here at Ibrox was irrefutable proof that Celtic supporters could en masse engage in those very behaviours that Submari was set up to eliminate. Their sad conclusion was that the Old Firm experience was more akin to two tribes preparing for war rather than a game of football. They were distressed by the palpable level of hate that filled all sections of the ground encompassing both sets of supporters.

Both Ernesto and Pepe had quickly grasped the indisputable fact well know to all honest Scottish observers, but often fudged, obscured or downright denied in polite Scottish establishment circles. The hatred generated at Old Firm games is not that of a small minority, but is actually the behaviour of the vast majority, on both sides of the divide. Even people you know to be intelligent, with well established values based on decency and respect for others, will, in this context ,turn into hate filled purveyors of vile bile. Then assure you in reasonable discussion over a pint after the game that of course they don't hate the other side, it was all just harmless fun.

Ernesto is a fair minded man who does not wear green tinted glasses. Because of that, he was able to see that the prevalent atmosphere of hatred was generated by both sets of supporters rather than just the home set, the Rangers supporters. He had been warned that Old Firm games were not pleasant occasions and that he might find aspects of them unpleasant. Pepe Mansilla, the poet philosopher of friendship, was particularly appalled by the total absence of friendship on display. The mutual hatred demonstrated on both sides was not the way it should be, not the way it would be, under Pepe's model of friendship to everyone.

I am not saying every single Rangers supporter shows hatred of Celtic and every single Celtic supporter displays hatred of Rangers. But with the eye of an outsider, Ernesto and Pepe were able to see a truth seldom spoken in Scottish circles, but the truth of which is known to many. For at least the 90 minutes of the game, it is the majority rather than a small minority that become ardent haters of the opposition. If a chant starts "If you hate the fucking Rangers, hate the fucking Rangers, clap your hands" what percentage of Celtic supporters will join in 1%, 5%, 25%? No the correct answer is much nearer 100%, including many sane adults who would be appalled by the notion that they are haters. And the other unfortunate reality is that while the intensity diminishes after the game, a residue simmers constantly as barely suppressed bigotry. Their motto, shared equally with the Rangers supporters, might be summarised as "Haters for 90 minutes, Bigots for Always"

On their return home to Vila-real, Ernesto and Pepe and the other shocked attenders had many long conversations with Saul Ramos, Vicente Arneu and many others about what they had seen, what it meant, and how the Celtic Submari should respond. The consensus was that when it comes to Rangers games, Celtic supporters somehow lose sight of the key central fact that it is only a game of football and the truly important thing is to respect all human beings.

Ernesto loves Celtic supporters, all of them, and still believes they are among the greatest, most generous people in the world. He is a Celtic supporter, for every game they will ever play except against Villarreal. Ernesto knows Celtic supporters are wonderful. He saw irrefutable proof of that in April 2004 and over the 7 years since then, as we have seen in this book, it has been fully reinforced time and time again in Spain and in Glasgow. But he now also knows that some of these wonderful people can act in a less than wonderful way in the twisted context of their rivalry with Rangers. The Celtic Submari consensus was that this was a major Paradox, brilliant behaviour in most contexts, poor behaviour on their own doorstep. The Submari people are not blinkered idealists. They saw there was no short term solution to the problem they encountered, that it would require a great deal of education over a long period of time.

Ernesto is too sensible a man to become a preacher or an evangelist. He is not going to be a lecturer to Celtic supporters. He and the other key members of the Celtic Submari are going to continue to implement their own mission, implement their own motto, but continue also to make it clear that it applies to all football supporters, not just Celtic supporters. Ernesto hopes many Rangers supporters will take up the offer to visit Vila-real and his Penya contained at the end of this book. Ernesto will rigorously ensure that all the many welcome Celtic supporters in the Penya show the respect he advocates to Glasgow Rangers, and will even more vigorously ensure there are no abusive chants, no offensive scarves and no ripping of the Rangers-Villarreal scarf from its place of honour on the Penya wall.

If Ernesto Boixader has a message for Celtic supporters, if they are to learn from his magnificent example, then it is that they have to begin to apply the crucial Celtic Submari motto, "Rivals for 90 minutes, Friends for Always" to Rangers as much as to Villarreal. Ernesto's example challenges Celtic supporters to reject the hatred in their heart for Rangers and replace it with respect. (Rangers supporters of course need to do the same in regard to Celtic).

The issue for Celtic supporters can be simply put. Stop letting yourself down. You are betraying the wonderful and true face you present to the rest of the world as generous caring friendly giving people, by the displays of hate-filled bigotry in your own backyard. Stop singing "If you hate the fucking Rangers, hate the fucking Rangers, clap your hands". Learn from the lessons and examples available from the likes of the Villarreal Celtic Submari abroad, which was after all created by your own very positive example. Learn also from organisations like Sense Over Sectarianism at home. They have demonstrated it is possible for Scottish Catholics and Protestants to play together, sing together, laugh together, enjoy football together.

The Celtic Submari can repay the favour they got from Celtic supporters in 2004 if the example of Ernesto Boixader can lead Celtic supporters to reconsider their behaviour in their own backyard, and implement there the lessons they taught the Celtic Submari in Vila-real, and indeed all over the football world. If his example can inspire change in that direction, then Ernesto Boixader truly will be a viable candidate for the Nobel Peace Prize.

Chapter Forty Two Can Celtic supporters be helped not to hate Rangers?

I wish to conclude with a brief look at what lessons the Celtic Submari experience can offer in the wider context of Scotland's response to the football related sectarian strife within its midst, and use that analysis to answer the question in the title of this chapter.

The history of sectarianism within Scotland is now well documented and will be known to most readers of this book. The works of authors like Professor Devine, Tom Gallagher, Steve Bruce and others have meant the whole background to sectarian strife in Scotland is well known.

The history of the particular and unique impact of sectarianism in Scottish society on Scottish football became the subject of much academic and popular study in the 1990s, led almost single-handedly by Bill Murray from the relative safety of Australia, with books like "The Old Firm" and "Bhoys, Bears and Bigotry". Again the fruits of this study will be very familiar to readers of this book.

It is necessary to acknowledge that there was institutionalised social and economic discrimination against Catholics in Scotland from the middle of the 19th Century right up to the middle of the 20th Century when it finally disappeared in the 1970s and 1980s, under the influence of the Scottish welfare state, and the growth of a well-educated Catholic population. The fact that occasional lingering traces of anti-Catholic feeling persist in certain sections of Scottish society is not the same as institutionalised discrimination.

It is also necessary to acknowledge that strong anti-Celtic discrimination did exist in Scottish football in its early years, and persisted right up until its final flourish in the early 1950s when certain forces within the SFA tried to expel Celtic over the Irish flag issue. It was actually Rangers Football Club, conscious of their entwined financial interests in the Old Firm rivalry, that finally put an end to that piece of nonsense.

After more than a century of institutional discrimination there was bound to be a general legacy of dislike and distrust, tension and negative feelings between the two communities. The role of the two Old Firm clubs as standard bearers for their respective communities ensured that all that generalised negativity found a focus in bitter football rivalry, engendering a hatred on each side that was if not rational at least very understandable. However, as the serious discrimination disappeared from Scottish society and the Catholic community became fully integrated and accepted, it might have been expected that the related football hatred would diminish and, if not disappear, at least subside to the more normal levels of antipathy found in other parts of the football world between traditional rivals. But this did not happen in Scotland.

The explanation for this failure can be found with Rangers Football Club. From the early 1960s Scottish society moved towards a position where discrimination disappeared as a factor, and integration became the norm. There was one major exception to this trend. The refusal of Rangers to sign Catholic footballers, or have any Catholic employees at all, in the 70 years from the end of the first World War. This blatant sectarian discrimination should have made them total pariahs in any civilised country but, for a variety of reasons, all the major Scottish religious, political and social institutions colluded with the continuation of this flagrant discrimination. It caused problems for the vast number of Scottish Protestants who cared about decent values and social justice but an alarmingly large number of them continued to give their loyalty to the Ibrox club, if in a slightly shamed manner.

But for Catholics the situation was simple. Rangers were the enemy, a total disgrace. How could anyone like, far less support, a team that would never let them play for them no matter how talented they were, solely on the basis of their religion? Indeed Scottish folklore is full of tales of many promising Protestant players who were denied the opportunity to play for Rangers because of sloppy assumptions about their name, their school or the foot they kicked with, Daniel McGrain being one of the more prominent casualties of this syndrome. It is certainly understandable that all Catholics would have a strong dislike for an organisation that proved so consistently biased against them. They did hate Rangers, and that feeling was understandable.

The hatred of Rangers took place at two levels. The first was the intense negative feelings towards an institution that practiced such blatant discrimination against fellow citizens solely on the basis of their religion. The second level was a revulsion that such blatant discrimination should not only go unpunished, but was actively colluded with by every major political, religious and social institution in Scotland.

The Labour Party, who might have been expected to lead the fight against such a brazen example of discrimination, feared too much antagonising the Protestant working class vote they had come to rely upon since the 1960s to make them Scotland's natural party of government. They also feared a concerted campaign against Protestant discrimination would open up the can of worms of Catholic school segregation, a can they preferred to remain firmly closed.

The Conservative Party refused to countenance the risk of alienating what was left of their core Protestant support by challenging the social institution, Rangers FC. In addition there was a remnant anti-Catholic prejudice around the Scottish Tory Party that was not finally organisationally erased until the 1980s.

As for the SNP, the existence of two separate and antagonistic religious communities in Scotland always caused difficulties for a party committed to independence. It tended to respond to those difficulties by avoiding any issue which might be seen as offering support to one of those communities at the expense of the other.

The Church of Scotland in the years between the two World Wars had been extremely concerned about the threat to Scottish identity caused by the Irish Catholic community in their midst. The more positive post war climate lead to much better and more positive relationships between the two religions. Some attempts were made in the 1970s and early 1980s for the Church of Scotland to disassociate itself from the religious discrimination practiced by Rangers FC, but these weak attempts faded away in bland acceptance of the assurance by Rangers FC that "they did not see what else could practically be done".

The Catholic Church in Scotland took a political decision not to partake in any concerted campaign against this last vestige of highly visible employment prejudice against Catholics in Scotland. The roots of their long relative silence on this contentious issue lay in the central compromise they made in the early 20th Century to tolerate certain forms of discrimination against the Catholic community in return for not risking opening up the segregated schools issue, the defence of which was their dominant aim. The Catholic Church and the community it led, who all generally hated and despised Rangers, stayed largely silent about their enemy while privately relishing the moral high ground given to them by the differences in policy and practice between the two clubs.

The STUC, the Scottish Trades Union Council, might have been expected to be the leading force in the fight against brazen employment discrimination on religious grounds by a major Scottish institution. But the bald fact is that it never did so. Partly because it was a prisoner of its own past, where most Scottish Trade Unions were Protestant organisations defending their members against the Catholic threat to their jobs (leading to the jibe that it was not really 'Red' Clydeside but 'Not green at any price' Clydeside). By the 1970s, the STUC, with a large Catholic trade union membership, did not support religious discrimination but neither did it campaign actively against it. So despite many individual Trade Union members and leaders, Protestant and Catholic, privately loathing Rangers, there was no concentrated campaign to commit the STUC to apply pressure on Rangers to abandon their employment discrimination.

It is interesting to consider the failure of one Union in particular to make this an issue, the Scottish Professional Footballers Association, given that many of their members were directly affected. But the reality was that the SPFA never undertook any campaign against Rangers and their policy of refusing to sign Catholic players. One Rangers player told me on the record in interview, that most Protestant players were happy with the status quo as it increased their chances of playing for Rangers; and all Catholic players recognised that it helped Celtic and hindered Rangers, and they wouldn't want to play for that hated club anyway. So the SPFA joined the ranks of organisations willing to collude with what should have been seen as totally unacceptable.

For most of its first 100 years the SFA leadership was in the hands of Protestants and Masons who hated Celtic and favoured Rangers. However by the late 1970s, the positive changes in Scottish society had affected the composition of the SFA, and greatly diluted the influence of the old Masonic elite. In 1980, for the first time ever, the SFA finally acknowledged that "sectarianism was the root cause of the hatred and bitterness which has existed between the two sets of supporters for decades." The SFA concluded in its report into the 1980 Cup Final riot that "we (the SFA) are not satisfied with Rangers' assertion that its present policies are in keeping with the Association's wishes." However, reaching this conclusion did not lead to any action to produce change. The SFA did not contemplate taking action against Rangers for their flagrant breach of the FIFA regulations preventing "discrimination against an individual for reasons of religion". The SFA chose to collude with this breach rather than take on Rangers FC in a direct manner.

Celtic FC also ended up colluding on the issue of Rangers refusing to sign Catholic players. Instead of demanding justice for the community they represented, they preferred the dual benefits of moral superiority and a practical monopoly over Catholic youth footballers. Many individual Celtic supporters, including future Club Historian and Board member Brian Wilson, urged them to do the morally correct thing and publicly campaign against Rangers and their policy of discrimination, but they consistently refused to do so, preferring the quieter easier route of colluding while wallowing in moral superiority.

So the undeniable reality is that as recently as less than 25 years ago, one of the most important Scottish social institutions, Glasgow Rangers Football Club, employed a sectarian and discriminatory employment practice that was an absolute disgrace and should have been regarded as intolerable by all sections of the community. It says a great deal about what a small minded and mean spirited country Scotland was then, that all the other major social institutions of Scotland colluded in the existence and operation of this policy. There was never a serious campaign mounted to end this stain of shame. That failure in itself should be a source of further shame.

That discrimination, and the collusion of all the major institutions of society in its continuation, are the linked reasons why in 1988 almost every Celtic supporter hated Glasgow Rangers and could not be said to be acting unreasonably in doing so. Rangers were the problem and the appropriate object of ire right up until 1989, when Graeme Souness and David Murray saved them from the inevitable consequences of their sectarian past.

All the dire predictions that had made for years as to the loss of support Rangers would suffer if they abandoned their Protestants only stance proved to be totally incorrect. Any loss of diehard support proved minimal, and was more than compensated for by the increased ability of decent minded people to re-embrace a non-discriminating Rangers.

Both Rangers and Celtic have, since the 1990s, accepted their responsibility to take a lead role in tackling bigotry and sectarianism within their club and amongst their supporters. The Celtic Bhoys Against Bigotry campaign and the Rangers Pride Over Prejudice campaign have both been welcome attempts by these two great clubs to live up to their wider moral and social responsibilities.

The actions of Graeme Souness and David Murray, from 1989 onwards, have brought Rangers Football Club into the modern world with all its demanding values. Since then, Rangers have become a socially responsible institution and have stood up to and opposed the worst excesses of its own supporters. This institution now deserves support and respect not hatred. Rangers are a genuine legitimate partner in the fight for a fairer and more decent Scottish society.

The range of forces colluding with their enemy reinforced the sense of paranoia traditionally felt by Celtic supporters, and gave it some kind of rational basis as late as the 1980s. However in modern Scotland there is no longer any rational basis at all for the strong sense of paranoia felt by most Celtic supporters. There is no wholesale range of Scottish social institutions lined up against Celtic and for Rangers. Every major institution is now on the same side as both Celtic and Rangers. But the hatred induced by the previous persecution persists, and has become learned behaviour for new generations brought up under a healthier, fairer Scotland, where the behaviour and causes which made the feeling understandable have disappeared. So despite all that social progress, most Celtic supporters still hate Rangers.

Rangers supporters have more than a century's history of hating Celtic. While this Rangers hatred of Celtic may be less justified than the Celtic hatred of Rangers, in terms of not being derived from a genuine sense of persecution and discrimination, it is still very understandable, historically speaking. This hatred has its origins in the decades of anger and fear generated in the native Protestant community in Scotland against the dangers, both real and imagined, posed to them by the growth of the immigrant Irish Catholic community. Rangers' role as the Protestant standard bearer of the fight against the major social representative organisation of this community, Glasgow Celtic, meant that their supporters easily transferred their generalised fears into a specific hatred of Celtic. The violent part of the hostility felt to Celtic could be put down partly to the phenomenon explained by Carol Craig as bicycling, where the second bottom tier of a violent and aggressive macho society hit out against the bottom tier, the new immigrants. But there should be no doubt that hatred of Celtic permeated every social tier of Protestant Scotland, from the boardrooms and drawing rooms to the backstreet pubs and cafes. There is also no doubt that the very public policy and practice of the Ibrox club in refusing to sign Catholic players, maintained right up until the end of the 1980s, gave generations of Rangers supporters 'permission' to hate Catholics and Celtic. The dramatic ending of that discriminatory policy in 1989 did have an impact both in removing that 'permission' and in generating a sense of identity between Rangers supporters and their growing number of Catholic players. However it did not result in any major reduction in the hatred felt by Rangers supporters in the mass towards Celtic. This has long been, and has remained, irrational learned behaviour passed on from generation to generation.

It is important to understand why in the very recent past there has been a resurgence in the vehemence of the hatred felt by at least some Rangers supporters, against the general trend of the past 50 years in the dying down of collective hatreds. It is no coincidence that this resurgence has occurred in a period when Rangers supporters have suffered a massive double humiliation. The first humiliation dates from Manchester in 2008. Almost all Rangers supporters saw the success of their team in getting to the Final of the UEFA Cup in 2008 as an opportunity to surpass the experience of Celtic in Seville in 2003, a collective celebration that brought the Celtic Football Club praise and recognition throughout the world. But history repeated itself, as both tragedy and farce. In 1972 Rangers' winning of a European club competition was diminished in comparison with the Celtic memory of Lisbon 1967, by scenes of rioting that besmirched rather than enhanced the reputation of Rangers. So even more

Rangers supporters made a point of honour of making it to Manchester than Celtic had attracted to Seville. But the contrast between Seville 2003 and Manchester 2008 was even greater, with the whole world being horrified at the scenes broadcast endlessly about Rangers supporters behaving disgracefully amid scenes of rioting and carnage. Not only did they lose the game, but psychologically more importantly, they lost the image war and suffered a major humiliation that confirmed in them, especially the 95% that had behaved impeccably, the sense that "no one loves so we don't care".

That sense of humiliation and despair and defiance has been the primary explanation of why Rangers supporters have reverted in the last few years to exhibiting their previously suppressed sectarian based behaviour that has set them on a collision course with both UEFA and the Scottish government. If that behaviour, especially the sectarian singing based on their identification with the Billy Boys, continues in 2011-12, it is almost certain Rangers will end up banned by UEFA, despite the transformation of the club itself into a force for good rather than darkness.

The second humiliation suffered by Rangers supporters has been the down grading of the status of their club due to debt difficulties. Rangers should be, have been until recently, one of the great Clubs of the world. They have a wonderful modern stadium they can fill every game with 50,000 committed supporters, and a massive world wide fan base. Yet over the past 3 years this great club has been almost paralysed by a relatively small debt. Rangers have been rapidly reduced from a great club to a mediocre club unable for the past few years to enter the transfer market and increasingly reduced to the humiliating status of taking promising youngsters on loan from real big clubs to allow them to gain experience. Murray's era ended in miserable humiliation. Even with new owners, Rangers have proved unable to compete with Championship teams for players that would relatively recently been seen as not good enough for Rangers. Rangers debt to Walter Smith is incalculable. His achievement over these troubled recent years in leading a vastly depleted and diminished squad to successive championships, is a truly phenomenal act of football management skill.

Any competent social psychologist would have been able to predict that such a massive double dose of humiliation would produce emotional regression, and a reversion to old habits of transferred hatred and aggression. This regression also largely explains the other strange phenomenon of the past months, the irrational hatred shown by many Rangers supporters to Neil Lennon. In the reawakened regressed Rangers psyche, Neil Lennon has become the personification of what similar Southern USA rednecks would call "an uppity nigger". With his shaved red hair, his aggressive posture and hardness, his often contorted face, Lennon fits the almost forgotten stereotype of the Irish Catholic danger to decent Scottish Protestant men and women, a threat to their jobs, their livelihood, their women, their very identity.

For all these reasons, almost all of the offensive sectarian behaviour that has recently generated the current political crisis; the bullets and bombs, the death threats, the incitements to violence, the actual physical aggression, the singing about "being up to our knees in fenian blood", has been from the Rangers side of the divide. But while this is undeniable, it is important to be clear that Celtic supporters have no grounds for complacency or moral superiority. As outsiders like Ernesto Boixader and Pepe Mansilla were able to see on Easter Sunday 2011, the sectarian hatred that so disfigures Old Firm games is contributed to by Celtic supporters in equal hate filled measures.

This chapter has argued that most Celtic supporters hate Rangers, and most Rangers supporters hate Celtic. And that in most cases, it is based on learned behaviour rather than current grievances. In asserting these truths I am not saying that this hate is exhibited every moment of every day. Most Celtic supporters I describe as 'hating' Rangers, have perfectly friendly relationships with Rangers supporters as colleagues, friends, social acquaintances and increasingly even as family members. But on days like Old Firm games, they hate Rangers. Too often an excess of alcohol mixed with a high dose of tribal fervour, creates a powerful cocktail that overcomes the normal restraints against the expression of hatred. The same pattern applies for Rangers supporters. Anyone who has ever been to the toxic experience that is an Old Firm game will find it hard to deny the truth of that assertion.

Many intelligent sensitive Celtic supporters join in chants of "If you hate the fucking Rangers, hate the fucking Rangers, clap your hands". These same people would not allow anyone who chanted "If you hate the fucking darkies, hate the fucking darkies, clap your hands" to deny they were racist, but they seem incapable of applying the same logic to themselves, while peppering their own conversations with references to Huns and Bluenoses.

UEFA were right in 2006, following the behaviour of Rangers fans in the two games against Villarreal, to point out that both the Scottish Football authorities and the Scottish Government had some responsibility for colluding in the sectarian behaviour of Rangers supporters, but that such collusion could not be used as a defence for the unacceptable behaviour of these supporters. UEFA did accept that Rangers Football Club had taken steps to control the behaviour of their fans, but what the governing body were clearly saying was that such steps required to be accompanied by effective action at a national level.

This message was heard and understood both within Rangers, and within the Scottish FA and Scottish political circles. One result was that tackling sectarian behaviour in football became a major item on the Scottish political agenda and has remained as such ever since. Both Labour and SNP administrations have led concerted cross party campaigns to tackle sectarian behaviour in Scottish football. From the 2006 Scottish Government 18 Point Action Plan to the 2011 40 recommendations of the Joint Action Group. Despite these efforts, season 2010-11 saw sectarian related misbehaviour within Scotland rather than abroad, become a major domestic issue. The various confrontations at Rangers Celtic games and the public hostility directed against Neil Lennon, the sending of bullets and letter bombs to Lennon and other prominent Celtic supporters, and the physical assault on Lennon at a Hearts game, lead the whole issue to feature as a major one in the Scottish election campaign of 2011, and a mad rush to seek workable solutions that would 'solve' the problem.

The Scotland of 2011 is less of a small minded, mean spirited country than it was in 1988. The development of its own Parliament has lead to an increase in maturity and confidence on behalf of Scots and the main institutions that represent them. This increased confidence and maturity means that it is inconceivable that ever again there would such a widespread collusion in ignoring the right and decent thing to do, as occurred previously with regard to the pre 1989 Rangers.

There is a further major difference from the position in 1988 that has transformed the whole nature of the political debate. Rangers are now officially, and correctly, seen as on the side of the good and righteous. The whole collusive apparatus created by the implications of their being on the dark side has been removed. Now every single major Scottish institution can be on the right side too, on the side of equality and justice and social care. All four political parties, both Churches, the STUC and the SPFA, Celtic and Rangers are all full partners in seeking positive solutions to the problems of sectarianism. One major implication of this is that root causes of the hostility and antipathy to Rangers have disappeared. Hating Rangers is no longer a rational or at least understandable act for Celtic supporters. It is a learned behaviour which has outlived its original causes. The rational response for Celtic supporters is to respect Rangers and the efforts they are making to contribute to a Scotland free of the worse excesses of sectarian strife.

Given that all the major Scottish institutions are on now the same side, can we reasonably expect a quick and decisive victory in the battle against sectarianism in Scottish football? And have the Government and their Joint Action Group got the solutions right? Unfortunately the answer to both questions has to be a resounding 'no'.

This is where the reality spotted by Ernesto Boixader and Pepe Mansilla becomes very important. The current Government supported proposals are a classic case of attacking the symptoms of a problem in preference to the slower, less glamorous process of addressing the causes. The main proposals focus on punishing displays of sectarian hate. They use a rhetoric of "Zero Tolerance" for all such displays. Now such a policy would be fine in a situation where displays of sectarian hate were confined to dangerous and damaged individuals who represented a real threat to society. However they become disastrously socially disruptive in situations where such displays are 'learned behaviour' acts of the majority. Ernesto and Pepe quickly grasped a truth that the Scottish establishment has preferred always to deny. Namely that the hate displayed at Old Firm games is not the preserve of a dangerous and isolated minority, but the behaviour of the majority, the vast majority. For each club we are probably talking about at least 40,000 game attending supporters plus about three times as many home based supporters. Meaning that if you rigorously apply the new proposals in a Zero Tolerance manner you could be facing imprisoning over 300,000 Scots for periods of up to 5 years. The reality is that those 'offenders' certainly do not require 5 years in prison, rather they require a course in Sectarian Awareness training.

I keep remembering my experience in Vila-real in September 2008 when 4,000 decent Celtic supporters acted magnificently throughout the day, mixing on friendly terms with Villarreal supporters and raising a great deal of money for local charities. Yet almost all of these 4000 people did something, in chanting "If you hate the fucking Rangers, hate the fucking Rangers, clap your hands", that under the terms of the proposed legislation would render them liable to jail sentences of 5 years. It is lunatic folly to introduce legislation that would make criminals out of, and even imprison, such decent and generally socially responsible people. Equally, on the Rangers side, many, indeed most, of those who sing "Hello, hello, we are the Billy Boys" are decent, generally social responsible citizens.

It is imperative that the Scottish Government and its all party and all organisation consensus grasp, accept and act on a recognition of the reality witnessed by Ernesto and Pepe at the Old Firm game last April. The reality that has been known for a long time by most people involved in Scottish football but a reality denied by the respectable Scottish establishment who have preferred to ignore its implications. Namely that sectarian hatred at Old Firm games is not the preserve of a small virulent minority but the normal behaviour, at least in that context, of the great majority.

Failure to accept that reality will send the Scottish Establishment stumbling down a disastrous, irrelevant and unworkable road of criminalising and imprisoning decent responsible Scottish citizens. Accepting that reality opens up a two pronged approach that will at last offer a real possibility of bringing football related sectarian behaviour down towards levels of antipathy tolerated in other civilised societies.

Full Zero Tolerance needs to be maintained for the top end of the range of unacceptable behaviour. The truly dangerous and objectionable offences, like the sending of bullets and bombs, the making of death threats, the physical assaults, the incitements to violence are all adequately covered by existing legislation. There will always be remnants of emotionally damaged, hate filled scumbags on both sides who find the notion of respect for the opposition too challenging to the only certainties they have ever known, that the enemy are scum to be abused. Tackling those kinds of offenders, on both sides of the Old Firm divide, is the proper and realistic task for the local Police forces and special units like the National Football Policing Unit. There is no need to introduce other major "offences" that will potentially bring so many normal members of Scottish society into contact with Courts and danger of penal servitude. And put ludicrous unworkable pressure on Strathclyde Police to arrest 40,000 people for singing a song or chanting a chant.

For the rest, the great decent majority who will never cross the line into violent anti-social behaviour, the goal should be to help move them towards football relationships based on respect rather than hatred, bitterness and sectarianism.

Indeed the written objectives of the Celtic Submari might well serve as the template for the model of behaviour desired.

People cannot be bullied, threatened, punished or legislated into showing respect. Respect comes from education and good role models rather than imposition from above. That is the real importance of the Celtic Submari. The Celtic Submari under the leadership of Ernesto Boixader has been showing for over 7 years that a new model of football relationships based on affection and respect not hatred, bitterness and sectarianism is perfectly possible, does exist, actually works and attracts and converts people everywhere they are exposed to it. But such a position is not achieved by threatening hundreds of thousands of Scots with long jail sentences. The Government needs to move away from hammering the symptoms of the problem and start the long slow process of actively addressing the causes.

This is where the second prong of the strategy should come in, aimed at tackling the hate demonstrated by a large percentage of existing supporters on both sides, generally through sectarian songs and chants. Yes, there should be action, maybe even laws, against such sectarian abuse by adults. But the action should be proportionate, and imaginative, based more on remedial education than punishment. Persistent or extreme offenders should be dealt with by bans from grounds, short-term and linked to Football Banning Orders, and orders made with compulsory attendance at Sectarian Awareness Educational events.

Rangers Football Club, with full support from Parliament and society, must make it clear to all its supporters that the singing of "Hello, Hello, we are the Billy Boys" will not be tolerated within Ibrox, in any of its versions. This song is too identified with the anti-Catholic hatred and violence that marred the 1920s and 1930s, as well as the older Loyalist references, to ever be anything but gratuitously offensive to Catholics. Measures like the temporary closure of parts of the stadium where its singing persists, perhaps for one game at a time, might be required but Zero Tolerance will be required to remove this song as the preferred anthem. As well as its negative impact in Scotland, this is the song that could well get Rangers expelled from UEFA, so the Ibrox club has an additional incentive to see it completely eliminated from the Rangers repertoire.

Celtic have successfully removed almost all pro IRA songs from Celtic Park, and their supporters do not sing anti-Protestant songs, but anti-Rangers chants must be treated with the same Zero Tolerance. Some agreed Panel must be established to monitor the development of any new offensive songs or chants, and clubs and supporters must be given clear and unambiguous guidance as to exactly what songs and chants are deemed unacceptable.

In calm discussion outwith Old Firm games, most individuals on both sides who practice this learned behaviour, will claim it is not the real them, that they do not actually hate in the way their words and actions in the heat of the game might appear to indicate they do. And that that are open to the notion of respect rather than hate. Educational efforts to change this behaviour will largely be pushing at an open door.

At the same time resources should be found by the Government and by relevant other bodies to institute a massive educational programme aimed at preschool, primary and secondary school children to prevent future generations of Old Firm supporters blindly adopting the same negative behaviours as their predecessors. The good news is that there is already evidence that such efforts can be remarkably effective. The Mark Scott Awards spawned by Nil by Mouth, and the work of Sense Over Sectarianism in Glasgow and the West of Scotland have shown that education directed at the young can have dramatic positive results within short timescales.

Perhaps at this point the elephant in the room can be addressed. As was recently forcibly pointed out, the existence of segregated Catholic schools did not cause the bitter sectarian hatred between the two communities that exists in Scotland. However it is at least open to argument that its continued existence might be a factor in perpetuating sectarian division and difference in a harmful way. In the long run, a constantly maturing Scotland will decide, with the full consent of both religious communities and secular society, whether it continues with the current rigid divisions or moves in some way towards a more integrated system. In the short run there can be little rational argument against a campaign to provide remedial sectarian awareness education to both sets of school communities together.

One other lesson from the Celtic Submari experience that would help create a better more respectful atmosphere is the appreciation of the civilising influence of families, women and children in the active world of football support. Villarreal CF have women as no less than 30% of their season ticket holders, a record in the world of top class football. Women and children between them form a majority both of Villarreal CF crowds and of active members in the Celtic Submari, leaving adult males as a minority. Trouble, drunkenness and aggressive behaviour are unknown in both locations. This membership reality initially shocked the Celtic supporters with whom the Celtic Submari were first in most touch, but over time the Celtic audiences have adapted and changed to begin to reflect back these realities in their joint social gatherings. Domestic violence and abuse is as big a problem within macho Spain as it is in macho Scotland, but within Vila-real and within the Celtic Submari it is effectively non-existent.

Carol Craig in her remarkable, haunting and uncomfortable book. "The Tears that made the Clyde" has graphically demonstrated in terms painful to read how miserable and fractured and low in self esteem are the lives and relationships of far too many men and women in the West of Scotland. Stuck in relationships seldom based on love, Scottish men on both sides of the sectarian divide lead narrow powerless lives filled with anger, aggression and barely concealed self loathing. Football is often the only outlet for emotional expression and is used as an escape from domestic unhappiness rather than a shared experience. The failure to receive emotional satisfaction, related to painful defeats, is then feed back negatively into the domestic situation explaining the much remarked links between Old Firm games and domestic as well as other forms of violence. There is an old Glasgow joke I first heard in the 1960s that has persisted because of the essential if sad truth it contains. The wife of an avid Celtic supporter says to her husband "I think you love Celtic more than you love me!" Her husband shakes his head and replies "No, hen, I love Rangers more than I love you!" The joke works equally well for Rangers couples.

Celtic are proud of the fact that women represent 12.5% of their season ticket holders, reputedly the highest percentage in Scotland. The percentage for Rangers would appear to be somewhat lower. If we can learn from the lessons of Villarreal CF and Celtic Submari, then maybe both clubs can be set a target of 20% female season ticket holders, and a range of imaginative schemes set up to help progress towards this, like 'buy one, get one for the wife at half price', and realistically priced family season ticket schemes. If women and children could become 33% of the Old Firm crowds, then think what impact this would have on the atmosphere and behaviour at Scottish football games. The evidence from Vila-real, anecdotal but powerful, would suggest such greater involvement in active football support leads not only to improved behaviour at football games, but to significantly improved family mental health.

The Celtic Submari members have seen a remarkable transformation over the 7 years of their existence. In 2004 they were the supporters of a wee team from a small town unknown in Europe, and Celtic and Rangers were two of the biggest and most respected clubs in Europe. Now, in 2011, their club Villarreal CF, from the town of less than 50,000 inhabitants, smaller than the average crowds of both Rangers and Celtic, are rated in the Top Twenty Clubs in Europe while Rangers and Celtic have slipped down the hierarchy to the point where they struggle to qualify for Europe and domestically fail to compete financially with clubs in the English Championship (second tier).

For the sake of the two clubs, and for the collective mental health of Scotland, the Old Firm have got to be released from the confines of competing only against each other, as effectively is the current case. It is like placing two trout in small bowl with 10 goldfish. There is bound to much unhealthy threshing and thrashing, and no equilibrium. The need to integrate Celtic and Rangers into a bigger, more competitive league is now very urgent.

It is an intellectual and moral challenge to the internationalism and interdependence in Europe that the SNP advocate, to accept the urgency of this need for the greater good of Scotland and to use their political influence as the government of Scotland to achieve it. Alex Salmond and Kenny MacAskill are football people and will understand the football realities. It has not harmed Welsh national identity, or the viability of their Parliament, that Swansea City will play in the English Premiership League in 2011-12 and that they may well be soon be joined there by Cardiff City. Likewise Scottish determination of their own affairs within devolved arrangements, or through moving to greater independence, will not be adversely affected by Rangers and Celtic joining the Premiership Division Two.

Indeed it will be a challenge for all 4 Scottish political parties to see the social importance of this as part of the bipartisan policy against sectarianism, and use their links with their UK organisations to bring pressure for this to become a reality. Only a move to the English Leagues can restore Rangers and Celtic to their rightful places as major clubs on the European scene.

To force the Old Firm to remain artificially stuck in a situation where they are only competing against each other, will ensure that their seasons are dominated by the 4, 5, 6 or 7 games a season they will play against each other, games that will thereby remain a focus for the unhealthy expressions of hostility that so marred Scotland last season. To leave them in a situation where their international competitiveness will continue to decline will exacerbate the current problems of sectarian strife. The relative decline of the last few years has knocked the confidence and self esteem of both sets of supporters. Since their peak of 2004, fewer Celtic supporters now believe they are the best supporters in the world, of the best club in the world. Rangers supporters have felt diminished and humiliated. The continuation of both these declines will adversely affect the public behaviour of both, and make the task of moving them towards a more respect based approach consequently harder.

A move to a more competitive situation, where they only play each other twice a season in a context of 40 odd other competitive games, will create a much more healthy dynamic and allow the attempts to steer both sets of supporters from hatred to respect to have a much greater chance of success. If these moves are not successful, it is likely the relative decline in European competitiveness of Rangers and Celtic will continue, and the Celtic Submari members will continue to enjoy the irony of their team being much superior to the two Scottish giants on the field, while being dwarfed by them off it.

Is it realistic to expect Celtic supporters not to hate Rangers? The vast majority of Celtic supporters are decent honourable people. The magnificent behaviour they have consistently displayed abroad has been much more in keeping with their values and their concept of themselves than is the hateful behaviour they can exhibit at home in relation to Rangers. There was a justifiable basis for that hatred until as recently as 1989 but not now. In the years since then, Rangers have transformed themselves into full partners in the fight against sectarian excesses in Scottish football. This transformation has meant there is no longer a rational justification for that hatred. It has become a learned behaviour that can easily be unlearned and jettisoned. Celtic supporters can adopt behaviour more in tune with their own concept of themselves and the positive face they proudly present to the rest of the world. Respect for Rangers is possible and the Celtic Submari offer a model of how to deliver behaviour based on that concept.

Rangers supporters have a harder challenge, both to relinquish the old ingrained habits of a never justified hate, and to overcome their anger, resentment and shame at the poor image of themselves presented to the wider world, and present a better one. But the great majority of Rangers supporters are decent people who care about the good name of their club.

It would be grossly naïve and unrealistic to except a mass outbreak of mutual love any time soon, but at least, under the right framework of Government supported sticks and carrots, with an appropriate balance of punishment and education resource investment, progress can be made in moving both sets of supporters away from sectarian based hatred towards a degree of acceptance. Full respect may take a little longer, but the publicising of examples like the Villarreal Celtic Submari of how relationships based on respect and affection can be achieved, will help that process.

Ernesto Boixader saw the very best of Celtic supporters in action in 2004 and was inspired to develop a new model for all football relationships based on that inspiration. He has succeeded magnificently through the Celtic Submari in putting that philosophy and its related motto, "Rivals for 90 minutes, Friends for Always", into effective action in Spain and throughout Europe. Hopefully in turn his example can now inspire Celtic supporters to end the paradox whereby they act magnificently when abroad but less positively on their own doorstep. If Ernesto and the model of the Celtic Submari can help Celtic supporters bring these positive principles home to their relationship with Rangers, then the circle of goodness will be complete.

An Open Invitation to all Readers

I discussed with Ernesto the issue that as a result of reading this book some people, maybe even many people, and not just Celtic supporters, would decide they would quite like to be a part of all this, and would want to come to Vila-real. He was very clear that he wanted this to be one outcome of the book and that he would guarantee everyone in that position a great welcome. I thought he would add "and unlimited free beer", which has been the reality until now, but in a cautious moment he restricted himself to guaranteeing that the first few drinks in the Penya would be free for all such travellers.

There would be two main ways for intending visitors to approach implementing a desire to visit.

One would to come en masse at the two Fiesta weeks, mid May and mid September. That is when the larger groups of Celtic supporters have tended to come, and the whole town, not just the Celtic Submari Penya, rallies round to offer hospitality to as many visitors as come. There are always organised events, Bull runs, street parties, processions, mass meals, dances, fireworks, church celebrations and the like.

If people wanted to come at other times, individually or in small groups, that would be fine too, and the Penya would guarantee they would be looked after and entertained. Anyone planning to do this, should first check the fixture list to ensure Villarreal are playing at home, then notify the Penya website, www.celticsubmari.com of their intended arrival, so arrangements could be made to welcome them. Ernesto confirmed the Penya always have at least two season tickets available for every home game, so that visitors can get into the ground free and be sitting beside Submari members. Priority goes to Celtic supporters who have never been before.

The people described in the book are real, are as wonderful and as friendly as described, and love having visitors, so please give serious thought to coming out, meeting them and having the experience of a lifetime. Remember, too, that since welcoming visitors is part of the club mission, the decision to come can be seen as a selfless act! Friday night is always open night in the Penya and games tend to be on Saturday or Sunday, so plan to be there at least mid-Friday to early Monday.

Most of the never ending succession of friends of mine that have visited Naquera over the past 3 years have been exposed to this experience, and can testify to the friendliness and generosity of the Submari members and the unforgettable nature of time spent in their company. The many Celtic supporters who have made the trip to Vila-real over the past 6 years can also testify to the wonderful reception every Celtic supporter receives.

But Ernesto was clear, that while Celtic supporters are, and always will be, particularly welcome, the invitation and the guaranteed warm welcome are open to supporters of any club, and any nationality. Ernesto would be delighted if any Rangers supporters reading the book decided to test this out for themselves and sign up to make the trip. Ernesto would welcome visits from Rangers supporters in any numbers, and guarantees they would be made very welcome by everyone.

I hope at least some Rangers supporters decide to put this offer to the test. I know they will be treated very well, and have a trip they will long remember positively.

Flights can be arranged to Reus, Barcelona, Girona, Valencia and Alicante Airports. Thanks to the ceaseless efforts of the club benefactor Carlos Fabra, there may even soon be flights direct to Castellon Airport. The Palace and Azul Hotels, and La Masia Boarding House in Vila-real welcome friendly visitors and the Penya will help with advice on travel and accommodations arrangements.

So please, if reading this book has been a positive experience, give serious thought to coming out and enjoying the phenomenon yourselves with family and friends. You are guaranteed "the experience of a lifetime."

Companion Volume
"Yellow Submarine   the Miracle of Villarreal CF

"Yellow Submarine" is essential reading for all football fans who believe that integrity and community can and should matter even at the highest levels in modern football.

It is exceptional value, offering Two Stories for the Price of One

Story One   The Miracle of Villarreal CF

The explanation of how a wee club from a small town of 50,000 inhabitants became a major force, not just in Spain but in Europe, including becoming Semi-Finalists in the Champions League, the UEFA Cup and the Europa League, and Runners Up in La Liga. The amazing success of Villarreal offers supporters of clubs, both large and small, throughout Europe a model of how they too might live the dream, without having to rely on Russian or American billionaires or Arab dynasties.

Story One reveals the component parts of this miracle transformation of a club used to life in the lower leagues. **"Yellow Submarine"** explores how this on field success and equally remarkable high degree of community involvement has been created, and offers its **Ten Secret Ingredients** as a model for other clubs throughout Europe, both big and small, to emulate.

Story Two The Inside Account of a three year voyage on the Yellow Submarine as they set sail in search of further European glory in the Champions League, Europa League and La Liga, encountering teams like Manchester United and Arsenal, Celtic, Barcelona and Real Madrid, and Porto on the way.

Story Two follows the Yellow Submarine through three seasons from 2008-2011 as they compete in both the Champions League and the Europa League, while striving to maintain the success in La Liga that will allow the European adventures to continue until the ultimate dream comes true and Villarreal win the Champions League.

It explores how the miracle ingredients identified in Book 1 are applied in practice, and examines the **Catch 64** question that threatens the continuation of the dream.

"Yellow Submarine - the Miracle of Villarreal" (ISBN 978-1-901514-02-5) is available from Ringwood Publishing and can be ordered online from the Ringwood website. www.ringwoodpublishing.com for £11.99 or by post from Ringwood Publishing at PO Box 16298 Glasgow G13 9DD

Information about the author and his other books
The Author
Sandy Jamieson, a Clyde supporter, was born in Glasgow and still lives there, having returned after three years in Spain. He gave up his job as a Senior Manager with Strathclyde Regional Council to concentrate on writing books. After producing 3 books in 7 years, he returned to fulltime social work to found and lead INCLUDEM, an organisation devoted to providing intensive support and supervision to Scotland's most troubled young people.

In 2007 he retired from this work, for which he received an OBE, to resume his writing career.

He is currently Director of SISIF, the Sherbrooke Institute for the Study of International Football.

He is also the Editor of two international football websites, **Greengreenworld**, international football for Celtic supporters (www.greengreenworld.co.uk) and **SISIF News**, dedicated to comment and analysis of world football (www.sisifnews.co.uk)

The Books
Graeme Souness   The Ibrox Revolution and the Legacy of the Iron Lady's Man   Mainstream 1997
This book, which was serialised over 3 days in the Herald, tells how an unloved Thatcherite revolutionised Scottish football, changing its face forever and removing one of its ugliest warts. Along with a fellow Thatcherite David Murray, Souness applied Thatcherite theories in a country that had rejected Thatcherism, and achieved great success. They had the courage to end forever the appalling employment discrimination practiced by Glasgow Rangers for 70 years. In ending this discrimination, Souness saved Rangers from the inevitable consequences of their long term actions, and allowed the Ibrox club to begin to become a force for good in Scottish society.

Own Goal   Ringwood Publishing 1997
Set in Glasgow in 1990, this book tells of one Glaswegian's dramatic contribution to Glasgow's Year as European City of Culture as he seeks revenge first on the Headmaster who had scuppered his most precious dream many years previously. Then, when that goes badly wrong, he is driven to seize the political destiny that will make him immortal, as the lucky Scot who got That Bloody Woman in the sights of a high powered rifle.

The Great Escape?   Ringwood Publishing 1997
This book is that rarity, an intelligent and readable novel about football and families. It follows the managerial debut of Derek Duncan, a Scottish international football player, in his attempt to start to make himself an immortal football manager by trying to save Griston City from seemingly inevitable relegation.

'Own Goal' and 'The Great Escape?' can be obtained via the Ringwood Publishing website www.ringwoodpublishing.com or ordered by post.

Acknowledgements

I have received the help of a great number of people in writing this book.

At the Vila-real end I received help from many more people than I can name here. Special thanks are due to Ernesto Boixader, his wife Maria Dolores, his brothers Jose Manuel and Julio. Also to Vicente Andreu, Saul Ramos, Angel and Encarnita, Jose Luis Broch, Luis Broch, Domingo Broton, Ioan Nelu Bordean, Estrella and Pablo, Sisi Nunes, Javi Vilar, Fermin and Claudia Font, Jesus Del Amo and Javi Serralbo.

In many visits to the Celtic Submari Penya I received nothing but kindness and support and I would like to thank all the members of the Celtic Submari for that support.

In two different senses there would be no book but for the massive contribution of Gerry Martin. Also he helped me with a great deal of information about the background to and development of the Celtic Submari, and he helped me communicate with its members.

At the Scottish end, I owe particular thanks to Derek Rush and Damien Kane who willingly shared with me details of their massive contribution to facilitating the trips of the Celtic Submari to Scotland.

Pat McGorry, her husband Francis, and friend Martin Kane provided me with much assistance, as did the other two key members of the 67 Bhoys, Hope and Willie Wightman. Their enormous contribution, particularly that of Pat and Hope, to the development of the friendship with the Celtic Submari, is I hope fully reflected in the content of the book.

Linda Orr and Tosh McLaughlin from John Ogilvie High School, Hamilton helped me a great deal, with information, insights and stories, as did Linda's brother Tam McCabe.

I would like to thank all the many hundreds of Celtic supporters who willingly talked to me during the course of the book. I would particularly thank all those whom I have quoted directly, but I would also like to thank the many more who gave me wonderful stories and insights I have been unable to squeeze in.

I am also very grateful to the many Rangers supporters who agreed to talk to me about the subjects covered in the book.

Many of the photographs used in this book are from private collections and I am grateful to all those who willingly provided these images.

Perhaps most importantly, my editors, Isobel Freeman and Lynsey Smith, went well beyond the call of duty and worked hard and long to render my prose more readable, more relevant and more concise. Any problems of longwindedness and irrelevancy that remain are solely the fault of the stubborn author. Andy McKeown provided specific editing advice.

Louise Colquhoun and Joanne Durning acted as Proof Readers.